BRUCE ENNIS has been involved with litigation on behalf of mental patients since 1968. He argued the landmark case of O'Connor vs. Donaldson, the first major Supreme Court decision defining the rights of mental patients. Currently serving as legal director of the American Civil Liberties Union and as a trustee of the A.C.L.U. sponsored Mental Health Law Project, Mr. Ennis is also the author of PRISONERS OF PSYCHIATRY: Mental Patients, Psychiatrists, and the Law.*

RICHARD EMERY is currently staff counsel with the New York Civil Liberties Union. For the last four years he has been director of the Institutional Legal Services Project for the state of Washington, the agency responsible for representing all mental patients institutionalized in the state. Mr. Emery was a principal drafter of Washington State's civil commitment law and has brought major test case litigation regarding patients' rights before the courts of that state. Both Mr. Ennis and Mr. Emery have published and lectured extensively on mental health law throughout the country.

*(Available from Avon Books   19299 $1.65)

Also in this Series

AN AMERICAN
CIVIL LIBERTIES
UNION HANDBOOK

THE
RIGHTS OF
MENTAL
PATIENTS

The Revised Edition of
THE BASIC ACLU
GUIDE TO A MENTAL
PATIENT'S RIGHTS

Bruce J. Ennis
Richard D. Emery

General Editors of this series:
Norman Dorsen, *Chairperson*
Aryeh Neier, *Executive Director*

 A DISCUS BOOK/PUBLISHED BY AVON BOOKS

THE RIGHTS OF MENTAL PATIENTS is an original publication of Avon Books. This work has never before appeared in book form. *

AVON BOOKS
A division of
The Hearst Corporation
959 Eighth Avenue
New York, New York 10019

First Discus Printing, February, 1978
Second Printing

DISCUS TRADEMARK REG. U.S. PAT. OFF. AND IN
OTHER COUNTRIES, MARCA REGISTRADA,
HECHO EN CANADA

Printed in Canada

ACKNOWLEDGMENTS

I would like to acknowledge the help, support, and assistance of several people during the preparation of this book. They include Debbie Lambrecht, Danette Roberson, John Jensen, Ann Cockril, Allen Ressler, and Greg Dallaire and other members of the Institutional Legal Services Project who made their expertise available to me. I am also indebted to Charles Morris, Milton Burdman, and Richard Mattsen, whose foresight in funding representation for institutionalized persons in the state of Washington not only helped the institutions to treat their residents more fairly, but also provided me with the opportunity to understand and write about some of their legal problems.

—Richard D. Emery

I would like to acknowledge the assitance of my colleagues at the New York Civil Liberties Union and the Mental Health Law Project, and the assistance of Kathy Durkin and Debbie Stead.

—Bruce J. Ennis

TABLE OF CONTENTS

INTRODUCTION   13

CHAPTER I.   Some Basic Facts About "Mental
              Illness" and Psychiatry   15
    Section 1. What Is "Mental Illness"?   15
    Section 2. How Is Mental Disorder Treated?   16
    Section 3. How Reliable Are Psychiatric
                Diagnoses?   19
    Section 4. How Valid Are Psychiatric
                Predictions of Dangerous
                Behavior?   20
    Section 5. What Are the Implications of
                the "Medical Model"?   22
    Section 6. What Is the Proper Role for
                Mental Health Professionals?   24

CHAPTER II.   Involuntary Hospitalization   35
    Section 1. What Theoretical and Practical
                Objections Can Be Raised Against
                Involuntary Hospitalization?   35
                Parens Patriae
                Police Power
    Section 2. Is Danger to Self a Justifiable
                Basis for Involuntary
                Hospitalization and Treatment?   49

CHAPTER III. The Civil Commitment Process   57
    Section 1. What Are the Emerging Standards
                for Civil Commitment?   57
    Section 2. What Is the Doctrine of the Least
                Restrictive Alternative?   57
    Section 3. What Are the Emerging
                Procedural Rights in the Civil
                Commitment Process?   60

CHAPTER IV. "Voluntary" Hospitalization 90
Section 1. Who Are the "Voluntary" Patients in Mental Hospitals? 90
Section 2. What Rights to Release Do "Voluntary" Patients Have? 93
Section 3. What Rights Do Minors Have When They Are "Voluntarily" Hospitalized by Their Parents? 95

CHAPTER V. Mental Patients in the Criminal Process 98
Section 1. How Are Persons Who Are "Incompetent to Stand Trial" Committed? 100
Section 2. What Rights Do Allegedly Incompetent Defendants Have? 103
Section 3. What Happens to Defendants Who Are Found Not Guilty by Reason of Insanity? 109
Section 4. What Are the Rights of Defendants Who Plead Not Guilty by Reason of Insanity? 110
Section 5. How Are Convicted Prisoners Committed to Mental Institutions? 110
Section 6. What Rights Do Convicted Prisoners Have to Contest Transfers Between Prisons and Prison Mental Hospitals? 111
Section 7. How Do So-called Sexual Psychopaths and Defective Delinquents Get Committed to Prison Mental Hospitals? 112
Section 8. What Rights Do Sexual Psychopaths and Defective Delinquents Have to Resist Commitment? 114

CHAPTER VI. Rights in the Institution 121
Section 1. What Is Life in a Mental Hospital Like? 121
Section 2. What Rights Do Involuntarily Hospitalized Patients Have to Periodic Review and Release? 127

Section 3.　Is There a Maximum Period of Time Beyond Which Mental Patients Cannot Be Involuntarily Confined?　130

Section 4.　May Mental Patients Refuse Treatment?　132

Section 5.　What Is the Relationship Between Consent and the Right to Refuse Treatment?　135

Section 6.　What Have Courts Said About Consent to, Or Refusal of, Specific Treatments?　137

Section 7.　What Rights Do Mental Patients Have to Be Protected from Restraints, Loss of Privileges, and Punishments?　142

Section 8.　Do Involuntarily Confined Mental Patients Have a Right to Treatment?　144

Section 9.　Do "Voluntary" Mental Patients Have a Right to Treatment?　153

Section 10.　Do Mental Patients Have a Right to Communicate with People Outside the Mental Hospital?　153

Section 11.　What Privacy Rights Do Hospitalized Mental Patients Have?　154

Section 12.　Do Hospitalized Mental Patients Have a Right to Spend or Control the Disposition of Their Money or Other Assets?　155

Section 13.　Must Involuntarily Hospitalized Patients Pay the Costs of Their Hospitalization?　156

Section 14.　What Rights Do Hospitalized Patients Have to Refuse to Work, or to Be Paid for Work?　159

CHAPTER VII.　Rights in the Community　170

Section 1.　What Rights Do Ex-Patients Have to Stay in the Community?　171

Section 2. What Rights Do Patients and Ex-Patients Have to Be Protected from Discrimination Because of Present or Past Mental Disorder? ... 172

Section 3. What Rights Do Persons Have in Proceedings to Declare Them Mentally Incompetent to Manage Their Assets or Affairs? ... 175

Section 4. What Rights Do Patients or Ex-Patients Have to Prohibit Disclosure of Information About Their Hospitalization or Treatment? ... 176

CHAPTER VIII. Lawyers and Mental Patients ... 181

Section 1. What Is the Proper Role for the Lawyer? ... .181

Section 2. What Trial Techniques Can Lawyers Use to Provide Effective Representation for Mental Patients? ... 184

Section 3. What Should Lawyers Know Before Undertaking "Right to Treatment" Lawsuits? ... 194

Appendix A   Statistical Information About the Mental Health System. ... 197

Appendix B   Psychoactive Drugs. ... 199
  I. Major Tranquilizers or "Anti-Psychotic" Drugs.
  II. Antiparkinsonian Drugs.
  III. Lithium Carbonate.
  IV. Antidepressants.
  V. Antianxiety Drugs or Minor Tranquilizers.
  VI. Sleeping Pills.
  Drug Chart

Appendix C   Advocacy Systems

Preface

This guide sets forth your rights under present law and offers suggestions on how you can protect your rights. It is one of a continuing series of handbooks published in cooperation with the American Civil Liberties Union.

The hope surrounding these publications is that Americans informed of their rights will be encouraged to exercise them. Through their exercise, rights are given life. If they are rarely used, they may be forgotten and violations may become routine.

This guide offers no assurances that your rights will be respected. The laws may change and, in some of the subjects covered in these pages, they change quite rapidly. An effort has been made to note those parts of the law where movement is taking place but it is not always possible to predict accurately when the law *will* change.

Even if the laws remain the same, interpretations of them by courts and administrative officials often vary. In a federal system such as ours, there is a built-in problem of the differences between state and federal law, not to speak of the confusion of the differences from state to state. In addition, there are wide variations in the ways in which particular courts and administrative officials will interpret the same law at any given moment.

If you encounter what you consider to be a specific abuse of your rights you should seek legal assistance. There are a number of agencies that may help you, among them ACLU affiliate offices, but bear in mind that the ACLU is a limited-purpose organization. In many communities, there are federally funded legal service offices which provide assistance to poor persons who cannot afford the costs of legal representation. In general, the rights that the ACLU defends are freedom of inquiry and expression; due process of law; equal protection of the laws; and privacy. The authors in this series have discussed other rights in these books (even though they sometimes fall outside the ACLU's usual concern) in order to provide as much guidance as possible.

These books have been planned as guides for the people directly affected: therefore the question and answer format. In some of the areas there are more detailed works available for "experts." These guides seek to raise the largest issues and inform the non-specialist of the basic law on the subject. The authors of the books are themselves specialists who understand the need for information at "street level."

No attorney can be an expert in every part of the law. If you encounter a specific legal problem in an area discussed in one of these handbooks, show the book to your attorney. Of course, he will not be able to rely *exclusively* on the handbook to provide you with adequate representation. But if he hasn't had a great deal of experience in the specific area, the handbook can provide helpful suggestions on how to proceed.

Norman Dorsen, Chairperson
American Civil Liberties Union

INTRODUCTION

This book is not a revised edition of the *Rights of Mental Patients*. It is essentially a new book. In no other area of the law has so much changed, so fast. Five years ago, when the *Rights of Mental Patients* was published, there were very few court decisions defining the legal rights of mental patients. Today there is a very substantial body of mental health case law. Over two-thirds of the cases cited in the extensive notes to this edition were decided since the first edition was written, and almost 90 percent were decided in the past ten years. Five years ago there were very few lawyers with substantial experience representing mental patients in test case litigation. Today there is a large and growing mental health bar. So much is happening that the American Bar Association's Commission on the Mentally Disabled now considers it necessary to publish a bimonthly *Mental Disability Law Reporter* to report current judicial and legislative developments.*

Many important legal questions remain to be decided, and we cannot with certainty predict the answers to those questions. But the trend of decisions over the past four years has been so uniform, and so widespread, that we can at least make educated guesses about future legal developments.

In addition to the substantial body of case law, there is now an enormous body of relevant legal and professional literature. A comprehensive work on the legal rights of mental patients would today require several volumes, and several thousand pages. This book is not a comprehensive treatise; it is a concise reference work for patients, law-

* The *Reporter* can be ordered from the ABA Commission, 1800 M Street N.W., Washington D.C. 20036; Tel: 202-331-2200.

yers, and mental health professionals. We have tried to keep the text as short and simple as possible.* Persons interested in particular points should consult the cases, books, and articles cited in the notes following each chapter.

The law is changing fast in this area and it would be a mistake for the reader to rely on this book as the final word. Important court decisions, statutes, and professional studies will appear even as this book is being printed. So consider this book a starting point—a good starting point, we hope, but only that.

Bruce J. Ennis
Richard D. Emery
September, 1976

---

* For that reason, we have decided not to use "him or her," "s/he," and similar terms. We regret the inability of our language to express neutral concepts in a simple but nondiscriminatory way, and hope that readers will understand the reason for our use of the traditional "he" and "him."

I

Some Basic Facts About "Mental Illness" And Psychiatry

What is "mental illness"?

No one knows for sure what "mental illness" means, what it is, or what causes it. Many people, including psychiatrists, believe the term "mental illness" is not a descriptive term in the same sense as "cancer" and "tuberculosis," but is only an <u>unproven *theory* used to "explain"</u> <u>behavior or thought processes we do not understand</u>, in much the same way the term "bewitched" was used to explain behavior our ancestors did not understand.[1] Other people, including psychiatrists, believe that "mental illness" is either <u>a physical disease or a disease of the psychological process</u> that can be diagnosed and treated in much the same way we diagnose and treat physical illness.[2] Those who hold that <u>"mental illness" is a theory</u>, not a thing, believe it would be <u>more accurate to use the term "problems</u> <u>in living."</u>[3] Even those who hold that "mental illness" is a physical or psychological disease disagree about its causes. <u>Some believe that "mental illness" is caused by chemical,</u> <u>hormonal, or other</u> physiological disorders; others that it is caused by <u>genetic defects</u>; and still others that it is caused by <u>environmental factors</u>, particularly by early childhood problems and traumas.

For the purpose of this book it does not matter whether an individual's problem is defined as a "mental illness," a "physical illness" that causes changes in thought and behavior, or a "problem in living." The legal rights are the same. But in order to avoid identification with implied en-

15

dorsement of any particular theory, for the most part we have used the inadequate but neutral term "mental disorder."

How is mental disorder treated?

It should not be surprising, given the disagreements about the causes of mental disorder, that mental health professionals, including psychiatrists and psychologists, also disagree about the best methods for "treating" mental disorder.[4] Some advocate psychoanalysis, which usually involves a long-term examination by a therapist of the individual's childhood, dreams, and "free associations" as a means of discovering and thereby alleviating the presumed unconscious causes of the individual's problems. People who undergo psychoanalysis do so voluntarily.

Other mental health professionals advocate psychotherapy. This is usually a shorter and less detailed examination of the individual's life to help him understand the causes of his problems. Psychotherapy usually involves an individual who voluntarily seeks that method of treatment.

Still other mental health professionals advocate chemotherapy, which relies on the use of various drugs, including tranquilizers and antidepressants, to control symptoms and behavior. It is rarely claimed that chemotherapy "cures" mental disorder. Rather, the claim is that chemotherapy lessens the "symptoms," or stabilizes the individual's thinking and behavior so that other therapies can be used. Chemotherapy is widely used for both voluntary and involuntary patients.

Still others advocate the use of electroconvulsive therapy (ECT), during which electric current is applied to the patient's temples. The current induces convulsions or seizures and is believed, by those who advocate this method, to help patients, particularly severely depressed patients. ECT is used on both consenting and nonconsenting patients.

Other mental health professionals, more likely to be psychologists than psychiatrists, advocate behavior therapy, sometimes called behavior modification. This method usually uses rewards or punishments to teach or condition the individual to change his behavior. Unlike psychoanalysis or psychotherapy, behavior therapy does not regard an understanding of the causes of the individual's problems as essential to their elimination. Behavior therapy is usually used for individuals who want or consent to that therapy, but it is also used to change the behavior of individuals who do not consent.[5]

There are other forms of treatment, but the only other form hospitalized patients are likely to encounter is called "milieu therapy." In theory, milieu therapy is an attempt to change the individual's behavior by changing the environment, or milieu, in which he lives, or by placing him in systematically and progressively different environments. The reactions of the individual to the new environment are closely monitored, and changes are then made in order to foster desired reactions. Milieu therapy is similar to some forms of behavior modification, particularly token economies (see p. 139), but it usually does not involve direct rewards and punishments. It can be used on both consenting and nonconsenting patients. Although milieu therapy is, in theory, a sophisticated method of behavior change, it requires extraordinary resources because different environments must be created, and constantly modified, to meet the changing problems and reactions of individual patients. A real milieu therapy program would require far more staff, and cost a great deal more money, than any other common form of treatment. For that reason, "milieu therapy" in most mental hospitals is simply a fancy term for custodial care. Providing a "structured environment,"— usually the same for all patients—together with food, clothing, and shelter, is not milieu therapy, although some unsophisticated mental health professionals claim that it is.

Surprisingly, there is very little empirical evidence about the effectiveness of particular treatments, or of psychiatric treatment in general. A substantial number of persons do get "better" after a short period of hospitalization and treatment. But whether they get better *because of* hospitalization and treatment, or simply because of the passage of time or some other reason, is not clear. There is no known "treatment" for the common cold. If persons with common colds were hospitalized and given tranquilizing drugs, ECT, or other psychiatric treatments, most of them would probably recover from their colds, but it would be wrong to conclude they recovered *because of* hospitalization and treatment.

In order to measure the effectiveness of psychiatric treatments, it would be necessary to have matched control groups of patients—using the treatment on one group but not on the other—and to observe the results. But very little research of that type has been conducted. Much of the research that has been conducted indicates that the recovery rates for control groups who receive drugs, psychotherapy, or nothing are about the same.[6]

On the other hand, there is a small but growing number of studies comparing the effectiveness of psychiatric treatment in a hospital with the effectiveness of psychiatric treatment in the community. Those studies indicate that persons treated in the community recover faster, suffer fewer relapses, deteriorate less from dependency fostered by hospitalization, maintain employment better, and cost the state about half as much money as similar patients treated in hospitals.[7] (see Chapter III). In this important sense, hospitalization can itself be viewed as antitherapeutic.[8]

There is another important point to consider. Even the most vigorous advocates of psychiatric treatment will admit that particular treatments do not always work. Let us assume, for example (though we know of no evidence to support such an assumption), that electric shock treatment benefits 60 percent of all persons on whom it is used. It would not benefit the remaining 40 percent, who would suffer the harmful or unpleasant effects of ECT without gaining any benefit. Obviously, if a patient knew in advance that he would be one of the 40 percent, he would not consent to ECT. The problem is that mental health professionals are not very good at predicting the outcome of a particular treatment on a particular person.[9] That is, even if mental health professionals could say in advance that ECT would benefit 60 percent of all "depressed" patients, they cannot say in advance whether a particular depressed patient will be one of the 60 percent or one of the 40 percent. Until there is evidence that a particular treatment will benefit the great majority of persons on whom it is used, or evidence that mental health professionals can predict the outcome of a particular treatment on a particular person, it would not necessarily be "irrational" for individuals to refuse that treatment, nor would it be justified to force the treatment on them.

How reliable are psychiatric diagnoses?

A great deal has been written on this subject.[10] Diagnoses of "organic" mental disorders, in which there is actual physical disorder of the brain or nervous system, are reasonably reliable. That is, a clear majority of all psychiatrists—say 80 to 90 percent—would probably agree whether a particular patient does or does not have an organic mental disorder. But diagnoses of "functional" mental disorders, in which there is no apparent physical disorder of the brain or nervous system, are far less reliable. In fact, mental health professionals are likely to agree whether a particular patient has a specific functional disorder—such as "schizophrenic reaction, paranoid type," "depressive reaction," or "passive-aggressive personality" —only about 40 percent of the time. This means that if one mental health professional testifies that a prospective patient has that disorder, it is more likely than not that a second mental health professional, chosen at random, would *disagree* with the first mental health professional's diagnosis.

It is important to understand that there is a major difference between the reliability of a diagnosis and the validity of a diagnosis.[11] If all the psychiatrists in the world agreed that a prospective patient was schizophrenic, that would be a very reliable diagnosis, but it might nevertheless be wrong, or an invalid, diagnosis. On the other hand, a low rate of reliability indicates a low rate of validity. For example, if 50 percent of all psychiatrists believed the prospective patient was schizophrenic, and 50 percent disagreed, the reliability, or rate of agreement, on that diagnosis would be 50 percent. But although both groups of psychiatrists might have been wrong, they cannot both have been right—the prospective patient was either schizophrenic or he was not. Thus, if a diagnosis is not very reliable, it is almost certainly not very valid.

We have talked about the reliability of psychiatric diagnoses rather than about their validity because there are very few studies of validity. The few that exist, however, strongly suggest that psychiatric diagnoses are quite often wrong. In fact, some studies indicate that psychiatrists cannot correctly distinguish even between people who are "normal" and those who are mentally disordered. For example, Rosenhan and several "mentally healthy" colleagues feigned mental disorder and were admitted to public and private mental hospitals.[12] Immediately after admission they began to act quite normally. Nevertheless, the mental health professionals on the staffs continued to believe the pseudopatients were mentally disordered, and "treated" them for several weeks. None of the pseudopatients was described as recovered, and none was discharged by the hospitals.

How valid are psychiatric predictions of dangerous behavior?

Much has been written on this subject, too.[13] Despite popular belief to the contrary, it now seems beyond dispute that mental health professionals have *no* expertise in predicting future dangerous behavior, either to self or to others. In fact, predictions of dangerous behavior are wrong about 95 percent of the time. Even when those predictions are based on a history of dangerous behavior in the recent past, they are still wrong about two-thirds of the time.

The point of concern to prospective mental patients is that mental health professionals almost always err by overpredicting, rather than by underpredicting, dangerous behavior. This is not only the fault of mental health professionals who make such predictions, but is also a statistical fact of life. For example, even if there were a test for dangerousness that was 90 percent accurate (and we know of no such test), if 1,000 people were tested and 10 among the 1,000 were dangerous, testing the 1,000 to find the 10 would result in 90 percent of the 990 persons who were nondangerous accurately being called "nondangerous," or 891; 90 percent of the 10 persons who were dangerous accurately being called "dangerous," or 9; 1 of the 10 dangerous persons inaccurately being called "nondangerous"; and 99 of the 990 nondangerous persons inaccurately being called "dangerous." Thus, if, as in our example, the "base rate" of dangerous behavior in a population of 1,000 persons is 1 percent (or 10 persons), a test that is accurate 90 percent of the time will necessarily result in 99 incorrect predictions of danger for every 9 correct predictions of danger. And 99 of the 100 incorrect predictions will be *overpredictions* of danger, that is, will predict danger when in fact no danger would occur. So 99 harmless persons would have to be confined in order to confine 9 dangerous persons. If the "base rate" of dangerous behavior is even lower, or if the test is less accurate than our hypothetical 90 percent test, there will be even more incorrect predictions of danger for every correct prediction of danger.

In the real world, the "base rate" of dangerous behavior (including suicide[14]) committed by persons diagnosed as mentally ill is very low, and the tests currently in use are far less than 90 percent accurate. This means that psychiatric predictions of dangerous behavior will be wrong far more often than they are right. And it means that committing people to mental hospitals because of such predictions will confine a great many harmless people for every dangerous person.

Two other factors contribute to overpredictions of dangerousness. First, mental health professionals are less likely to be criticized or held responsible for damages for confining harmless people than for releasing people who turn out to be dangerous. Mental health professionals would make many more accurate predictions if they predicted that all mental patients would be nondangerous. But they are more likely to be protected from lawsuits claiming damages for negligence, and from embarrassing newspaper headlines such as "Dr. X Releases Mental Patient Murderer," if they predict that their patients will be dangerous.

Second, most mental health professionals are not interested in dangerousness. Many view it as a technical and inappropriate legal requirement for commitment. They desire to "treat" patients, and when they see a person whom they feel needs treatment, many are willing to say he is "dangerous" if that is what it takes to provide treatment. The consequence is overprediction of dangerousness when need for "treatment" is the real reason for confinement. (See Chapter II "Police Power.")

A prestigious task force of the American Psychiatric Association has recognized the inability of psychiatrists to predict dangerousness. It concluded that "neither psychiatrists nor anyone else have reliably demonstrated an ability to predict future violence or 'dangerousness.' Neither has any special psychiatric 'expertise' in this area been established."[15]

The unreliability of psychiatric diagnoses and the inability of psychiatrists to predict dangerous behavior are critically important. Much of the recent case law can best be understood as an attempt by judges to protect patients and prospective patients from errors of psychiatric diagnosis and prediction.[16] Anyone seriously interested in the legal rights of mental patients should therefore study the authorities cited in the notes to this and the preceding answer.

What are the implications of the "medical model"?

Many state mental hospitals are functionally indistinguishable from prisons. Patients live on locked wards, with bars on the windows, and receive the same food, clothing, and "structured environment" they would receive in a prison. Society prohibits the involuntary commitment of mentally disordered noncriminals to places called "prisons," but authorizes their commitment to functionally indistinguishable places called "hospitals." Mental institutions are called "hospitals" rather than prisons, are staffed by "doctors" rather than guards, and care for "patients" rather than prisoners.

The terminology employed conveys the impression that mental institutions are more like general hospitals than like prisons. The impression is not accidental. For years, doctors have been saying that "mental illness" is an illness just like any other illness.[17] Of course, this is not true in at least one very important sense. With few exceptions, persons with physical illnesses cannot be involuntarily hospitalized and treated. If proponents of the medical model would really follow it, involuntary civil commitment would end. But the belief that mental disorder is essentially a medical problem to be dealt with by doctors makes it easier to ignore the legal, ethical, and social issues raised by involuntary hospitalization and treatment.

The "medical model" of mental disorders therefore legitimizes practices that would be much more controversial if they were described in nonmedical terms.

This is a relatively recent model for dealing with mental disorder. In many ways, the earlier models were more barbaric; in some ways, they were more humane. Historically, "lunatics," "madmen," "fools," and "witches" were not thought of as "mentally ill," or even as "sick." It was believed that their condition was caused by evil spirits or ungodliness. They were said to have strayed from God (or the gods) or to have fallen under the influence of the moon—hence the word "lunatic."

Rich "fools" and harmless "lunatics" were kept by their families. The poor roamed, begged, and scavenged. Frequently they were banished. "Witches," and those thought to be possessed by evil spirits, were either punished for criminal law violations or burned at the stake under religious authority. Rarely were mentally disordered persons confined to poorhouses or prisons. When they were, it was because of poverty or conviction of crime, not because of mental disorder.

In Europe and America, mental disorder was not a common cause for institutionalization until early in the nineteenth century.[18] One doctrine of the Enlightenment was the belief that an "asylum," architecturally designed for solitude and quite routine, could cure mental disorder. The treatment then was not medication but meditation. The asylums were operated by doctors or clergy, who claimed that relief from pressures of the outside world would "cure" the vast majority of their "patients." Many wealthy families, and later those who could afford only state-supported institutionalization, sent their mentally disordered relatives for meditation, "moral treatment," and the promise of "cure." Long stays were common.

At that point in history, mental disorders were believed to be caused by a turbulent society, disordered family life, and, in some instances, oppressive religious indoctrination. Yet despite the presumed social causes, doctors asserted that mental disorder was a physical "disease" like any other. They claimed that the brain reacted to social and economic stress in the same way the liver reacts to excessive consumption of alcohol. They also claimed there would be physical evidence of those brain reactions. "Every general practitioner in the pre-Civil War era agreed that insanity was a disease of the brain and that the exam-

23

ination of tissues in an autopsy would reveal organic lesions, clear evidence of physical damage in every insane person."[19] The lesions were never detected, but the doctors continued to claim that with better equipment, they would be. Thus the medical model of insanity was based on a claim for which there was no evidence.

The medical superintendents of the asylums formed an association that later became the American Psychiatric Association.[20]

What is the proper role for mental health professionals?

Because of the prevalence of the medical model, and for other reasons to be discussed in this section, psychiatrists—and to a lesser extent psychologists—have been given, or have assumed, enormous power in the mental health system. Although such laws are increasingly being declared unconstitutional, many states authorize any two physicians to invoke the power of the state to compel the involuntary hospitalization and treatment of any individual whom they believe requires such care. No state authorizes any two laymen—a grocer and a typist, for example—to exercise such power. Mental health professionals are given this enormous power because of the incorrect assumption that involuntary hospitalization and treatment involve only medical issues. But every civil commitment proceeding also involves major legal, ethical, and social issues, and those issues clearly predominate over any purely "medical" issues.[21] There is no evidence that mental health professionals can make more reasonable or more informed or more accurate judgments about legal, ethical, or social issues than can laymen. Little or no evidence exists that mental health professionals are more "expert" than laymen at making *any* of the judgments and predictions relevant to a civil commitment proceeding.[22]

Some mental health professionals are beginning to question the propriety of their deciding legal, ethical, and social issues for which they have no demonstrated expertise. They are starting to think about these issues because now, for the first time, there is an organized movement of patients and ex-patients beginning to raise them. Because of the stigma of "mental illness" and the effects of treatment (particularly ECT and tranquilizing medication), mental patients have been reluctant, or unable, to organize. That is changing rapidly. There are now well-established patient and ex-patient organizations in almost every state. There are even regular patient and expatient publications, one of the best of which, *Madness Network News*, is distributed nationwide.[23]

These organizations stress the *real* function, not the ostensibly medical function, of many mental health professionals. Particularly in the civil commitment context, mental health professionals often act as quasipolice, as agents of society, deciding and enforcing societal norms of behavior, and facilitating the removal from society of persons whose behavior causes fear, disgust, embarrassment, annoyance, inconvenience, pity, or guilt. Unlike other doctors, psychiatrists (and other mental health professionals) treat patients against the patients' wishes, but in accord with society's demands. As one knowledgeable commentator has said, "If all the mental hospitals in a given region were emptied and closed down today, tomorrow relatives, police, and judges would raise a clamor for new ones; and these true clients of the mental hospitals would demand an institution to satisfy their needs."[24] Thus coercive psychiatry serves very real and substantial social interests under the guise of serving the interests of patients.[25]

This point merits elaboration. No statute authorizes involuntary hospitalization and treatment of mentally healthy individuals, even if their behavior is seriously abnormal. Ostensibly, no one is committed simply because his behavior is bizarre or abnormal. In theory, individuals are committed only when their abnormal behavior is "caused by" or is "the result of" a mental disorder. For example, if a concededly sane individual were to say "I have decided that I wish to spend the rest of my life sitting cross-legged in a corner," that individual would not, theoretically, be subject to commitment, even though his behavior would be quite abnormal. But in practice, it is very easy for a mental health professional to say that any abnormal behavior is "caused by" mental disorder, and very difficult for anyone else to disprove such opinions because, as already explained, mental disorders are not verifiable in the same ways as physical disorders. A mental health professional could say, for example, that no sane person would choose to sit in a corner forever—that such a decision must be caused by a mental disorder[26]—and no one could "disprove" that opinion.

This tension between theory and practice creates ethical conflicts for mental health professionals. The conflicts would be easier to perceive if statutes expressly authorized the involuntary hospitalization and treatment of concededly mentally healthy individuals who have chosen to behave in abnormal ways. In that event, mental health professionals would be performing not a medical function, but the social and ethical function of deciding which behaviors are sufficiently abnormal to warrant deprivation of liberty. And they would be performing that function without standards or guidelines, on the basis of their own judgments of what is normal or abnormal, or of what society would deem normal or abnormal. (At least in the criminal law context, the standards and guidelines for determining which behavior is sufficiently abnormal to be called "criminal" are predetermined as specifically as possible by legislatures, and are not devised on an ad hoc basis by police.)

Human behavior is so complex, and so little understood, that it is almost never possible to say with certainty that an individual behaves in an abnormal way "because of" mental disorder, and would not behave in that same way if sane. Human behavior is the cumulative product of an almost infinite number of familial, educational, biological, social, environmental, and economic factors. Singling out mental disorder as "the cause" of abnormal behavior is almost always a gross oversimplification. The many different schools of thought about the causes and treatment of mental disorders show that no one explanation is adequate. But because mental disorder is such a broad and elastic concept, and such a convenient "explanation" for behavior we cannot easily understand, it is possible for mental health professionals to make and enforce, knowingly or unknowingly, ethical judgments about normal and abnormal behavior simply by saying that behavior is "the result" of mental disorder.

In our view, mental health professionals should avoid the substantial conflicts of interest inherent in serving society and serving patients at the same time by refusing to participate in involuntary hospitalization and treatment decisions. They should acknowledge the unreliability and invalidity of psychiatric diagnoses, and should refuse to make the legal, ethical, and social judgments required by every involuntary deprivation of liberty. For example, they should candidly say, "Judge, I have no expertise at predicting dangerous behavior. That's a problem for you or for a jury." In criminal proceedings, they should acknowledge that they cannot know what a defendant was thinking during a crime and that they know less about defendants' competence "to stand trial" than do defense attorneys (see Chapter V).

If mental health professionals do not acknowledge the limitations of psychiatry, judges will. The basic point of tension between judges and psychiatrists is the growing judicial recognition that psychiatry is an art, not a science.[27] As that point becomes clearer, judges become more reluctant to defer to psychiatric expertise.

The insanity defense is one area in which psychiatrists have actively sought power, and have not simply had it thrust upon them. Organized psychiatry bitterly criticized the traditional standard for the insanity defense—the right-wrong test—because it allegedly prevented the utilization of modern psychiatric knowledge. Responding to that criticism, Judge David Bazelon, an extremely distinguished judge, a past president of the American Orthopsychiatric Association, and a genuine friend of organized psychiatry, wrote an opinion[28] that abandoned the old standard and expanded the courtroom role of psychiatrists. Under that opinion, a criminal defendant is considered insane, even if he *did* know that his act was wrong, if that act was the "product" of a mental disease or defect.

Over the years Judge Bazelon became increasingly disillusioned with the ability of psychiatrists to provide relevant and useful knowledge under the new standard. Finally, thirteen years after his original decision he concluded that "there is no justification for permitting psychiatrists to testify on the ultimate issue" in an insanity defense proceeding, and therefore precluded psychiatrists from "testifying whether the alleged offense was the 'product' of mental illness . . ."[29] As Judge Bazelon subsequently wrote, for a psychiatric audience, that decision was made necessary because "psychiatrists did not ac-

27

knowledge the limits of their expertise."[30] He made the same point in another case: "In practice, however, under *Durham* [the earlier case] and its progeny psychiatrists have continued to make moral and legal judgments beyond the proper scope of their professional expertise."[31] Finally, in a civil case Judge Bazelon wrote:

> As the record in this case and others like it strongly suggests, conclusory psychiatric opinion tends to dominate the criterion for determination. We have criticized this expert dominance in other contexts and see no reason for not extending this concern to the present circumstances: in both cases, psychiatric judgments may disguise, wittingly or unwittingly, political or social biases of the psychiatrist; and excessive reliance on diagnosis will preempt the primary role of legal decision-makers. (Footnotes omitted).[32]

Thus, the judge who was once considered the leading proponent of increased judicial reliance on psychiatric testimony is now skeptical, and even critical, of psychiatric testimony.[33]

Similar skepticism turns up in many recent decisions. Because diagnosis of mental disorder is so subjective, judges are requiring proof of dangerousness. And because psychiatric predictions of dangerouness are so inaccurate, judges are requiring evidence of recent overt acts of a dangerous nature (see Chapters II and III).

The medical model of civil commitment is now being rejected even by judges who are not antagonistic to that model. In a recent case,[34] for example, the judge who struck down Hawaii's mental health law, which closely followed the medical model, was quite sympathetic to the virtues of the medical model. He had personally chaired the committee that, six years earlier, had drafted the law. But though "fully aware of the implications of a return to the 'legal model' as opposed to the 'medical model,' " he felt compelled to declare the law unconstitutional. In concluding his opinion, he summarized the *real* reasons why judges throughout the country are rejecting the medical model: "The overriding consideration behind recent cases . . . has been that personal freedom is involved. A close

28

second consideration has been that the diagnosis and treatment of mental illness leave too much to subjective choices by less than neutral individuals."[35]

In short, most judges believe that personal freedom is more important than mental health. They are unwilling to limit that freedom on the basis of a subjective opinion expressed by a mental health professional acting as an agent of society rather than an agent of the client whose interests he professes to serve.

Justice Brandeis' famous statement in *Olmstead v. United States* illustrates the currently prevailing judicial view:

> (E)xperience should teach us to be most on our guard to protect liberty when the government's purposes are beneficent. . . . The greatest dangers to liberty lurk in insidious encroachment by men of zeal, well-meaning, but without understanding.[36]

Or as the judge in the Hawaii case put it, "Limiting a person's constitutional rights on the theory that it is in his best interests is questionable philosophy and bad law."[37]

NOTES

1. Szasz, *The Myth of Mental Illness* (1961), *The Manufacture of Madness* (1970), *Ideology and Insanity* (1970), *Law, Liberty and Psychiatry* (1963); Laing, *The Politics of Experience* (1967); Cooper, *Psychiatry and Anti-Psychiatry* (1967); Scheff, *Being Mentally Ill: A Sociological Theory* (1966); Rogow, *The Psychiatrists* (1970), 21-30. See, in general, Brandt, *Reality Police* (1975); Donaldson, *Insanity Inside Out* (1976); Gotkin, *Too Much Anger, Too Many Tears: A Personal Triumph over Psychiatry* (1975); Kesey, *One Flew over the Cuckoo's Nest* (1962); Piercy, *Woman on the Edge of Time* (1976); Torrey, *The Death of Psychiatry* (1974).
2. For example, Reiss, "A Critique of Thomas Szasz's *Myth of Mental Illness*," 128 *Am. J. Psychiat.* 1081 (1972); Ausubel, "Personality Disorder Is Disease," 16 *Am. Psychologist* 69 (1971).
3. Szasz, *supra* n. 1.
4. For example, see the theories and methods described in

Mischel, *Introduction to Personality* (1971); Ziskin, *Coping with Psychiatric and Psychological Testimony* (2nd ed., 1975).

5. For a more precise definition of behavior therapy, see Friedman, "Legal Regulation of Applied Behavior Analysis in Mental Institutions and Prisons," 17 *Ariz. L. Rev.* 39 (1975); and Brenner, "Behavior Modification," 12 *Crim. Def. Tech.* 73-1 (1976).

6. See generally, Schwitzgebel, "The Right to Effective Mental Treatment," 62 *Calif. L. Rev.*, 936 (1974); Katz, "The Right to Treatment—An Enchanting Legal Fiction," 36 *U. Chi. L. Rev.* 755 (1969); Ennis and Litwack, "Psychiatry and the Presumption of Expertise: Flipping Coins in the Courtroom," 62 *Calif. L. Rev.*, 693 (1974); Chambers, "Alternative to Civil Commitment: Practical Guides and Constitutional Imperatives," 70 *Mich. L. Rev.* 1108 (1972); Ennis, "Civil Liberties and Mental Illness" 7 *Crim. L. Bul.* 101, p. 105, fn. 15 (Mar. 1971); Rappaport, Hopkins, Hall, Belleza, and Silverman, *Schizophrenics for Whom Phenothiazines May be Contraindicated or Unnecessary*, Langley Porter Neuropsychiatric Institute, Agnews State Hospital, San Jose, Cal. 94114 (1975); May, *Treatment of Schizophrenics: A Comparative Study of 5 Treatment Methods* (1968); Eysenck, "Behavior Therapy, Spontaneous Remission and Transference in Neurotics," 119 *Am. J. Psychiat.* 867-71 (1963): "Neurotics tend to get better without any form of specific psychiatric therapy," citing Denker, "Results of Treatment of Psychoneurosis by General Practitioners," *N.Y. State J. Med.* 46, 2164-66 (1946); Levitt, "The Results of Psychotherapy with Children: An Evaluation," 21 *J. Consult. Psychol.* 189-96 (1957); Shepherd and Gruenberg, "The Age for Neurosis," 35 *Millbank Mem. F. Quart. Bull.* 258 (1957). See also Hoffer and Osmond, *How to Live with Schizophrenia* (1966), p. 3: "The natural recovery rate of schizophrenia has remained unchanged throughout the years . . . the natural course of the disease accounted for recovery of fifty percent of the patients." See also pp. 7, 127-28, and 139-40. And see Ennis and Friedman, *Legal Rights of the Mentally Handicapped* (1973), PLI Vol. I, pp. 437-50, 514-20; Vol. II, pp. 749-55.

Commitment to a mental institution has special *harmful* effects on children. See, for example, De Meyer, "New Approaches to the Treatment of Very Young Schizophrenic Children," in *The Mental Health of the Child*, (Public Health Service Pub. No. 2168, 1971), 424; Hammond, "Parental Interest in Institutionalized Children: A

Survey," 20 *Hosp. & Comm. Psychiat.* 338 (1969); Kaufman, "The Effects of Institutionalization on Development of Stereotyped and Social Behaviors in Mental Defectives," 71 *Am. J. Men. Def.* (1967); Klaber and Butterfield, "Stereotyped Rocking—A Measure of Institution and Ward Effectiveness" 73 *Am. J. Men. Def.* 13 (1968); Lipsius, "Judgments of Alternatives to Hospitalization," 130 *Am. J. Psychiat.* 892 (1973); Lyle, "The Effect of an Institution Environment upon the Verbal Development of Imbecile Children" 1 *J. Men. Def. Res.* 1 (1960); Reiger, "Changing Concepts in Treating Children in a State Mental Hospital," 1 *Int'l. J. Child Psychotherapy* 89 (1972); Sternlight and Siegel, "Institutional Residence and Intellectual Functioning," 12 *J. Men. Def. Res.* 119 (1968); Stimpson *et al*, "Effects of Early Institutionalization on Growth and Development of Young Children with Down's Syndrome," 67 *Mich. Med.* 1213 (1968); Tizard and Rees, "The Effect of Early Institutional Rearing on the Behavior Problems and Affectional Relationships of Four-Year-Old Children," 16 *J. Child Psychol-Psychiat.* 61 (1975); Youngelson, "The Need to Affiliate and Self-Esteem in Institutionalized Children," 26 *J. Personality & Psychol.* 280 (1973).

For information on the inadequacy of mental hospitals, see Solomon, "The American Psychiatric Association in Relation to American Psychiatry," 115 *Am. J. Psychiat.* 1 (1958); Joint Information Service of the American Psychiatric Association and the National Association for Mental Health, *Fifteen Indices: An Aid in Reviewing State and Local Mental Health Programs* (1966); American Psychiatric Assoc. Task Force on the Right to Care and Treatment, Draft Position Paper on the Right to Adequate Care and Treatment for the Mentally Ill and Mentally Retarded (4th Draft, Oct. 1974); American Bar Foundation, *The Mentally Disabled and the Law*, 1-14 (Brakel and Rock 1971); Rothman, *Discovery of the Asylum* (1971); Rock, Jacobsen, and Janopaul, *Hospitalization and Discharge of the Mentally Ill* (1968); Goffman, *Asylums* (1961); Joint Commission on Mental Illness and Health, *Action for Mental Health* (1961); Deutsch, *The Mentally Ill in America* (1949); *Hearings on the Constitutional Rights of the Mentally Ill Before the Subcommittee on Constitutional Rights of the Senate Committee on the Judiciary*, 87th Cong., 1st Sess. 1 (1961) and 91st Cong. 1st and 2nd Sess. (1969-70) (hereafter cited as Hearings—87th or Hearings—91st").

7. See Ennis and Litwack, *supra* n. 6; Chambers, *supra* n. 6;

Hearings—87th and 91st, *supra* n. 6; Goffman, *supra* n. 6; Bouton, *Institutional Neurosis* (1966); Gruenberg, "Social Breakdown Syndrome—Some Origins," 123 *Am. J. Psychiat.* 1481 (1967); Belknap, *Human Problems of State Mental Hospitals* (1956); Schwartz and Schwartz, *Social Approaches to Mental Patient Care* (1964); Wing and Brown, *Institutionalization and Schizophrenia* (1970); *In re Ballay*, 482 F.2d 648 (D.C. Cir. 1973); and *Hawks v. Lazaro*, 202 S.E.2d 109, 121 (W. Va. 1974).

8. See authorities cited *supra* nn. 6 and 7.
9. See Ennis and Litwack, *supra* n. 6.
10. See studies compiled in Ennis and Litwack, *supra* n. 6; Ziskin, *supra* n. 4; Comment, "The Language of Involuntary Mental Hospitalization: A Study in Sound and Fury," 4 *Mich. J. L. Ref.* 195, 204 (1970), *supra* n. 4. See also, Rosenhan, "On Being Sane in Insane Places," 179 *Science,* 250 (1973), and 13 *St. Cl. Lwr.* 379 (1973); Roth, Dayley, and Lerner, "Into the Abyss: Psychiatric Reliability and Emergency Commitment Statutes," 13 *St. Cl. Lwr.* 400 (1973); Beck *et al.* "Reliability of Psychiatric Diagnosis: A Study of Consistency of Clinical Judgments and Ratings," 119 *Am. J. Psychiat.* 351 (1962); Shah, "Crime and Mental Illness: Some Problems in Defining and Labelling Deviant Behavior," 53 *Ment. Hyg.* 21 (1969).
11. See Ennis and Litwack, *supra* n. 6.
12. Rosenhan, *supra* n. 10.
13. See studies compiled in Ennis and Litwack, *supra* n. 6; Stone, *Mental Health and the Law: A System in Transition* (1975), Ch. 2; Livermore, Mahlmquist, and Meehl, "On the Justifications for Civil Commitment," 117 *U. Pa. L. Rev.* 75 (1968); Peske, "Is Dangerousness an Issue for Physicians in Emergency Commitment?" 132 *Am. J. Psychiat.* 825, 828 (1975); American Psychiatric Association Task Force Report 8, *Clinical Aspects of the Violent Individual* (1974).
14. Note, "Developments in the Law of Civil Commitment of the Mentally Ill" 87 *Harv. L. Rev.* 1190-1227 and fn. 141 (1970) (hereafter cited as Harvard Article); Enki Research Institute, *A Study of California's New Mental Health Law* 1970-71 (1972), p. 152; Greenberg, "Involuntary Psychiatric Commitments to Prevent Suicide," 49 *N.Y.U. L. Rev.* 227 (1974); Rosen, "Detection of Suicidal Patients: An Example of Some Limitations of the Prediction of Infrequent Events," 18 *J. Consult. Psychol.* 397 (1954); Piotrovske, "Psychological Test Prediction of Suicide," in Resnick, *Suicidal Behaviors: Diagnosis and Management* (1968); Lester, "Attempts to Predict Suicidal

Risk Using Psychological Tests," 74 *Psychol. Bull.* 1 (1970); Murphy, "Clinical Identification of Suicidal Risk," 27 *Arch. Gen. Psychiat.* 356 (1972).

15. Task Force Report 8, *supra* n. 13, p. 28.
16. See *Greenwood v. United States*, 350 U.S. 366, 375 (1956); *Drope v. Missouri*, 420 U.S. 162 (1975); *O'Connor v. Donaldson*, 422 U.S. 563, 579 (1975) (Burger, C.J., concurring); *In re Ballay*, *supra* n. 7; *Smith v. Schlesinger*, 513 F.2d 462 (D.C. Cir. 1975); *Lessard v. Schmidt*, 349 F. Supp. 1078, 1094 (E.D. Wisc. 1972) (subsequent cites in *Ch. II*, n. 2); *Suzuki v. Quisenberry*, 411 F. Supp. 1113 (D. Ha. 1976); *In re Quesnell*, 83 Wn.2d 224, 517 P.2d 568 (1973); *In re Levias*, 83 Wn.2d 253, 517 P.2d 588 (1973); *Doremus v. Farrell*, 407 F. Supp. 509 (D. Neb. 1975); *Lynch v. Baxley*, 386 F. Supp. 378, 393 (M.D. Ala. 1974); *Bartley v. Kremens*, 402 F. Supp. 1039, 1052-53 (E.D. Pa., 1975), *vacated on other grounds*, —— U.S. ——, 97 S. Ct. 1709 (May 16, 1977); *Tippett v. Maryland*, 436 F.2d 1153, 1165 (4th Cir. 1971); *Hicks v. United States*, 511 F.2d 407, 415 (D.C. Cir. 1975); *Washington v. United States*, 390 F.2d 444 (D.C. Cir. 1967); *United States v. Brawner*, 471 F.2d 969 (D.C. Cir. 1972); *State ex rel. Finken v. Roop*, 339 A.2d 764 (Pa. Super. Ct. 1975); *State v. Krol*, 344 A.2d 289, 310 (N.J. Sup. Ct. 1975); *People v. Burnick*, 535 P.2d 352, 364 (Cal. Sup. Ct. 1975); *Sarzen v. Gaughen*, 489 F.2d 1076, 1086 (1st Cir. 1973); *Tarasoff v. Regents of Univ. of Cal.*, 551 P.2d 334 (Cal. Sup. Ct. 1976).
17. Goffman, *supra* n. 6; Wales, "The Rise, the Fall, and the Resurrection of the Medical Model," 63 *Geo. L.J.* 87 (1974); Bazelon, "Psychiatry and the Adversary Process," *Scientific American*, Vol. 320 (June 1974); Ziskin, *supra* n. 4; Szasz and Torrey, *supra* n. 1.
18. The historical information in this section is from Rothman, *The Discovery of the Asylum* (1971); Deutsch, *The Mentally Ill in America* (2nd ed., 1949); Kittrie, *The Right to Be Different* (1971), pp. 8-11, 56-65.
19. Rothman, *supra* n. 18, p. 110.
20. See Szasz, "Foreword" in Ennis, *Prisoners of Psychiatry* (1972).
21. See Szasz, *supra* n. 1; Livermore et al., *supra* n. 13; Roth et al., *supra* n. 10; Siegel, "The Justifications for Medical Commitment—Real or Illusory?" 6 *Wake For. L. Rev.* 21 (1969); Dershowitz, "Psychiatry in the Legal Process: A Knife that Cuts Both Way," 51 Judicature 370 (1968); *In re Ballay*, *supra* n. 7; Friedman and Daly, "Civil Commitment and the Doctrine of Balance: A Critical Analysis,"

13 *St. Cl. Lwr.* 503 (1973); Kittrie, *supra* n. 18; Morris, "Institutionalizing the Rights of Mental Patients: Committing the Legislature," 62 *Calif. L. Rev.* 957 (1974).

22. Ennis and Litwack, *supra* n. 6, p. 696.
23. *Madness Network News,* P.O. Box 684, San Francisco, California 94101. See Appendix C for list of publications produced by ex-patient organizations.
24. Goffman, *supra* n. 6, p. 384.
25. Braginsky and Braginsky, "Psychologists: High Priests of the Middle Class," *Psychology Today* (Dec. 1973); see also *supra* n. 21.
26. For real life examples, see *In re Sealy,* 218 So.2d 765 (D. Ct. App. Fla. 1969) ("hippie" commitment challenged); and *American Psychiatric Association Press Release on Homosexuality,* (Dec. 15, 1973).
27. *Supra* n. 16.
28. *Durham v. United States,* 214 F.2d 862 (D.C. Cir. 1954).
29. *Washington v. United States,* 390 F.2d 444, 456 (D.C. Cir., 1967).
30. Bazelon, "The Perils of Wizardry" 131 *Am. J. Psychiat.* 1317, 1320 (1974); see also Bazelon, *supra* n. 17.
31. *United States v. Brawner,* 471 F.2d 969, 1019 (D.C. Cir. 1972) (concurring and dissenting).
32. *Smith v. Schlesinger, supra* n. 16, p. 476.
33. See generally Wales, *supra* n. 17.
34. *Suzuki v. Quisenberry, supra* n. 16.
35. *Ibid.* p. 1135.
36. *Olmstead v. United States,* 277 U.S. 438, 479 (1928) (Brandeis, J., dissenting).
37. *Suzuki v. Quisenberry, supra* n. 16, p. 1130.

II

Involuntary Hospitalization

The states have traditionally exercised broad power to commit persons found to be mentally ill. . . . Considering the number of persons affected, it is perhaps remarkable that the substantive constitutional limitations on this power have not been more frequently litigated.[1]

What theoretical and practical objections can be raised against involuntary hospitalization?

Although no court has yet entirely prohibited involuntary hospitalization, many courts are moving in that direction. Recent decisions have substantially restricted the power of the state to hospitalize persons against their will.[2]

Those restrictions are important, and they will be discussed in the next chapter. In this chapter, however, we will summarize the arguments that can be made not only to restrict but to prohibit involuntary hospitalization.[3]

There are very strong arguments against involuntary hospitalization and treatment as it exists in the United States. Our ability to define, distinguish, and cure those whom, for convenience, we label "mentally ill" is poor.[4] By contrast, the social and family pressures to find some solution, however inadequate, for individual and social problems are so great that inappropriate hospitalization—that is, hospitalization that is not truly more beneficial for the persons hospitalized than it is detrimental—is inevitable.

Respect for individual difference and personal autonomy

is the distinguishing characteristic of Western democracy. It has accurately been said that "the right to be let alone" is perhaps the most fundamental of all rights.[5] Involuntary hospitalization destroys that right and also abridges the right to physical liberty, to associate with persons of one's choice, to travel, to speak and read what one wishes, to work at a job of one's choice, and to be free from unreasonable searches of one's person, or seizure of one's papers and personal effects.[6] As the Supreme Court has noted, involuntary hospitalization and treatment are a truly "massive curtailment of liberty."[7]

When judged against the severity and sweep of these abridgements, the theories relied upon to justify involuntary hospitalization seem weak. Historically, involuntary hospitalization has been justified by reliance on the state's *parens patriae* power or its police power. Substantial arguments can be made against reliance on either of those powers.

A. PARENS PATRIAE

Parens patriae means "Father of his country; parent of his country. In England, the King. In the United States, the state as sovereign—referring to the sovereign power of guardianship over persons under disability . . . such as minors and insane and incompetent persons."[8]

The concept of *parens patriae* power developed in feudal England not so much to protect insane persons as to protect the king's property interests. The king, as sovereign, had claims on the property administered by lords and barons. In order to prevent "insane" noblemen from squandering their property, and thus diminishing the king's revenues, the king asserted a power, as the "father" of his country, to directly control the property of insane noblemen, much as a real father would control the property of a very young child. Eventually, as the power of the English kings began to decline, they began to justify the *parens patriae* power as necessary to protect the property of the noblemen from their own insane acts. The focus thus shifted from protection of the king's property interests to protection of the insane person's property interests. But it was still *property* that was the concern. The *parens pa-*

triae power was not invoked to justify sovereign interference in the day-to-day lives of the insane poor—they were simply abandoned, or banished, or locked in basements.[9] Nor was the *parens patriae* power invoked to justify the involuntary "treatment" of insane noblemen. So long as their property was secure and could not be squandered, they were free, with few exceptions, to do as they pleased.

It is only comparatively recently that the *parens patriae* power has been invoked to justify not only sovereign control of the insane person's property, but also involuntary hospitalization and treatment of the insane person. In the United States, the *parens patriae* power began to be used as a justification for involuntary treatment only in the latter part of the nineteenth century, a period when physicians were claiming that "moral treatment" in a remote institutional setting could "cure" almost all insanity[10] (see Chapter I).

Today, the historical justifications for the *parens patriae* power have been forgotten or ignored. The *parens patriae* power is now used to justify state interference in the lives of individuals whenever the state believes those individuals are not capable of protecting their own interests.

Unlike the "police power," which is used to protect *society* from harm, the *parens patriae* power is used to protect *individuals* who cannot or will not protect themselves. The essence of the *parens patriae* power is that it authorizes the state to substitute and enforce its decisions about how individuals should live, even when those individuals are causing no direct harm to others or to society.

Statutes that permit civil commitment under the *parens patriae* power typically permit involuntary hospitalization of individuals who do not have "sufficient insight or capacity to make responsible decisions concerning hospitalization," or who are "so impaired that they are unable to understand the need for such care and treatment." Vague and circular standards such as these are used to distinguish between people who are allowed to decide for themselves about treatment and those who must accept it.[11]

There is now a discernible trend among legislatures and courts to question the constitutionality or propriety of commitments based on the *parens patriae* power. Several courts and legislatures have ruled, in effect, that *parens patriae* is not sufficient authority for commitment.[12]

In 1975, in *O'Connor v. Donaldson*,[13] a case in which a harmless patient was confined, allegedly for his own good, for nearly fifteen years, the Supreme Court ruled:

A finding of "mental illness" alone cannot justify a State's locking a person up against his will and keeping him indefinitely in simple custodial confinement. Assuming that term can be given a reasonably precise content and that the "mentally ill" can be identified with reasonable accuracy, there is still no constitutional basis for confining such persons involuntarily if they are dangerous to no one and can live safely in freedom.

. . . [T]he mere presence of mental illness does not disqualify a person from preferring his home to the comforts of an institution. Moreover, while the State may arguably confine a person to save him from harm, incarceration is rarely if ever a necessary condition for raising the living standards of those capable of surviving safely in freedom, on their own or with the help of family or friends. . . .

Mere public intolerance or animosity cannot constitutionally justify the deprivation of a person's physical liberty. . . .

In short, a State cannot constitutionally confine without more a nondangerous individual who is capable of surviving safely in freedom by himself or with the help of willing and responsible family members or friends. Since the jury found, upon ample evidence, that O'Connor, as an agent of the State, knowingly did so confine Donaldson, it properly concluded that O'Connor violated Donaldson's constitutional right to freedom.

In *Donaldson*, the Court declined to specify what reasons, if any, would justify involuntary civil commitment. The case did not raise those issues. However, on the basis of the language and reasoning of the *Donaldson* case, other federal courts that have had to face those issues in Hawaii, Iowa, Nebraska and Pennsylvania have found state laws unconstitutional because they rely only on *parens patriae* authority.[14]

Even before *Donaldson*, the Supreme Court said in *Humphrey v. Cady*[15] that it was reasonable for a state to condition confinement

> not solely on the medical judgment that the defendent is mentally ill and treatable, but also on the social and legal judgment that his potential for doing harm, to himself or others, is great enough to justify such a massive curtailment of liberty.[16]

Relying on this language, federal and state courts in Wisconsin, Pennsylvania, Michigan, Washington, Alabama, West Virginia, and Kentucky have either eliminated *parens patriae* as a basis for involuntary commitment, or have ruled that even though *parens patriae* commitments are in theory justifiable, the standard is so vague, meaningless, and unreviewable that it violates due process.[17]

In *Hawks v. Lazaro*, for example, the West Virginia Supreme Court explicitly rejected the *parens patriae* power as a basis for civil commitment[18]:

> In much the same way that the Tower of London has endured as an architectural monument since medieval times, the doctrine of *parens patriae* has endured from pre-medieval times as a monument to the state's power over the private lives of its citizens; however, in the face of constitutional principles which are antithetical to the doctrine of *parens patriae*, mere endurance no more commends the logic of that doctrine to our favorable attention than a similar endurance commends the lurid history of the Bloody Tower. . . . It can be seen that the doctrine of *parens patriae* has been suspect from the earliest times. While well-meaning people frequently attempt to operate under it for the benefit of their fellowman, it has as often been used as a justification for greedy actions on the part of relatives or for the removal of unwanted or troublesome persons. . . .[19]
>
> The standard for hospitalization for the benefit of the individual leaves an entirely subjective determination

for the committing authority which violates due process because it forecloses meaningful appeal and places an individual in jeopardy of losing his freedom without providing an objective standard against which the committing authority's determination can be measured.[20]

In other words, we allow people to drink, smoke, squander their money, work when they are physically ill, and fly balloons across the Atlantic without interference. Why should people who are called mentally disordered forfeit similar personal autonomy when their behaviors are often less harmful than the "strange" behaviors of "normal" people? As John Stuart Mill said in *On Liberty*:

The only freedom which deserves the name, is that of pursuing our own good in our own way, so long as we do not attempt to deprive others of theirs, or impede their efforts to obtain it. Each is the proper guardian of his own health, whether bodily, mental or spiritual. Mankind are greater gainers by suffering each other to live as seems good to themselves, than by compelling each to live as seems good to the rest.[21]

Second, courts recognize that the circular reasoning on which *parens patriae* commitments are based (that refusing treatment is a "symptom" of an "illness" that therefore requires forced treatment) relies on two false assumptions: (1) the mentally disordered cannot make rational decisions, and (2) if they could, they would choose treatment. Rarely are persons so disordered that they cannot function in a reasonably "normal" manner. Crisis periods and specific disabilities associated with mental disorders come and go.[22] That is, even persons labeled mentally disordered function in a reasonably "normal" manner— eating, sleeping, washing, dressing, working—most of the time. Even many involuntary commitment laws recognize this fact.[23] For example, involuntarily committed mental patients are frequently authorized to transact business, make family decisions, advise their attorneys, sign welfare applications, draft wills, and conduct their lives as best they can inside institutions. They can even choose to be voluntary instead of involuntary patients. In fact, the great majority of mental patients are at least ostensibly voluntary patients [24] (see Chapter IV). No one contests the rationality or wisdom of an individual's decision to seek psychiatric treatment. Why, then, should the same individual's decision to refuse psychiatric treatment be ignored?

Even if it were true that a particular person could not make a rational choice about treatment, why should we assume that, if capable, that individual would choose treatment? Considering all the factors—including the possibility of lifelong confinement and of treatments such as electroshock or drugs or lobotomy, the widespread failure of mental health professionals to inform mental patients about the risks and effects of treatments, the stigma of the label "mental patient," the loss of privacy, the uncertainty that cure will result from treatment, the likelihood that prolonged hospitalization will aggravate mental disorders, and the unavailability to most patients of adequately staffed and equipped facilities[25]—refusing treatment would not necessarily be an irrational choice.

Even if we could assume that a brief period of hospitalization and treatment would actually benefit the individual by improving his mental condition, after discharge the now "cured" individual may be unable to find a decent job or a decent place to live because of the ex-patient label. Given the enormous stigma of that label, it might well be more rational to refuse hospitalization and hope that the passage of time will bring improvement. Thus the old adage: "You'd have to be crazy to sign yourself into a mental hospital." When courts hear evidence of the grim custodial reality of most institutions, they question the propriety of a commitment standard that relies on a "rational" choice about the need for "treatment" because they realize the patient is not likely to receive much treatment.[26]

Finally, and perhaps most important, courts recognize that the *parens patriae* justification for involuntary hospitalization is little more than an "expert" disagreeing with a layperson about what is best for the layperson.[27] Such disagreements are necessarily subjective and therefore difficult to evaluate in judicial proceedings (see Chapter I). As a practical matter, it is nearly impossible for courts to judge the validity of a psychiatrist's opinion that a prospective patient's refusal of hospitalization is "irrational." There are simply too many variables to make objective scrutiny of such opinions possible. For example, if, after hospitalization, the prospective patient's employer would continue to promote the individual and give him positions of responsibility, refusing hospitalization might not be rational. But if the employer would lose confidence in the individual and either fire or refuse to promote him, that fact alone might make the refusal rational. There are so many variables of this type, and they vary so greatly from individual to individual, that objective evaluation of the rationality of a decision to refuse hospitalization is almost impossible. In fact, even if the prospective patient gives clearly irrational or totally incoherent reasons for refusing hospitalization ("A bird told me to refuse," "I can't go in the hospital now because my niece will be 15 next year"), the refusal might nevertheless be "rational" for other unexpressed reasons.

Recently, Professor Alan Stone offered a slight variation on "inability to make a rational choice about treatment" as a justification for involuntary commitment.[28] According to Stone, forced treatment is justified because most mental patients who are treated involuntarily will be "thankful" for the treatment when it is completed. He believes most ex-patients would say, in effect, "I am glad you treated me when I was unable to choose treatment. *Thank you* for forcing treatment on me."

One problem with this theory is that there is little or no empirical evidence to support it. Our experience suggests that Stone is wrong, and that most ex-patients deeply resent their involuntary hospitalization and treatment. But even if he is right in some cases, it is impossible prior to hospitalization to predict which persons will later say "thank you." Disregarding an individual's decision because of a psychiatric prediction that the individual will later say "thank you" is an unjustified and circular procedure, which, in practice, simply legitimizes the psychiatrist's opinion of what should be done.

The "thank you" theory, however, raises two interesting possibilities. If the only justification for involuntary treatment is that the individual will later say "thank you," and if empirical study demonstrated that the vast majority of ex-patients would *not* say "thank you," then there would be no justification for involuntary hospitalization and treatment. Also, an individual could indicate, while in a period of undoubted mental "health," that he would *not* be grateful for involuntary treatment. The individual could execute what is coming to be known as a "living will."[29] The living will would state that should the individual ever in the future be deemed by others to be mentally disordered, the individual nevertheless would not wish to be involuntarily hospitalized or treated, or would not wish to be given specific treatments such as psychosurgery or shock therapy. The living will should recite the reasons for that decision and should show that the individual clearly understands the possible benefits of treatment, the risks and consequences of refusing treatment, and the possible effects of serious mental disorder. A doctor's statement attesting to current sanity could also be included. If such living wills became common, they would eliminate any remaining arguments that a *parens patriae* or "thank you" commitment could be justified.

Largely because *parens patriae* standards for commitment are so vague and subjective, and because *parens patriae* cannot escape the circular trap of calling a refusal to be treated a symptom of a disease that requires forced treatment, courts are beginning to require proof that commitment is justified under the somewhat more objective standards of the police power.

B. POLICE POWER

The police power is distinguished from the *parens patriae* power by its purpose, which is to protect society rather than to protect individuals.[30]

Because the police power lacks the ostensibly beneficent purpose of the *parens patriae* power, it is easier to perceive that a proposed commitment under the police power creates an adversary relationship between the proposed patient and society. Of course it is often claimed that police power commitments, like *parens patriae* power commitments are "in the best interests" of the proposed patient. For example, "If Smith is not hospitalized he will assault his ex-girl friend and then he will be sent to prison, and that is not in his best interests." Analytically and realistically, however, the individual's true interests are irrelevant. It is *society's* interests that take precedence under the police power.

Because the police power is correctly perceived as pitting the state against the individual, courts and legislatures have recognized the necessity for substantive and procedural safeguards to protect the individual from a misguided or excessive exercise of state power. For example, the criminal law, which is the most severe and extensive application of the police power, requires precise standards and elaborate procedures for evaluating whether its invocation is justified in a particular case. Persons are sent to prison not because of the subjective judgment that they are "criminal types," but because of the objective judgment that they have committed specific predefined criminal acts. Those acts must be proved "beyond a reasonable doubt," to the satisfaction of a jury, under rigorous procedures (counsel, cross-examination, privilege against self-incrimination, and so forth). In short, when the police power is used in a criminal law context, the focus is not on the defendant's status, or condition, but on his acts.

On the other hand, when the police power has been used in a mental health context, the focus has been not on the prospective patient's acts, but on his status. And strict procedural safeguards equivalent to the procedures available to criminal defendants have not traditionally been available to persons said to be mentally disordered (see Chapter III). Thousands of individuals have been committed to mental hospitals not because it was proven at a trial that they committed dangerous *acts*, but because they were labeled dangerous *types* who might (or might not) commit dangerous acts in the future. Thus, until recently, the standards used for commitment under the police power and the procedures used to implement those standards have allowed judgments nearly as subjective as those on which confinement has been authorized under the *parens patriae* power.

This is changing rapidly. Courts and legislatures are now

requiring more objective standards and stricter procedures for police power commitments (see Chapter III).

The use of more objective standards and stricter procedures limits commitments under the police power, but does not totally prohibit such commitments. Actually, a strong argument can be made for prohibiting police power commitments entirely.

Although the wording varies, most states authorize involuntary hospitalization under the police power only if the prospective patient is in some way "dangerous" to others, or to himself. Some statutes simply require a finding of "dangerousness"[31]; others, a finding of "danger to the public"[32]; still another, a finding that "physical harm will be inflicted by an individual upon another, as evidenced by behavior which has caused such harm or which places another person or persons in reasonable fear of sustaining such harm."[33] Regardless of the precise wording of these statutes, the important point is that they authorize confinement of persons who have not violated the criminal law, on the basis of a finding that these persons are in some way dangerous or likely to be dangerous in the future.

Except as applied to mental patients, preventive detention is still considered an improper exercise of the police power. Society is reluctant to confine persons solely because of what they might do in the future. Probably 50 to 80 percent of all ex-felons will commit crimes after release from prison.[34] But when their sentences expire, we let them go, and do not "civilly" commit them as dangerous. Ghetto residents and teenage males are also much more likely to commit dangerous acts than the "average" citizen,[35] but we do not confine them. Of all the identifiably dangerous groups in society, only the mentally disordered are singled out for preventive detention, and they are the least dangerous group of the groups here mentioned. In fact, the evidence overwhelmingly indicates that the mentally disordered, as a class, are not more dangerous than the sane.[36]

Why should society confine a person if he is dangerous and mentally disordered, but not if he is dangerous and sane?[37] If a sane man can be dangerous, then by definition, "rationality" and awareness of the consequences of apprehension do not deter dangerous acts. It is not enough to say that the mentally disordered and dangerous person might be treated and rendered nondangerous. That argument assumes the person is dangerous *because* he is mentally disordered and would not be so if sane. Courts have difficulty enough in deciding whether a *past* act, under known circumstances, was the "product" of a mental disease, or was, instead, the product of cultural, educational, economic, familial, or other factors. Psychiatrists have not been very helpful in that regard,[38] and it is both naive and disingenuous to assume they can be more helpful in predicting whether an unspecified *future* act, under unknown circumstances, will be the "product" of a mental disease. Preventive detention of persons who are thought to be both dangerous and mentally disordered may appear to be more reasonable than preventive detention of the "sane," but it is not.

In fact, as we noted in Chapter I, psychiatrists simply cannot predict future dangerous behavior. Such predictions are wrong far more often than they are right. Accordingly, commitments based upon such predictions will necessarily be arbitrary and capricious.

There are, of course, other objections to police power commitments based on dangerousness. First, most statutes do not specify what they mean by *dangerousness*, how likely it must be or how imminent. Is danger to property enough? Must the danger be "probable," or "likely," or only "possible?" Must it be expected within the next day, or week, or year? And so on. (see Chapter III.) Because the statutes are typically vague on these points, mental health professionals rely upon their own definitions of these critical points, usually without explaining their definitions to the prospective patient or the judge. Even if cross-examination reveals what the professional's definitions are, it is impossible to determine whether those definitions were intended by the legislature to be sufficient to authorize deprivation of liberty and forced treatment.[39]

Because statutory definitions of dangerousness are usually vague, it is easy for mental health professionals to call people dangerous. As we noted, many professionals consider dangerousness a mere technicality, a magic word that must be uttered in order to "get patients the treatment they need." Psychiatrists often label prospective patients "dangerous" in order to achieve *parens patriae* purposes. In almost every commitment hearing where "dangerousness" is supposedly the major legal and factual issue, the testimony is predominantly about how "sick" the person is and how much help he needs. Only rarely do commitment decisions actually turn on whether the person's behavior constitutes a sufficient danger to satisfy the statutory requirements.[40]

Second, committing people to mental hospitals because of dangerousness makes little sense because, in general, dangerousness is not treatable.[41] Most of the mental patients who are considered dangerous do not have mental disorders, as that term is commonly understood, but personality disorders. They would more properly be diagnosed as "sociopaths." As Dr. Stone has noted:

> It is a truism in psychiatry that treatment success with personality disorders, particularly sociopaths, is quite limited. . . . Few psychiatrists are motivated or interested in treating the dangerous personality disorder. These patients are neither amenable to psychotropic drugs, nor to brief individual psychotherapy.[42]

As Dr. Stone puts it, "why confine dangerous persons to mental hospitals at all? . . . If they are truly dangerous, and if treatment is unlikely to succeed, or will take years, then surely a prison is better than a community mental health center."[43]

Accordingly, there are substantial objections to police power commitments because of dangerousness. In the short run, we believe that judicial insistence on physical dangerousness, evidenced by an overt act, is a sensible method for narrowing the class of persons subject to commitment, and thereby limiting abuse of the commitment power. In the long run, however, preoccupation with dangerousness makes little sense. We have the criminal law to confine people who commit dangerous acts. If dangerous conduct is not sufficiently dangerous to warrant criminal proscription, it is not sufficiently dangerous to warrant hospitalization.

Actually, a strong argument can be made that a finding of dangerousness should *preclude*, rather than authorize,

47

civil commitment. Dangerous people, as a class, are much more difficult to treat than nondangerous people; their presence on a ward certainly restricts the freedom of others on the ward; and associating dangerousness with psychiatric treatment further stigmatizes the nondangerous mentally disordered.

But for now, as we said, requiring proof of dangerousness as a condition of involuntary commitment seems appropriate, and whether sensible or not, seems to be, in the opinion of most judges, constitutionally required. Although the Supreme Court has not definitively resolved this issue, it has ruled that the constitution prohibits the custodial confinement, without treatment, of a mentally disordered but nondangerous individual. In *O'Connor v. Donaldson*,[44] the Court said that "a State cannot constitutionally confine without more . . . a nondangerous individual who is capable of surviving safely in freedom by himself or with the help of willing and responsible family and friends." Similarly, said the Court, "the mere presence of mental illness does not disqualify a person from preferring his home to the comforts of an institution. . . . Incarceration is rarely if ever a necessary condition for raising the living standards of those capable of surviving safely in freedom, on their own or with the help of family or friends."

A fair reading of *O'Connor v. Donaldson* suggests the following. First, the Supreme Court apparently believes that involuntary confinement simply because of mental illness and need for treatment is not constitutionally justified. There must be proof of some degree of danger to self or others. Second, the Supreme Court apparently believes that an individual cannot be considered dangerous to *self* if that individual is *surviving*—a word used three times by the Court. The important point here is that the Court has clearly rejected a "welfare" standard in favor of a "survival" standard. Thus, even if hospitalization would promote a person's welfare or be in his best interest, involuntary hospitalization will not be constitutionally permissible if the individual is surviving.

We believe that involuntary hospitalization and treatment cannot be justified on *parens patriae* or police power grounds. And we believe that, on balance, involuntary hospitalization and treatment do more harm than good.[45]

48

Proponents of civil confinement quite correctly argue that its abolition would cause much human degradation and social harm—but less, we believe, than its retention. For every man who, if at liberty, would take his life or assault his neighbor, there are thousands in confinement who would not. For every man who, if at liberty, would embarrass or destroy his career, there are thousands whose careers are destroyed because of confinement.

Accordingly, we urge courts and legislatures to begin to think seriously about alternatives other than involuntary hospitalization and treatment.

Is danger to self a justifiable basis for involuntary hospitalization and treatment?

Threatened or attempted suicide presents unique problems. There is substantial disagreement, for example, whether commitment because of suicidal behavior is based on the *parens patriae* power or on the police power. Logically, it is based on the *parens patriae* power and should be analyzed accordingly. But because the consequences of suicide are so much more substantial and irreversible for the individual than the consequences of the other types of behavior that result in *parens patriae* commitments, and because suicide creates such direct and substantial consequences for others, particularly for the family of the deceased, many authorities think of commitment because of suicidal behavior as an exercise of the police power. Whether regarded as an exercise of the *parens patriae* power or of the police power, there are substantial objections to commitment because of threatened or attempted suicide.

The first point to consider is that most people who commit suicide are not mentally disordered, or at least have not previously been diagnosed or considered to be mentally disordered. There are, after all, "rational" reasons for suicide—terminal illness, the loss (particularly in later life) of a loved one or sole companion, extreme poverty and degradation with no realistic expectation of improvement. In fact, there is some evidence that correlates "mental health" with suicide.[46]

Second, a diagnosis of mental disorder, even if reliable and valid, tells us almost nothing about whether the person so diagnosed will or will not commit suicide. It is often said that "depressed" persons are more likely to commit suicide than nondepressed persons. But of the many persons who are considered depressed,[47] few commit suicide,[48] so an accurate diagnosis of depression provides no assistance in predicting suicide. Actually, the "base rate" for suicide, even among persons who have actually attempted or threatened it, is astonishingly low. The literature suggests that only about 1 percent of all persons who have attempted suicide actually kill themselves within the following year.[49] And the base rate for suicide among people who merely talk about committing suicide is no doubt lower still. As we stated in Chapter I, accurate prediction of any event with a low base rate is almost impossible, even if the test used to make the prediction is very accurate.[50] It should not be surprising, therefore, that "prediction of the infrequent event of suicide is poor."[51] After surveying the literature, one authority concluded that "a method for distinguishing persons who will suicide from those who will not with a measure of accuracy sufficiently high to permit its use in psychiatric commitments simply does not exist at present."[52] This means that in order to hospitalize one individual who really would commit suicide if at liberty, we must hospitalize many individuals who really would not commit suicide if at liberty.[53] One authority has estimated that even using a test that is 80 percent accurate (and no suicide test we know is nearly that accurate), for every 10 truly suicidal persons we "correctly" confine, we must confine at least 240 persons who would not actually kill themselves.[54]

Third, because the decision to commit suicide is perhaps one of the most subjective and personal decisions an individual can make, it is often impossible to evaluate the "rationality" of that decision. Events that prompt one individual to commit suicide might not prompt others to commit suicide, but that does not mean the first individual's decision was, for him, in his particular circumstances, irrational. Mental health professionals usually cannot judge the "rationality" of a suicide attempt on any medical or objective scale. They must rely, instead, on their own subjective determination of "normal" and "abnormal" responses to events, a function for which they are not specially qualified by training or experience.

Fourth, except in very clear cases (for example, slashed wrists), distinguishing behavior we will call suicidal from behavior not so labeled is a very arbitrary and subjective procedure. We allow people to jeopardize their lives in many ways without calling their behavior suicidal. People are allowed to fly balloons across the ocean, climb Mount Everest, race in the Indianapolis 500, and smoke cigarettes. When Supreme Court Justice Robert Jackson had a heart attack, his physicians told him that the stress of resuming his judicial duties would kill him. And it did. But Justice Jackson was not hospitalized for suicidal behavior. To the contrary, his choice was honored. As Simon Sobeloff, Solicitor General of the United States, remarked in the official memorial to Justice Jackson before the Supreme Court on October 11, 1954:

> Associate Justice Robert Houghwout Jackson died suddenly of a heart attack on Saturday, October 9, 1954, at the age of sixty-two and at the height of his brilliant judicial career. . . . Justice Jackson had suffered a previous attack in the spring of 1954. . . . His doctor gave him the choice between years of comparative inactivity or a continuation of his normal activity at the risk of death at any time. With characteristic fortitude he chose the second alternative . . . he returned for the present term of the Court and sat at its opening session on Monday, October 4.[55]

Five days later he was dead.

Fifth, there is very little evidence that involuntary treatment reduces the rate of suicide, and there is some evidence that such treatment may even increase it.[56] There is "reason to believe that tranquilizers are ineffective in preventing suicides," and the studies of the effectiveness of ECT and other therapies "have been either inconsistent or negative."[57] On the other hand, if drugs *do* work, they too, might increase the rate of suicide: "If psychosis is . . . an escape from intolerable stresses of reality, perhaps the partial easing of the psychotic state through medication or

51

tranquilizing drugs brings these patients to a state of painful insight before they are able to cope with new insights."[58] Finally, many people kill themselves because they think of themselves as worthless human beings. To the extent that involuntary hospitalization and treatment confirms or exacerbates those thoughts, commitment may itself increase the likelihood of suicide.[59]

Courts have uniformly upheld commitments based on "danger to self" without even discussing the justification for such commitments under the police power or the *parens patriae* power. Even courts that have rejected "need for treatment" as a justification for civil commitment have upheld involuntary treatment because of danger to self.[60] Several courts have limited such commitments somewhat by ruling that an "overt act" of self-danger must be proved. [61] And some legislatures have limited the maximum permissible duration of involuntary treatment because of "danger to self."[62]

NOTES

1. *Jackson v. Indiana*, 406 U.S. 715, 737 (1972).
2. *Dixon v. Attorney General*, 325 F. Supp. 966 (M.D. Pa. 1971); *Lessard v. Schmidt*, 349 F. Supp. 1078 (E.D. Wis. 1974), *vacated on procedural grounds*, 414 U.S. 473 (1975), *reinstated* 379 F. Supp. 1376 (1974), *vacated on procedural grounds*, 421 U.S. 957, (1975), *reinstated* 413 F. Supp. 1318 (E.D. Wis. 1976); *Lynch v. Baxley*, 386 F. Supp. 378 (M.D. Ala. 1974); *Doremus v. Farrell*, 407 F. Supp. 509 (D. Neb. 1975); *Suzuki v. Quisenberry*, 411 F. Supp. 1113 (D. Ha. 1976); *In re Levias*, 83 Wn. 2d 253, 517 P. 2d 588 (1973); *In re Quesnell*, 83 Wn. 2d 224, 517 P. 2d 568 (1973); *State ex rel. Hawks v. Lazaro*, 202 S.E. 2d 109 (W. Va. 1974); *Stamus v. Leonhard*, 414 F. Supp. 439 (D. Iowa 1976); *Bell v. Wayne County Hospital*, 384 F. Supp. 1085 (E.D. Mich. 1974); *Bartley v. Kremens*, 402 F. Supp. 1039 (E.D. Pa. 1975); *vacated on other grounds*, —— U.S. ——, 97 S. Ct. 1709 (May 16, 1977); *Kendall v. True*, 391 F. Supp. 413 (W.D Ky. 1975); *Goldy v. Beal*, 429 F. Supp. 640 (M.D. Pa. 1976); *Pennsylvania ex rel. Finken v. Roop*, 339 A. 2d 764 (Pa. Super. Ct. 1975); *Suzuki v. Yuen*, —— F. Supp. ——, 46 U.S.L.W. 2181 (D. Ha.

Sept. 26, 1977); but see *Coll v. Hyland*, 411 F. Supp. 905 (D. N.J. 1976).

3. See also Szasz, *Ch. I*, n. 1; Siegel, *Ch. I*, n. 21; Roth *et al.*, *Ch. I*, n. 10; Laing, *Ch. I*, n. 1; Friedman and Daly, *Ch. I*, n. 21, Rogow, *Ch. I*, n. 1; Cooper, *Ch. I*, n. 1.

4. *Ch. I*, nn. 6 and 7.

5. *Olmstead v. United States*, *Ch. I*, n. 36, p. 478 (Brandeis, J., dissenting).

6. See Harvard Article, *Ch. I*, n. 14, pp. 1193-1201; *Lessard v. Schmidt*, *supra* n. 2; Hearings—91st, *Ch. I*, n. 6.

7. *Humphrey v. Cady*, 405 U.S. 504, 509 (1972).

8. *Black's Law Dictionary* (4th ed., 1951).

9. Jones, *Lunacy, Law and Conscience* (1955). Bethlem was "the only public hospital in England devoted to the care of the insane" (p. 11). And there the only "medical treatment . . . consisted in unvarying and indiscriminate use of weakening agents (bloodletting, forced vomiting, and so forth) to reduce violence, coupled with the frequent use of mechanical forms of restraint" (p. 16). Patients were kept in "near or complete nakedness" and were "chronically undernourished" in order to make them "more amenable" (p. 16).

10. Rothman, *Ch. I*, n. 18, and other authorities cited in note; see also Harvard Article, *Ch. I*, n. 14, pp. 1207-21; *Hawks v. Lazaro*, *supra* n. 2.

11. Brooks, *Law, Psychiatry and the Mental Health System*, (1974), Ch. 9, "Standards of Commitment"; Livermore *et al.*, *Ch. I*, n. 13.

12. *Supra* n. 2.

13. *O'Connor v. Donaldson*, 422 U.S. 563 (1975).

14. *Suzuki v. Quisenberry, Stamus v. Leonard, Doremus v. Farrell, State v. ex rel. Finken v. Roop, Goldy v. Beal*, *supra* n. 2.

15. *Humprhey v. Cady*, *supra* n. 7.

16. *Ibid.*, p. 509.

17. *Lessard v. Schmidt, Finken v. Roop, Bell v. Wayne County Hosp., In re Levias, In re Quesnell, Lynch v. Baxley, Hawks v. Lazaro, Kendall v. True*, *supra* n. 2.

18. *Hawks v. Lazaro*, *supra* n. 2, p. 117.

19. *Ibid.*, p. 119.

20. *Ibid.* p. 123.

21. J.S. Mill, "On Liberty," *The Philosophy of John Stuart Mill* (1961).

22. See generally Harvard Article, *Ch. I*, n. 14, p. 1214 and n. 80; Ennis, *Ch. I*, n. 6.

23. For example, see Rev. Code of Washington 71.05.060. (Throughout this book, many statutory examples will be

taken from the Washington State Civil Commitment Law, Rev. Code of Wash. 71.05 *et seq.* and 72.23 *et seq.* We chose the Washington statute because it was recently rated by mental health professionals as the best civil commitment statute presently in effect in the United States. Treffert and Krajeck, "In Search of a Sane Commitment Statute," *Psychiatric Annals*, p. 56/283 (June, 1976). See also Brooks, *supra* n. 11, pp. 820-23.

24. Ennis, *Ch. I*, n. 6; Wexler, "Forward: Mental Health Law and the Movement Toward Voluntary Treatment," 62 *Calif. L. Rev.* 671 (1974).

25. *Lessard v. Schmidt, supra* n. 2, p. 1094; Harvard Article *Ch. I*, n. 14, pp. 1193-1207.

26. For example, *Doremus v. Farrell* and *Hawks v. Lazaro, supra* n. 2.

27. See especially *In re Ballay, Ch. I*, n. 7, and *Lessard v. Schmidt, Stamus v. Leonard, Finken v. Roop, Kendall v. True, Bell v. Wayne County Hosp., Hawks v. Lazaro, Goldy v. Beal, In re Levias,* and *In re Quesnell, supra* n. 2; Coombs, "Burden of Proof and Vagueness in Civil Commitment Proceedings," 2 *Am. J. Crim. L.* 47 (1973).

28. Stone, *Ch. I*, n. 13, pp. 66-70.

29. Harvard Article, *Ch. I*, n. 14, p. 1218.

30. *Ibid.*, pp. 1222-40; Kittrie, *Ch. I*, n. 18, pp. 58-59.

31. For example, Cal. Wel. & Institutions Code §5150.

32. Minnesota, Minn. Stat. Ann. §253.07A subd. 17 (c) (Supp. 1973).

33. Rev. Code Wash. 71.05.020(3).

34. Not all of those crimes will be detected or prosecuted. But relying only on crimes that are detected, we can say that the recidivism rate in New York City is 73 percent. In New York federal institutions, the rate is 63 percent. And in New York State institutions the rate is 52 percent. "Albany Report Calls Jails 'Crime Breeding Grounds,'" *The New York Times,* Nov. 10, 1969, p. 30.

35. E.g., *Report of the National Advisory Commission on Civil Disorders* (1968), pp. 128-35; *Youth in the Ghetto* (Harlem Youth Opportunities Unlimited, Inc., 1964), pp. 137-60: juvenile delinquency rate for Central Harlem is two to three times higher than the New York City average; narcotics use in Central Harlem is ten times the city rate; and the homicide rate is six times the city rate. See also Livermore *et al., Ch. I*, n. 13, pp. 76-77: "By combining background environmental data, we can identify categories of persons in which we can say that fifty to eighty percent will engage in criminal activity within a short period of time. If social protection is a sufficient justifica-

tion for incarceration, this group should be confined as are those criminals who are likely to sin again."

36. Ennis and Litwack, *Ch. I*, n. 6, p. 716, n. 73, 74, and 145, and the authorities cited therein; Stone, *Ch. I*, n. 13, pp. 25-37; Gulevich and Borene, "Mental Illness and Violence" in Gilula and Ochberg, *Violence and the Struggle for Existence* (1970), p. 309; NIMH, *Schizophrenia—Is There An Answer?* (1972); Greenland, "Evaluation of Violence and Dangerous Behavior Associated with Mental Illness," 3 *Sess. in Psychiat.* 345 (1971); Schmideberg, "The Promise of Psychiatry: Hopes and Disillusionment," 57 *N. W. U. L.* Rev. 19 (1962).

37. Livermore *et al.*, *Ch. I.*, n. 13, pp. 76-77, 83, and 85. Dershowitz, "The Role of Law and the Prediction of Harmful Conduct," reprinted in Katz, Goldstein, and Dershowitz, *Psychoanalysis, Psychiatry and Law* (1967), p. 588: "If the function of involuntary hospitalization is the preventive detention of dangerous people, then why should it matter whether such people are, or are not, 'mentally ill.' If a 'mentally healthy' person is sufficiently dangerous, why should he not be confined?" Similarly, approximately 70 percent of all suicides are committed by persons who have not been considered mentally ill. Clinard, *Sociology of Deviant Behavior* (1957), p. 425. See also E. Durkheim, *Suicide* (1951), especially pp. 66-67. If prevention of a suicide is a legitimate social goal, why should we not confine all potential suicides, whether sane or insane?

38. See, for example, *Washington v. United States*, *Ch. I*, n. 16, in which the court ruled that psychiatrists should not be permitted to give an opinion on whether a criminal act was the "product" or "result" of mental illness.

39. Stone, *Ch. I*, n. 13, pp. 25-37.

40. *Ibid.*, pp. 34-35; Shah, *Ch. I*, n. 10.

41. Stone, *Ch. I*, n. 13, pp. 36-37.

42. *Ibid.*, p. 36 (footnotes omitted).

43. *Ibid.*, p. 37.

44. *O'Connor v. Donaldson, supra* n. 13.

45. See authorities cited in *Ch. I*, nn. 6 and 7.

46. See *Ch. I*, n. 14, especially Harvard Article, p. 1227 and fn. 141.

47. In 1975, between four and eight million Americans suffered from depressive disorders, and 350,000 Americans were hospitalized because of depressive disorders. (Provisional figures provided by Robert Hirschfeld, M.D., Depression Section, Clinical Research Branch, DERP, National Institute of Mental Health.)

48. One study of male veterans diagnosed as "depressives"

found the annual suicide rate to be 0.566 percent, Greenberg, *Ch. I*, n. 14, p. 260.

49. *Ibid.*
50. *Ibid.*, pp. 262-63, and authorities cited therein; Murphy, *Ch. I*, n. 14.
51. Murphy, *Ch. I*, n. 14, p. 357.
52. Greenberg, *Ch. I*, n. 14, p. 263.
53. See *Ch. I*, n. 14.
54. Greenberg, *Ch. I*, n. 14, p. 262.
55. 99 L. Ed. 1311-12.
56. Greenberg, *Ch. I*, n. 14, pp. 236, 250, 256-59.
57. *Ibid.*, pp. 256-57.
58. Pokorny, "Myths About Suicide," in *Suicidal Behavior: Diagnosis and Management* (H. Resnick, ed. 1968), p. 64.
59. Greenberg, *Ch. I*, n. 14, pp. 258-59.
60. *Supra* n. 2.
61. *Lessard v. Schmidt, Lynch v. Baxley, Bell v. Wayne County Hospital, Finken v. Roop, Doremus v. Farrell, supra* n. 2; see also Rev. Code Wash. 71.05.020(3).
62. See Rev. Code Wash. 71.05 *et seq.* (limit of 107 days); Cal. Welf. and Inst. Code §5150 *et seq.* (West, 1972) (limit of 17 days).

III

The Civil Commitment Process

What are the emerging standards for civil commitment?
As we said in Chapter II, courts and legislatures are limiting the *standards* under which people can be involuntarily hospitalized and treated. The clear trend is to require proof of physical danger to self or others,[1] based on evidence of overt acts, threats, or attempts of a dangerous nature in the recent past,[2] and to prohibit involuntary hospitalization if "need for treatment" is the only reason for hospitalization. In this chapter we will discuss the emerging *procedural* protections that prospective patients can use to resist involuntary hospitalization.

What is the doctrine of the least restrictive alternative?
One of the most important developments in recent years has been the application, in the mental health context, of the constitutional doctrine of the least restrictive alternative.[3] The doctrine, which originated in other types of constitutional cases,[4] means essentially that even if the government's purpose is legitimate, it must implement that purpose in the way that least restricts fundamental personal liberties. Under that doctrine, no one can be committed to a mental hospital if there are less restrictive alternatives. For example, if conditional release to family or friends, outpatient care in the community, or a period of residence in a halfway house would be sufficient to achieve the purposes of a particular commitment, forced treatment in a hospital would be unconstitutional.

The doctrine of the least restrictive alternative can also be used throughout hospitalization and after hospitalization. It can be used, for example, to test the appropriateness of particular forms of treatment. Similarly, a change in the mentally disordered person's condition, or a showing that the security of a hospital is no longer necessary for a particular patient, may require transfer to a less restrictive ward or other environment. Thus, even within a hospital, transfer from a secure ward to an open ward may be constitutionally required by this doctrine.[5] The argument for the least restrictive alternative is very powerful, especially when courts hear the convincing evidence in studies, experiments, and expert opinions that hospitalization is itself harmful, and that treatment in the community or in less severe conditions is almost always more appropriate.[6]

Several statutes incorporate this requirement explicitly.[7] But whether or not statutes spell out the requirement, most commitment statutes are sufficiently ambiguous about the right to the least restrictive alternative to allow judicial interpretation consistent with the right.[8] Some statutes and court decisions even require the state to prove affirmatively, after investigation, that no less restrictive alternative is available at the time of commitment.[9] And one court has ruled that the right to the least restrictive alternative requires the government to *create* less restrictive alternatives when none are currently available.[10]

The right to the least restrictive alternative thus gives even persons who are otherwise committable a powerful defense. Even if the criteria for forced treatment are otherwise satisfied, the state must nevertheless prove that the specific conditions of confinement are the least restrictive available for the prospective patient. Many witnesses, including nonexperts who have observed the person in the past, may testify on that issue. Persons who operate community facilities can compare their residents to the person being considered for commitment. And the person who faces commitment may thus be able to convince the court that hospitalization is unnecessary.

In the commitment process, the right to the least restrictive alternative often provides an opportunity to reveal the superficiality of many psychiatric judgments (see Chapter I). Rarely will state psychiatrists or other state witnesses thoroughly explore alternatives. Usually, an independent expert can be found to suggest viable alternatives to hospitalization.

Finally, it may even be argued that if a less restrictive facility would be appropriate but none is actually available because that type of facility is full or has not yet been built, commitment is unconstitutional. Although, as a practical matter, many courts will be reluctant to accept this argument, they can be reminded of the basic rule that lack of financial resources is no defense when state action or lack of action abridges a constitutional right.[11] Whether the right to the least restrictive alternative is a right only to available alternatives or to possible but nonexistent alternatives is at present unresolved. But one court has decided that a statute that guarantees a right to treatment requires that mental hospitals be responsible for creating alternatives to hospitalization.[12] If this view of the least restrictive alternative is widely accepted, a mental health system will be created which has so many alternative facilities that outpatient care may become attractive enough to diminish involuntary treatment to a fraction of what it is today.

For a time, an ambiguous Supreme Court decision, *State v. Sanchez*,[13] created doubt whether the Court would apply the doctrine of the least restrictive alternative to civil commitment. But as the National Association of Attorneys General has pointed out,[14] the Court's decision in *O'Connor v. Donaldson*,[15] a mental health case in which the Court cited *Shelton v. Tucker*,[16] the leading least restrictive alternative case, has now put that doubt to rest. In *O'Connor*, the Court relied on *Shelton v. Tucker* in ruling:

> [W]hile the State may arguably confine a person to save him from harm, incarceration [in a mental hospital] is rarely if ever a necessary condition for raising the living standards of those capable of surviving safely in freedom, on their own or with the help of family or friends.[17]

"Thus the Court for the first time indicated that persons may not be constitutionally 'incarcerated' if less restrictive alternatives would be sufficient. *O'Connor* ratified prior decisions ignoring or discounting *State v. Sanchez*. Courts now will be constitutionally obligated to find involuntary hospitalization impermissible if individuals can merely survive outside the hospital, either on their own or with the assistance of family or friends."[18]

What are the emerging procedural rights in the civil commitment process?

In addition to narrowing the permissible standards for civil commitment, courts and legislatures are expanding the procedural rights prospective patients can use to resist involuntary hospitalization. Although the procedures vary greatly from state to state, there is a common thread that runs through most of the recent statutes and decisions: courts and legislatures now seem willing to give prospective patients substantially the same procedural rights they would have if charged with a crime. In the following sections, we will discuss the emerging procedural rights.

The purpose of procedural rights is to assure that people who do not meet the *standards* for commitment will not be involuntarily hospitalized or treated. Narrowing the *standards* for commitment is meaningless unless there are procedures to prepare for, present, and evaluate evidence that tends either to prove or disprove that the standard is met in each case. Thus every procedural right assures that fewer people will be committed in violation of statutory or constitutional commitment standards.

A. THE RIGHT TO COUNSEL

Most states provide by statute that persons facing involuntary hospitalization have a right to be represented by a lawyer during the judicial hearing. And several courts have indicated that the Constitution requires the appointment of lawyers for patients who wish to contest hospitalization.[19] If the person does not have enough money to pay an attorney of his choice, a free lawyer will be provided by the court. But the right to a lawyer—the single most important right for ensuring that the prospective patient will benefit from other legal rights—is not nearly as comprehensive or straightforward as this statutory and constitutional guarantee might suggest. For example, having a free lawyer will not help the prospective patient very much unless the lawyer is appointed sufficiently in advance of the hearing to permit adequate preparation. Civil commitment hearings are actually quite complicated. A lawyer who meets his client only at or shortly before the hearing will not have time to read the hospital records, interview witnesses, decide on strategy (for example, should the prospective patient testify or not), or gain the confidence of his client.

Similarly, a great many important legal decisions must be made well before the judicial hearing. Often the patient must affirmatively request a judicial hearing or there will not be one. Patients need legal advice and assistance to make and implement that decision. There are different types of judicial hearings (for example, statutory review hearings are likely to be quite different from habeas corpus hearings), and patients need legal help in deciding which type of hearing to choose. Many other prehearing decisions require legal assistance. Should the patient talk with the staff? (See H. "Self-Incrimination"). Should the patient accept or refuse medication? (See G. The Right Not to be Drugged at a Hearing). And so on. For these reasons, courts are requiring the appointment of counsel as early in the proceedings as possible.[20] In our view, every person should automatically be assigned a lawyer either before deprivation of liberty or within 24 hours after hospitalization.

Most lawyers have little or no psychiatric expertise and tend to defer to the judgments of mental health professionals. They accept as "true" such diagnoses as "schizophrenia," "paranoid," and "manic." They also accept predictions of danger and conclusions about a person's competence without bothering to find out how superficial and inaccurate those judgments usually are (see Chapter I). They believe that treatment will work. They do not read ward charts or medication schedules, or question witnesses before hearings. And worst, but most common of all, they pay little or no attention to the wishes of their clients.[21]

Like most "normal" people, lawyers feel uncomfortable around a client whose thoughts or behaviors are difficult to understand. They often want to "help" the client by hospitalizing him against his wishes. Lawyers often trust the doctors, police, and prosecutor more than their client, and they rarely challenge or adequately cross-examine the testimony of persons recommending hospitalization. Very often, lawyers substitute their judgments for their client's, without any consultation. They believe that the hospital is the best place for their client and they therefore do little or nothing to prevent hospitalization (see Chapter VIII).

Many lawyers who represent prospective patients act not as lawyers ordinarily do (seeking to implement their client's wishes), but as "guardians *ad litem*." Guardians *ad litem* are permitted and encouraged to ignore their client's wishes if, in their opinion, the client's wishes would not be in the client's "best interests." Guardians *ad litem*, who in effect act as counsel *and* guardians at the same time for the same person, are appointed in this dual capacity before any judicial hearing. Their decision about the mental capacity of a client determines whether they act as advocate for their client, the traditional lawyer's role, or whether they simply waive their client's right to contest commitment. By acting both as guardians *ad litem* and as counsel, they have a conflict of interest. If a guardian *ad litem* believes treatment is necessary, he can ignore statutory and constitutional objections to hospitalization that the client would otherwise raise, and in effect consent to hospitalization. For example, guardians *ad litem* have often consented to the hospitalization of clients who were not at all dangerous to self or others.[22] To do this, the guardian simply waived the prospective patient's rights to the procedures available to contest commitment.

The client's right to a jury, proper notice, competent evidence, cross-examination, his own expert witness, statutory time limits, and other important procedural rights have been routinely waived by guardians. Under these circumstances, commitments went smoothly and "hearings" took five or ten minutes.[23] Clients often protested, but their protests were ignored or interpreted as additional evidence of "mental illness," "lack of impulse control," or "dangerousness."

But the use of guardians *ad litem* in civil commitment cases, in lieu of more traditional legal representation, is rapidly diminishing, and is now widely recognized as unconstitutional.[24] Lawyers who represent persons alleged to be mentally disordered must abide by the Code of Professional Responsibility.[25] They must follow their clients' wishes. In essence, courts are ruling that substituted judgments, whether by doctors or by lawyers, cannot be permitted when important substantive or procedural rights are at stake.

As one court said when a guardian *ad litem* waived a jury trial against the wishes of an allegedly mentally disordered person:

[T]he assistance of counsel, as guaranteed by both Federal and State Constitutions, amounted to a 15-minute conversation by the guardian *ad litem* with the appellant. No meaningful form of representation can occur (1) if the guardian *ad litem* does not provide the accused with an attorney other than himself, when he believes that his role as guardian does not contemplate acting as advocate, (2) if the guardian *ad litem* fails to call any witnesses on behalf of the alleged mentally ill person when the record indicates that witnesses are present at the hearing, (3) if the guardian honestly believes the "best interests" of the defendant will be served but the entire hearing is devoid of any instance of discussion between guardian and client to determine the best interests of the defendant. Such a passive role of an attorney as guardian *ad litem* becomes even more critical and suspect where this guardian must represent all other persons on the court's calendar for that day, and where on subsequent days different guardians *ad litem* are appointed for the accused, whose only actions on her behalf comprise waiving her right to trial by jury contrary to her timely demand therefore.[26]

Just like "normal" people, the mentally disordered and persons alleged to be mentally disordered need vigorous advocates when important rights are at stake in a legal proceeding. There is convincing evidence that when attorneys do actively represent persons alleged to be mentally disordered, fewer commitments occur.[27] Hospital personnel and psychiatrists do not like to have their judgments questioned and will often withdraw a commitment petition if they encounter substantial resistance (see Chapter VIII).

B. THE RIGHT TO JUDICIAL HEARINGS

Until recently, many people were involuntarily hospitalized for substantial periods of time without ever appearing before a judge for a judicial hearing on the propriety or legality of hospitalization. They were simply hospitalized on the authority of a "certificate of mental illness" signed by one or two physicians. Other states authorized commitment after a hearing before a special commission, usually composed of two or more doctors and perhaps an attorney. Many states still rely upon commission hearings rather than judicial hearings, and very few states mandatorily *require* judicial hearings prior to final commitment.[28] But though judicial hearings are not usually mandatory, they are usually authorized at the *request* of the prospective patient.[29] Of the very recent federal commitment cases, one court ruled that judicial hearings are required.[30] One suggested that commitment based only on a "commission" hearing would be constitutional.[31] But even in that case, the patient could obtain a "prompt *de novo* review by the district court" of the commission's decision. It is clear that patients have a constitutional right to a hearing before some independent tribunal—either a court or a commission—prior to final commitment. And though the point has not yet been resolved, most courts have ruled that judicial hearings, not just commission hearings, are constitutionally required. In our view, a view shared by most courts that have considered the issue, prospective patients should have a constitutional right to *judicial* hearings *prior* to hospitalization in nonemergency situations, and to *judicial* hearings *promptly* after hospitalization in emergency situations.

Whether the hearing is before a court or a commission, there are two kinds of hearings. The first is usually called a "probable cause" hearing, and the second is usually called a "final" hearing.[32] Many states provide only final hearings. The purpose of a probable cause hearing is to determine whether there is substantial evidence that the prospective patient meets the standards for involuntary hospitalization. If there is, the patient is usually hospitalized until a final hearing can be arranged. The major advantages of probable cause hearings are that they can usually be held more quickly than can final hearings, and if the patient loses, the loss does not constitute a decision that the patient actually meets the standards for commitment, but only that there is substantial evidence to that effect. The major disadvantages of probable cause hearings are that the patient and his lawyer have less time to prepare a defense, and less evidence of mental disorder or dangerousness will be required than at a final hearing.

It is not yet clear whether probable cause hearings are constitutionally required. And it is not entirely clear how quickly probable cause or final hearings must be held. It is clear, however, that patients who did not receive a hearing prior to hospitalization have a right to some form of hearing promptly after hospitalization.

One court has required a hearing within 48 hours,[33] to decide whether probable cause to hospitalize exists. Others have allowed slightly longer prehearing confinements.[34] Recent commitment statutes usually require a probable cause hearing within a few days after hospitalization[35] and a final hearing approximately two weeks after the probable cause hearing.[36]

It is usually to the patient's advantage to have a hearing as soon as possible. A great deal happens during the initial period of hospitalization. Patients are drugged, shocked, diagnosed, and dressed in hospital clothes. These facts may make it more difficult for the patient to convince a judge (or commission) that he does not require hospitalization. In addition, hospitalized patients may lose jobs, friends, property, or the custody of their children.

As noted, some states still authorize final commitments based only on the decision of a "commission." We believe that at least the final decision, and preferably all probable cause decisions, should be made by judges or juries. Commissions are usually composed of a panel of two or more doctors. Sometimes they include lawyers or other professionals, such as a psychologist.[37] The commission's jurisdiction is usually granted by statute and is generally under the supervision of a lower court. But no judicial officer empowered to deprive a citizen of liberty is present at commission hearings.

Naturally, commission hearings are less formal than court hearings. Usually commissions meet in hospitals in a room on the ward and the public is effectively, if not explicitly, excluded, even if the person who faces commitment wants a public hearing. Rarely are commission members familiar with the legal rights discussed in this section; and if they are, they often consider such rights to be ritualistic, technical, and nonessential. Sometimes they decide cases by majority vote.[38] Commissioners often permit and even encourage patients to waive important rights, even when the patient lacks the capacity to make a knowing and voluntary waiver (see L. Waiver). Even when procedural errors are recognized by commissioners, their response will often be that they are "technical," or "so what, let's proceed."

The use of commissions is consistent with the medical model (see Chapter I), but inconsistent with the legal model. In our view, allowing nonjudicial officials to deprive individuals of liberty is both unconstitutional and unwise. Judicial officers are trained to decide questions that involve mixed ethical, legal, social, and medical questions, whereas doctors' expertise is limited to medicine. Judicial officers are trained to decide facts and evaluate the credibility of witnesses, but doctors rarely have similar expertise. Commissions are more likely to commit than judges, both because they are more likely to believe in the medical model and because they are more likely to be influenced by the possibility of adverse public reaction if a noncommitted person should ever injure himself or others. For these reasons, we believe patients should have an opportunity for a *judicial* hearing at some point prior to final commitment.

C. NOTICE

Until recently, prospective patients were either given no notice that they were about to be committed, or were given only a very terse notice just hours, or even minutes, before commitment.

The rationale given for eliminating notice was the claim made by some mental health professionals, with little or no evidence to support it, that prior specific notice would traumatize or disturb a mentally disordered person. That claim presupposed that the person was mentally disordered, a fact not yet proven, and it assumed that notice would "aggravate" any mental disorder that did exist. In our opinion, however, and in the opinion of many psychiatrists, any trauma that might occur because of notice is inconsequential compared with the trauma of confinement without notice and opportunity to oppose.[39] At any rate, it is now clear that a meaningful form of notice well in advance of any judicial hearings is constitutionally required.[40]

Although the precise timing and content of the required notice vary from state to state, the following points seem clear. At least one day prior to a probable cause hearing, and several days prior to a final hearing, the person facing commitment should be given a written notice, in a language he understands, which states the time and place of the hearing, the name, address, and telephone number of the attorney who will represent him, the statutory standard under which he may be committed, the rights he has prior to the hearing and at the hearing, the reasons and *specific facts* that are alleged to justify commitment, the names of all persons who will testify in favor of hospitalization, and the substance of their testimony.[41]

D. THE RIGHT TO A FREE AND INDEPENDENT EXPERT WITNESS

As we indicated in Chapter I, we believe mental health professionals are not "experts" at making the kinds of judgments that are relevant in a civil commitment proceeding. Accordingly, we believe mental health professionals should not be permitted to testify as "experts" in civil commitment cases.[42] They should be permitted to give *factual* testimony, just like any lay witness (for example, "I saw Mr. Smith hit his wife"), but they should not be permitted to give *opinion* testimony (for example, "In my opinion, Mr. Smith will injure his wife if he is not hospitalized"). Courts are beginning to question the "expertise" of mental health professionals,[43] and we believe that, eventually, the role of the "expert" in civil commitment proceedings will be greatly diminished.

In most commitment cases in the near future, however, an "expert" will testify in favor of commitment, and it will therefore be important for prospective patients to rebut the effect of such testimony by presenting "experts" who will testify that hospitalization is not necessary, that less restrictive alternatives would suffice, that the prospective patient is not mentally disordered or dangerous, and so on. Otherwise, the court or jury will probably simply adopt the opinion of the "expert" recommending hospitalization.

Most prospective patients cannot afford to hire an "expert." Accordingly, the right to a free expert, appointed at state expense, is a very important right. Several courts, and at least two legislatures, have recognized a right to free expert witnesses.[44]

Prospective patients should be aware, however, that use of an "independent" expert may not always be to the patient's advantage. The independent expert may agree with the state's expert, or be unwilling to testify about the unreliability of psychiatric diagnoses and predictions. If the independent expert prepares a report, the persons recommending hospitalization may be able to obtain the report by discovery. And it is unlikely that the doctor-patient privilege will prevent disclosure of the independent expert's opinion.

On the other hand, an expert who opposes commitment, or is willing to explain the deficiencies of psychiatric diagnoses and predictions, is very helpful. And as a practical matter, the patient's chances of winning a commitment hearing will be substantially increased if he can call at least one independent expert. This means that prospective patients should use independent experts, but they should use care in the selection of those experts. Psychiatrists who tend to oppose involuntary hospitalization in all but a very few cases are now fairly common and willing to testify. Often experts with this "progressive" point of view are more effective in court than are the few psychiatrists who oppose all involuntary commitments. Judges view "abolitionists" as "kooks" because the judges themselves commit people every day. But "progressive" psychiatrists will almost always testify convincingly for some less restrictive "treatment" of which the expert has personal knowledge. Also, the "progressive" is usually aware of the professional literature on faulty diagnoses and predictions. At least he will say that involuntary hospitalization is, at best, only an unsatisfactory last resort, and that predictions that someone is *not* dangerous are much more likely to be correct than predictions that he is. If an expert will testify in any manner against commitment, it is likely that at least a sufficient doubt will be raised so that if the judge or jury follows the prescribed burden of proof (see J. "Burden of Proof"), commitment will be avoided.

The key is knowing the expert's general point of view and probable opinions beforehand. This takes savvy and experience. But the right to an expert will be much less valuable if the person who faces commitment does not have the right to choose that expert. Some statutes grant this right specifically.[45] Some courts permit it as a practical matter by their appointment procedures. But most statutes and courts limit appointment of an independent expert to psychiatrists the court chooses. Usually, these are experts who are not as "progressive" as those otherwise available to the person who faces commitment.

Thus, whether the right to an expert is an advantage depends on whether there is a realistic choice.[46] Courts so far have decided only that an independent expert is required, not that there is a right of choice.[47]

Substantial arguments can be made in support of a right to select an independent expert.[48] Due process (fairness) requires an independent judgment because, as we have shown (Chapter I), judgments made by mental health professionals, including those who recommend hospitalization, are not very reliable. If the state is permitted to use such unreliable testimony, the patient should have the same right. The state selects its expert, and the patient should similarly be allowed to select his expert. The right to the effective assistance of counsel may in turn require that counsel be assisted by an expert chosen by counsel to explain the basis of the state expert's opinion and to assist in preparing a defense. The constitutional right to present witnesses may also require that patients be permitted to choose expert witnesses. Equal protection may require that poor patients be able to choose experts just as rich patients can.

In our view, the state should provide each prospective patient with a reasonable amount of money, sufficient to retain at least one expert witness. The patient and his lawyer could then select an expert of their choice. Should it develop that the expert's testimony would not be favorable to the patient, the expert would not be called as a witness, and his report would be confidential. The patient would then have to retain another expert, with whatever funds were left, or go to trial without an expert.

One final note: As with the appointment of counsel, choosing and working with the independent expert must be done as early as possible. The patient's lawyer will need extensive contact with the expert in order to judge whether he will help or hurt. In most cases, at least two one-hour-long examinations of the person who faces commitment *and* two lengthy conversations with counsel are necessary to establish knowledge and credibility superior to the state's expert, and to prepare an effective defense.

E. DISCOVERY

Ordinarily, litigants in civil cases can use various legal procedures (subpoenas, requests to produce documents, depositions, interrogatories, and so forth) to learn, or "discover," information known to the other side. In most civil litigation, pretrial "discovery" is considered a very important part of the litigation process.

Involuntary hospitalization is considered to be a civil procedure, and there is every reason why the traditional discovery methods should be used in such proceedings. But in practice, few patients (or their lawyers) have even tried to use discovery methods in civil commitment cases. If they did, they could find out in advance much more about what the state's "expert" is likely to say at the hearing. They could examine all relevant hospital records. They could even find out if there were disagreements among the staff concerning the necessity for hospitalization.

Only a few courts have considered this issue, but there is growing recognition that prospective patients should be able to use the same discovery methods as other civil litigants.[49]

F. PRESENCE AT THE HEARING

Like any other party to a legal proceeding, whether civil or criminal, a person who faces commitment has a right to attend and participate in the hearing. The person also has a right to be present at all conferences, either in "open court" or "in chambers," where discussions take place that concern his case. Presence is necessary to preserve and implement other legal rights, including effective assistance of counsel and confrontation of adverse witnesses. For example, new allegations of fact may be made for the first time during courtroom testimony. The person who faces commitment may be the only one who can correct false allegations or, at least, give true allegations a different weight or perspective. Also, decisions about commitment will be more informed if the judge or jury has an opportunity to observe the prospective patient's appearance, demeanor, and behavior in the courtroom.

There are few commitment hearings where there is any reason even to consider excluding the prospective patient from the courtroom. Exclusion is based on the unsupported notion that a due process hearing will harm the person. This presumes that the allegation that the person is mentally disordered is true before the hearing to decide that issue is even held. It also assumes that mentally disordered people are harmed by fair hearings.

It is also possible that due process hearings might harm persons charged with crime, but no one has ever suggested the routine exclusion of criminal defendants from the courtroom. And we are aware of no studies that even claim that mentally disordered people are harmed more by fair hearings than are "normal" people. To the contrary, many mental health professionals believe that fair hearings are therapeutic for prospective patients.[50]

On occasion, persons who face commitment get angry during commitment hearings. Often they have legitimate complaints about the way the hearing is being conducted and are unable to restrain themselves from protesting. But the occasional difficulty caused by permitting patients to be present at their hearings is no reason to deny the right to be present to everyone who faces commitment. Guaranteeing meaningful exercise of the other legal rights discussed in this chapter often depends on the person's presence, and that fact is more important than the small possibility that harm will occur. Exclusion from the courtroom should occur only when the hearing actually cannot proceed because of the disruptive behavior of an unruly person.[51] At that point, as in any other case, the court may exclude the prospective patient if exclusion is absolutely necessary for the hearing to continue. Short delays or warnings should be tried before exclusion. If exclusion is ordered, the court should do everything it can to permit as much participation as possible by the excluded individual, including the continued assistance of counsel and access by microphone and television to the hearing.

We believe every prospective patient should be permitted to attend his commitment hearing unless and until his courtroom behavior so disrupts the proceeding that it cannot continue without his exclusion. With but one exception of which we are aware, every recent decision on this issue agrees with this position.[52]

G. THE RIGHT NOT TO BE DRUGGED AT A HEARING

By the first court appearance, most people who face civil commitment have been hospitalized for several days. Usually, doctors will already have administered powerful sedatives or other drugs that affect the way they think and act. Often the hearing is held before "correct" dosages are determined. As a result, many people who face civil commitment are overdrugged, and most are under the influence of drugs.

As anyone who has used alcohol or marijuana or any mind-altering drug knows, such drugs substantially affect an individual's ability to defend himself in a court proceeding. For some patients, mind-altering drugs used in mental hospitals make them feel as if they were "tipsy" from alcohol. For others, the drugs induce drowsiness and sleep. Drugs cause many patients to get very dizzy. They usually slow speech. In almost every case, the effects of drugs will be noticeable to the judge, lawyers, witnesses, and jury. (For more information on drugs see Appendix B.).

Of course, drugs may also calm agitated patients and may otherwise make a patient better able to function and present a stable appearance at a commitment hearing. (see Chapter VIII). But forced drugging prior to the initial hearing is, in our view, unjustifiable. It presumes that the allegation of mental disorder is true, and that drugs are an appropriate response, before there is an opportunity to contest either of those assumptions. The effects of drugs inhibit the exercise of all the procedural rights theoretically available to individuals who face commitment, and abridge privacy rights and the right to think and speak guaranteed by the First Amendment. (see Chapter VI). But worst of all, in the commitment process, drugging unduly influences the judge and jury. Even if the person can overcome this disadvantage, judges and juries often conclude that the only reason the person does not seem to be overtly crazy and dangerous is because he is "on drugs," which the psychiatrists claim are helping him, and which they say he will not continue to get unless he is committed.

The decision to accept or refuse drugs before a hearing is very difficult.[53] In our opinion, patients should have an option. They should not be prevented from taking hospital-prescribed drugs they believe will make them feel or appear better. But there is no justification for forced drugging before the appropriateness of commitment is tested at a hearing.

Federal courts in Michigan, Nebraska, Wisconsin, Alabama, and Hawaii have discussed the issue of prehearing drugging. The Nebraska court banned all prehearing treatment, including drugging.[54] The Michigan court prohibited prehearing drugging unless absolutely necessary to prevent physical injury.[55] The Wisconsin, Alabama, and Hawaii courts prohibited forced drugging that inhibits a meaningful opportunity to participate, because drugging to that extent interferes with the right to be "present" at hearings.[56]

H. SELF-INCRIMINATION

One of the most difficult questions considered by recent decisions is whether the privilege against self-incrimination applies in civil commitment proceedings.[57] The core concept of the privilege is clear: the state cannot compel an individual to testify against himself during a criminal proceeding. And with minor exceptions that are not here relevant, it is equally clear that even before criminal proceedings have begun, the state cannot compel an individual to say things that the state may later use against the individual in a criminal proceeding. Beyond this, the scope of the privilege is not entirely clear. For example, if there is no coercion, must the state warn the individual that he has a right to keep silent, or may the state itself keep silent and later use the individual's uncoerced statements against him? For present purposes, the major questions are whether the state may coerce an individual to say things that the state may later use against him, and whether the state may keep silent and later use an individual's uncoerced statements against him not in a criminal proceeding, but in a civil proceeding.

In the context of ordinary civil proceedings, where loss of liberty is not a possibility, the state can probably coerce an individual to say things that may be used against him, and can almost certainly use the individual's uncoerced statements without first warning the individual of his "right" to keep silent. The complicating factor, of course, is that involuntary hospitalization proceedings are not like ordinary civil proceedings. They involve deprivation of liberty, stigma, and other consequences comparable in seriousness to criminal proceedings. For this reason, several courts have decided, when considering the applicability in hospitalization proceedings of the privilege against self-incrimination and other constitutional rights, that the "civil" label should be ignored, and involuntary hospitalization proceedings should be analyzed as the functional equivalent of criminal proceedings.[58]

In criminal proceedings, the law is clear that a statement may be considered "coerced" even if the state does not use physical force to compel that statement. The general rule in criminal proceedings is that whenever an individual is in "the custody" of the police (is arrested or otherwise detained), the probability of subtle or indirect coercion is so great that the state must warn the individual that he has a right to keep silent. If it does not, coercion will be presumed, and statements made by the individual without such a warning cannot be used against him.[59]

In our opinion, the subtle and indirect coercive effects of hospital custody are at least as substantial as the coercive effects of police custody. Patients, like prisoners, have been deprived of liberty and separated from family and friends. They find themselves in an unfamiliar environment, at a time when they are likely to be agitated or depressed. Prisoners, at least, have a right to be released from custody on bail within a short period of time. But patients do not have a right to bail, and they are likely to be confined until the hospital staff decides to let them go. Prisoners are automatically given legal assistance within a matter of hours. Patients may not be assigned a lawyer unless they affirmatively ask for one, and even then, they are likely not to see an attorney for days or weeks. Prisoners are at least presumed to be mentally capable of protecting their own interests. Patients are in custody because they are alleged to be mentally disordered. Prisoners are not given mind-altering drugs, ECT, or other treatments that lessen their ability to remain silent or otherwise resist the coercive pressures of confinement. Patients are. Finally, and perhaps most important, prisoners know that the police are their adversaries. Patients are told, again and again, that the doctors are their friends and want only to help them. And the average mental health professional is probably much more adept and experienced at eliciting information from an uncooperative individual than is the average police officer.

Thus, at least with respect to the element of coercion, hospital custody is probably much more coercive than police custody. It just does not seem fair (even though mental health professionals are attempting to treat at the same time they are evaluating patients) to trick or induce patients into saying things that will later be used to justify their involuntary commitment. For these reasons, several courts have ruled that the privilege against self-incrimination should apply to involuntary hospitalization proceedings.[60] The extent to which the privilege will apply is not yet clear, but in our opinion, patients should at least be told that what they say may be used as evidence of mental disorder or dangerousness, and thus to justify involuntary hospitalization.

We also believe that if involuntarily confined patients are forced to speak with psychiatrists, or choose to do so, they should have the right to have their lawyer present during the interview. There is some judicial support for this position.[61]

Finally, lawyers should advise patients that they may have a constitutional right to remain silent. Whether it is advisable to exercise that right will depend on the circumstances of each case. If it is likely that a brief conversation with the psychiatrist will persuade the psychiatrist to release the patient, silence may not be advisable. Similarly, the patient might agree to talk with the psychiatrist but only if the psychiatrist promises not to testify against the patient or disclose the patient's statements to anyone else, including other staff members.

I. THE RULES OF EVIDENCE

Judicial hearings are usually conducted under specific rules of evidence that govern the use of documents and the admissibility of testimony. Although those rules of evidence could be applied to involuntary hospitalization proceedings, until recently this was rarely done. Usually there was no discussion of the applicability of the rules—no one raised the issue. When the issue was raised, mental health professionals would claim that use of the rules would cause trauma or psychological harm to the prospective patient. There is very little evidence to support that claim, and no evidence that more trauma would be caused by applying the rules than by ignoring them. Many mental health professionals believe that denying patients the protection of the rules of evidence is far more traumatic than applying the rules.[62]

Strict application of the rules of evidence would make it more difficult to prove that involuntary commitment is necessary. This is the real reason many mental health professionals oppose application of the rules. The problem with this position is that commitment should not be easy. Individuals should be deprived of liberty and subjected to involuntary treatment (if at all—see Chapters I and II) only as a last resort, and only if the need for hospitalization is fully and fairly established. If a person is not so disturbed as to be committable under the usual rules of evidence, he should not be committed at all.

The purpose of the rules of evidence is to assure that only reliable, accurate, and trustworthy evidence is the basis for judicial decisions. Only this type of "admissible" evidence should serve as the basis for decisions that affect the substantial interests of persons involved in civil commitment proceedings. Even if we could assume that persons recommending hospitalization never lie about the underlying facts, and are motivated by the prospective patient's "best interests," the rules should apply because they are designed to keep witnesses not only honest but careful.

The most common abuse of the rules of evidence is the routine use of "hearsay" evidence. Doctors and staff testify about what other staff told them in order to prove that the person who faces commitment did something or said something. Often hospital records (which may arguably be admissible as a business record exception to the rule against hearsay, or may be made admissible by statute) are used as evidence against the prospective patient. Hearsay is inadmissible in part because it is unreliable, but also because it deprives the opposing party of the right to cross-examine the person who made the statement. Without the right of cross-examination, the right to assistance of counsel and the right to confront witnesses are also impaired. For example, statements on a ward chart that a doctor said the prospective patient "threatened dangerous acts" or "was aggressive" will influence the judge or jury even though there may be no opportunity to show by cross-examination of the doctor that he was referring only to idle talk on the ward or boisterousness.

Five courts have recently considered the applicability of the rules of evidence to involuntary hospitalization proceedings, and have decided that the rules are applicable.[63] Other courts have ruled that specific rules of evidence (for example, the rule against hearsay) are applicable.[64] And at least one statute specifically guarantees application of the rules in involuntary hospitalization proceedings.[65]

J. BURDEN OF PROOF

It is generally accepted that the state must prove the prospective patient meets the standard for commitment.[66] The degree of proof required (or how convincing the proof must be on each element of the standard) is less clear.

Traditionally, the state had only to bear a burden of "preponderance of evidence." That is, if the fact finder believed that it was more probable than not that each element of the standard—usually mental disorder and dangerousness—was present, then the person could be committed. Recently, several courts have ruled that the "preponderance" burden is too lax,[67] and that the state must prove each element "beyond a reasonable doubt"—the burden the state must bear in every criminal case.[68] These courts viewed the loss of liberty through civil commitment as equivalent to criminal sanctions. They also believed that requiring proof "beyond a reasonable doubt" would somewhat compensate for the inherent unreliability of psychiatric testimony and for the vagueness of many commitment standards.

Other courts have also increased the burden of proof required in civil commitment, but they have required a slightly lower standard—"clear, cogent, and convincing" proof.[69] This burden is defined as somewhere between the "preponderance of the evidence" and the "beyond a reasonable doubt" burdens.[70]

The burden of proof is a rather abstract concept, but it can also be an important trial argument with crucial practical effect. Generally, the law imposes high burdens of proof when it is deemed desirable to reduce the number of wrong decisions in circumstances where wrong decisions are particularly intolerable.[71] For example, the "beyond a reasonable doubt" standard protects defendants in criminal cases in order to assure that as few as possible of the wrong decisions that are inevitably made will result in convicting innocent people. Thus "beyond a reasonable doubt" permits many defendants who are actually guilty to go free so that few defendants who are actually innocent will go to prison. The innocent are protected at the expense of society, which must suffer the consequences of allowing the guilty who are found not guilty to go free. The "beyond a reasonable doubt" standard is thus an expression in legal terms of the very high value we place on liberty. Society would rather suffer the consequences of criminals walking the streets than increase the chance that liberty will be unjustly deprived.[72]

By requiring higher standards of proof, courts are attempting to compensate for the arbitrariness of commitment. They are ruling that if mistakes are to occur, we should err in favor of liberty.

On a practical level, higher standards of proof can be a major protection for those who face civil commitment. Mental disorder, dangerousness, and the absence of less restrictive alternatives must all be proven to the required degree. In almost every case, powerful arguments can be made that danger and lack of less restrictive alternatives have not been proved even by "clear, cogent, and convincing" evidence, much less "beyond a reasonable doubt."

K. JURY TRIAL

In most criminal cases (including most misdemeanors), and in every civil case for damages where more than a small amount of money is sought, there is a constitutional right to a jury trial if requested. But most involuntary hospitalization proceedings are held before commissioners or judges.

It is unlikely that the Due Process Clause of the Constitution requires a right to a jury trial for persons who face commitment.[73] Juveniles who face indefinite detention do not have that right.[74] But the Equal Protection Clause requires that if other persons in similar situations have the right to a jury trial, then persons who face commitment do. Based on this reasoning, several courts have ruled that the Equal Protection Clause requires a jury trial for persons in the commitment process because other statutes guarantee jury trials for persons in other proceedings that cannot reasonably be distinguished from commitment proceedings.[75] Thus a constitutional right to a jury trial is probably limited to states in which juries are guaranteed by statute to people who face comparable legal proceedings. Many states, however, provide a *statutory* right to a jury trial in involuntary hospitalization proceedings.[76]

Whether a person who faces commitment should request a jury trial is a difficult question. The answer depends on the attitudes of people in the particular geographic area where the jury will be selected. The Supreme Court has said, "The jury serves the critical function of introducing into the process a lay judgment reflecting values generally held in the community, concerning the risks of potential harm that justify the state in confining a person for compulsory treatment."[77] But it is hard to judge whether prospective jurors will doubt or believe psychiatrists, or whether they will be willing to tolerate harmless mental disorders. Some lawyers with expertise in this area believe that jurors from very small towns and from big cities will be tolerant of deviance. Jurors from medium-sized towns and small cities may be more likely to emphasize normality and conformity. It is impossible, however, to make generalizations about jurors by geographical location, social class, sex, or race. In Washington, D.C., public defenders have been more successful representing people who face commitment before juries than before judges. In Seattle, Washington, the opposite is true.

L. WAIVER

The rights we have been discussing will not benefit prospective patients if they are waived. For example, if the patient or his lawyer does not object to the use of hearsay, failure to object will constitute a waiver of the rule against hearsay. Similarly, in many states even such important rights as the right to a lawyer or to a judicial hearing are not automatic. Unless the patient *affirmatively requests* a lawyer or a hearing, he will be *presumed* to have *waived* those rights.

In criminal cases, the Supreme Court has ruled that defendants cannot, by their inaction, be deemed to have waived such important constitutional rights as the right to a lawyer or to a hearing.[78] And the Supreme Court has ruled that a defendant in a criminal case does not, by mere inaction, waive his right to a hearing to determine his competence to stand trial.[79]

In our opinion, waiver of any of the important rights involved in a civil commitment proceeding should be considered invalid and of no effect unless the waiver meets the tests for a valid waiver that have long been applied in criminal cases. That is, the waiver must be affirmative—mere silence or inaction cannot be deemed a valid waiver. It should be voluntary—that is, without duress or coercion. And it should be "knowing and intelligent"—that is, based on full comprehension of the importance of the right being waived and of the consequences of waiver. Finally, the decision whether there has been a valid waiver under these three tests should be made, as in criminal proceedings, by a judge on the basis of actual evidence.

We also believe that unless the individual has already been adjudged mentally incompetent (not just mentally ill), no third party, including the individual's lawyer, should be permitted to waive the individual's constitutional rights.[80]

Recently, courts have become sensitive to the problems of waiver (either affirmative or by inaction) in civil commitment cases, and have specified much more stringent procedures for judging the validity of waivers.[81] Several courts have ruled that the right to be present at the hearing can *never* be waived,[82] and one authority believes that the right to a lawyer should not be waivable.[83]

We believe persons who have not been adjudicated incompetent should be permitted to waive *any* right, if a judge finds the waiver meets the three tests outlined above. Of course, some rights (such as the right to counsel) are more fundamental than others (such as the right to exclude hearsay). Waiver of the most important rights should be very thoroughly examined by the court after counsel has already been assigned and has consulted with the person who wants to waive the right. This means that the right to counsel, unlike other rights, should be waivable only after the individual has met with counsel.

Finally, in our opinion, the patient should always refuse

81

to waive any right, no matter what the judge or his attorney says, unless he understands specifically what will happen if he waives that right and how waiver will benefit his case. "Saving time," the most common reason for most waivers, is usually an inadequate reason for waiver.

M. RECORD OF THE PROCEEDINGS

As with any case that goes to court, it is essential for purposes of appeal to have a complete verbatim record of the proceedings. If crucial evidence or statements by the judge are missing from the record, it is likely that the right to appeal will effectively be lost. Without a record, it is impossible to verify whether alleged legal mistakes actually occurred. And without a record, it is often difficult to show that even admitted legal errors were prejudicial or resulted in the decision to commit. To assure that civil commitments are as reviewable as other cases, courts have specifically recognized the right to a record.[84]

As a practical matter, judges and lawyers sometimes talk "in chambers" and "off the record." These discussions may seem minor and irrelevant at the time, but often key decisions are made during these "off the record" conversations. Many lawyers are so intimidated by judges that they will not demand that decisions be made "on the record," or if they are made "off the record," the lawyer will fail to repeat the decision and the reasoning behind it "for the record" when record-taking is resumed. But if decisions are made "off the record," it is likely they will be unreviewable on appeal.

N. APPEAL AND OTHER POSTCOMMITMENT RIGHTS

As a practical matter, most appeal and similar postcommitment rights are useless because it will take more time to enforce them than the patient will probably be confined. But because many commitments are indefinite, and have lasting legal and practical effects even after release, postcommitment legal rights are nevertheless important remedies.

Appeal is the usual remedy for a dissatisfied party to a legal proceeding.[85] But appeal usually takes much too long. For an appeal, the entire transcript of the commitment hearing must be typed, and then appellate court procedures allow several months for briefs to be filed before oral argument. Even after oral argument, cases are rarely decided for several months.

Special remedies called "extraordinary writs" are the alternative. These include writs of habeas corpus, *certiorari, mandamus,* prohibition, and *coram nobis.* Each permits a challenge of the propriety of a public official's action, in this case the action of the committing judge. But before courts will accept these writs, the patient must show that no other remedy, including appeal, is meaningfully available. Thus the court must be convinced that an appeal will take too long.

These extraordinary writs are interchangeable in most jurisdictions. Often a state statute consolidates all of these remedies in one course of action. But regardless of the particular procedure, these writs may provide a quicker way to challenge the denial of rights that resulted in an unconstitutional or clearly unfair commitment by the committing judge. But even if another judge evaluates the proceedings that resulted in civil commitment, he will rarely change the committing court's decision unless the error was clear and contributed directly to commitment.

NOTES

1. *Ch. II,* n. 2
2. *Ch. II,* n. 61
3. Chambers, *Ch. I,* n. 6, *Lessard v. Schmidt, Lynch v. Baxley, Suzuki v. Quisenberry, Dixon v. Atty. General., Stamus v. Leonhard, Ch. II,* n. 2, *Welsch v. Likins,* 373 F. Supp. 487 (D. Minn. 1974); partially vacated on other grounds, 550 F.2d 1122 (8th Cir. 1977); *Covington v. Harris,* 419 F.2d 617 (D.C. Cir. 1969); *Wyatt v. Stickley,* 344 F. Supp. 373 (M.D. Ala., 1972); *aff'd sub nom. Wyatt v. Aderholt,* 503 F.2d 1305 (5th Cir. 1974). See also Justice Burger's concurring opinion in *O'Connor v. Donaldson,* 422 U.S. 563, 580-

89 (1975); and Harvard Article, *Ch. I*, n. 14, pp. 1245-53. *J. L. et al. v. Parham*, 412 F. Supp. 112 and 141 (M.D. Ga. 1976), *appeal pending*, ——— U.S. ——— (no. 75-1690, May 31, 1977); Ennis and Friedman, Vol. II, *Legal Rights of the Mentally Handicapped*, *Ch. I*, n. 6, p. 991; see also *Eubanks v. Clarke*, ——— F. Supp. ———, 46 U.S.L.W. 2026 (E.D. Pa. July 1, 1977).

4. *Shelton v. Tucker*, 364 U.S. 479 (1960).
5. *Covington v. Harris*, *supra* n. 3.
6. See *Ch. I*, n. 6 and 7.
7. See, for example, Rev. Code Wash. 71.05.230, 240, 290, 320; and N.Y. Mental Hyg. Law §31.27 (d).
8. See Chambers, *Ch. I*, n. 6, pp. 1138-45.
9. *Lynch v. Baxley*, *Ch. II*, n. 2; also *supra* n. 7.
10. *Dixon v. Weinberger*, 405 F. Supp. 974 (D.D.C. 1975); see also *NYSARC v. Rockefeller*, 393 F. Supp. 715 (EDNY 1975); *Morales v. Turman*, 383 F. Supp. 53 (E.D. Tex. 1975), *vacated on other grounds*, 535 F. 2d 864 (5th Cir. 1976), *reinstated*, ——— U.S. ———, 97 S.Ct. 1189 (Mar. 21, 1977).
11. See Ennis and Friedman, *Ch. I*, n. 6, Vol. III, pp. 1187-88.
12. *Dixon v. Weinberger*, *supra* n. 10.
13. *State v. Sanchez*, 457 P. 2d 370 (N. Mex. 1969), *appeal dismissed for want of a substantial federal question*, 396 U.S. 276 (1970).
14. Schmidt, *The Right to Treatment in Mental Health Law*, The National Association of Attorneys General (1976).
15. *Ch. II*, n. 13.
16. *Supra*, n. 4.
17. *O'Connor v. Donaldson*, *Ch. II*, n. 13, p. 575.
18. Schmidt, *supra* n. 14, p. 54 (footnotes omitted).
19. *Lynch v. Overholser*, 369 U.S. 705 (1962); *Specht v. Paterson*, 386 U.S. 605 (1967); *Heryford v. Parker*, 396 F.2d 393 (10th Cir. 1968); *Thornton v. Corcoran*, 407 F.2d 695 (D.C. Cir. 1969); *People ex. rel. Rogers v. Stanley*, 17 N.Y.2d 256 (1966); *Dixon v. Atty Gen'l, Lessard v. Schmidt, Bartley v. Kremens, Lynch v. Baxley, Bell v. Wayne County Hosp., In re Quesnell, Suzuki v. Quisenberry, Doremus v. Farrell, Stamus v. Leonhard*, *Ch. II*, n. 2; *Sarzen v. Gaughan*, *Ch. I*, n. 16; *In re Fisher*, 39 Ohio 2d 71 (1974); *Wisconsin ex rel. Memmel v. Mundy*, No. 441-417 (Cir. Ct. Milw. Wisc., 441-417 Sept. 1976), and *on appeal*, 249 N.W.2d 573 (1977). Harvard Article, *Ch. I*, n. 14, pp. 1283-91; Ennis and Friedman, *Ch. I*, n. 6, Vol. I, pp. 117-22, and Vol. III, pp. 1365-66. See also authorities in Hearings—91st, *Ch. I*, n. 6; and authorities cited

infra n. 27. See, in general, *Argersinger v. Hamlin*, 407 U.S. 25 (1972).

20. Early appointment of counsel was specifically required in *Lynch v. Baxley, Doremus v. Farrell, Suzuki v. Quisenberry, Bell v. Wayne County Hosp., Stamus v. Leonhard, Ch. II*, n. 2; also *Heryford v. Parker, Sarzen v. Gaughan supra* n. 19.

21. See, for example, the description of representation in Milwaukee ruled unconstitutional in *Memmel, supra* n. 19.

22. Wexler, *Ch. II*, n. 24, p. 676, fn. 17.

23. See *In re Quesnell, Ch. II*, n. 2, and Cohen, "The Function of the Attorney and the Commitment of the Mentally Ill," 44 *Tex. L. Rev.* 424, 427-30 (1966); Wexler and Scoville, "The Administration of Psychiatric Justice: Theory and Practice in Arizona," 13 *Ariz. L. Rev.* 1 (1971).

24. *Lessard v. Schmidt, Lynch v. Baxley, Hawks v. Lazaro, Suzuki v. Quisenberry, Doremus v. Farrell, In re Quesnell*, and *Bell v. Wayne County Hosp. Ch. II*, n. 2. All hold that prospective patients have a constitutional right to adversary counsel, not just to a guardian *ad litem*.

25. For example, *Hawks v. Lazaro* specifically requires attorneys to follow the Code of Professional Responsibility; see also American Bar Association, Special Committee on Evaluation of Ethical Standards, Code of Professional Responsibility, Canon 5 (1969).

26. *In re Quesnell, Ch. II*, n. 2, p. 575.

27. See studies cited in Andalman and Chambers, "Effective Counsel for Persons Facing Civil Commitment: A Survey, a Polemic, and a Proposal," 45 *Miss. L.J.* 43 (1974); Gupta, "New York's Mental Health Information Service: An Experiment in Due Process," 25 *Rutgers L. Rev.* 405, 437-38 (1971); Wenger and Fletcher, "The Effect of Legal Counsel on Admissions to a State Mental Hospital: A Confrontation of Professions," 10 *J. Health & Soc. Behav.* 66 (1969). See generally, for articles on the role of attorneys at commitment hearings, Litwack, "The Role of Counsel in Civil Commitment Proceedings: Emerging Problems," 62 *Calif. L. Rev.* 816, 838 (1974); Galter, "The Role of Defense Counsel in Civil Commitment Hearings," 10 *Am. Crim. L. Rev.* 385, (1972); Comment "A Constitutional Right to Court Approved Counsel for the Involuntarily Committed Mentally Ill: Beyond the Civil-Criminal Distinction," 5 *Seton Hall L. Rev.* 64 (1973); Mutnick and Lazar, "A Practical Guide to Involuntary Commitment," 11 *Willa. L.J.* 315 (1975).

28. Treffert, *Ch. II*, n. 23.

29. For example, N.Y. Ment. Hyg. Law §31.39 (34A McKinneys Supp. 1973).
30. *Suzuki v. Quisenberry, Ch. II*, n. 2.
31. *Doremus v. Farrell, Ch. II*, n. 2.
32. See, for example, Rev. Code Wash. 71.05.200, 310, and 320.
33. *Lessard v. Schmidt, Ch. II*, n. 2.
34. *Bell v. Wayne County Gen'l Hosp., Lynch v. Baxley, Bartley v. Kremens, Doremus v. Farrell, Suzuki v. Quisenberry, Stamus v. Leonhard, Ch. II*, n. 2, allow confinement from five to seven days before an initial hearing.
35. For example, Calif. Welf. & Institn's Code §5250 and Rev. Code Wash. 71.05.210 (72 hours); see generally, Roth et al., *Ch. I*, n. 21.
36. For example, Rev. Code Wash. 71.05.290, 300, 310; Calif. Welf. & Institn's Code §5250 (14 days); *Bell v. Wayne County Hosp., Lynch v. Baxley, Bartley v. Kremens, Doremus v. Farrell, Kendall v. True, Suzuki v. Quisenberry, Stamus v. Leonhard, Ch. II*, n. 2 (require "probable cause" hearings with a final hearing soon afterwards). See also *Thompson v. Hensley, —— F. Supp. —— (D.N.Mex., Civil No. 74-279, Memorandum Opinion of Dec. 23, 1975), summ. aff'd*, 45 U.S.L.W. 3305 (Sup. Ct. Oct. 18, 1976), approving a five-day period of emergency hospitalization without a judicial hearing, of persons certified to be dangerous by one physician and confirmed within 24 hours after hospitalization by a second physician.
37. See, for example, *Stamus v. Leonhard, Ch. II*, n. 2, for the Iowa practice.
38. *Ibid.*
39. See, for example, Deposition of Israel Zwerling, M.D., reproduced in Ennis and Friedman, *Ch. I*, n. 6, Vol. I, pp. 521-23. Kittrie, "Compulsory Mental Treatment and the Requirements of 'Due Process,'" 21 *Ohio St. L.J.* 28, 47 (1960).
40. *Dixon v. Atty Gen'l, Lessard v. Schmidt, Lynch v. Baxley, Bell v. Wayne County Hosp., Hawks v. Lazaro, Kendall v. True, Bartley v. Kremens, Suzuki v. Quisenberry, Doremus v. Farrell, Stamus v. Leonhard, Ch. II*, n. 2; see also Harvard Article, *Ch. I*, n. 14, pp. 1273-75.
41. *Ibid.*
42. See Ennis and Litwack, *Ch. I*, n. 6.
43. *Ch. I*, n. 16.
44. *Stamus v. Leonhard, Dixon v. Atty Gen'l, Ch. II*, n. 2; *Proctor v. Harris*, 413 F.2d 383 (D.C. Cir. 1969); *Miller v. Blalock*, 356 F.2d 273 (4th Cir. 1966); *Watson v. Cameron*, 312 F.2d 878 (D.C. Cir. 1962); see also Rev. Code Wash.

71.05.300, and N.Y. Judiciary Law §35; Farrell, "The Right of an Indigent Civil Commitment Defendant to Psychiatric Assistance of His Choice at State Expense," 11 *Idaho L. Rev.* 141 (1975); see Ennis and Friedman, *Ch. I*, n. 6, Vol. I, pp. 120-23.

45. Rev. Code Wash. 71.05.300.
46. Dershowitz, *Ch. I*, n. 21.
47. See cases *supra* n. 44.
48. Farrell, *supra* n. 44.
49. *Lessard v. Schmidt*, and *Lynch v. Baxley*, Ch. II, n. 2, contemplate discovery for prospective patients; *Bell v. Wayne County Hosp.*, *Hawks v. Lazaro*, *Kendall v. True*, *Suzuki v. Quisenberry*, *Doremus v. Farrell*, *Stamus v. Leonhard*, *Ch. II*, n. 2, require specific and detailed notice sufficiently in advance so that some discovery may take place; *Sas v. Maryland*, 334 F.2d 506, 512 (4th Cir. 1964), approves of discovery procedures available under state law prior to civil defective delinquency commitments; see also *Memmel v. Mundy*, *supra* n. 19.
50. See *supra* n. 39.
51. See *Bell v. Wayne County Gen'l Hosp.* Ch. II, n. 2; *Illinois v. Allen*, 397 U.S. 337 (1970).
52. *Lessard v. Schmidt*, *Lynch v. Baxley*, *Bell v. Wayne County Hosp.*, *Kendall v. True*, *Hawks v. Lazaro*, *Bartley v. Kremens*, *Doremus v. Farrell*, *Suzuki v. Quisenberry*, *Stamus v. Leonhard*, *Finken v. Roop*, *Ch. II*, n. 2; see also, *Specht v. Patterson*, *supra* n. 19; but see *Coll v. Hyland*, *Ch. II*, n. 2.
53. Kutner, "The Illusion of Due Process in Commitment Proceedings," 57 *Nw. U. L. Rev.* 383 (1962); Wexler et al., *supra* n. 23.
54. *Doremus v. Farrell*, *Ch. II*, n. 2.
55. *Bell v. Wayne County Hosp.*, *Ch. II*, n. 2.
56. *Lessard v. Schmidt*, *Lynch v. Baxley*, *Suzuki v. Quisenberry*, *Ch. II*, n. 2; see also Rev. Code Wash. 71.05.200, which allows patients to refuse drugs for 24 hours before an initial hearing.
57. Ennis, "Mental Illness," *1969-1970 Annual Survey of American Law*, New York University Law School, p. 29; Note, "*Miranda* on the Couch: An Approach to Problems of Self-Incrimination, Right to Counsel, and *Miranda* Warnings in Pre-Trial Psychiatric Examinations of Criminal Defendants," 11 *Colum J. Law & Soc. Prob.* 403 (1975); Aronson, "Should the Privilege Against Self-Incrimination Apply to Compelled Psychiatric Examinations?" 26 *Stan. L. Rev.* 55 (1973); Fielding, "Compulsory Psychiatric Examination in Civil Commitment and the Privilege

Against Self-Incrimination," 9 *Gonz. L. Rev.* 117 (1973); see also Harvard Article, *Ch. I*, n. 14, pp. 1303-13.

58. *Lessard v. Schmidt, Suzuki v. Quisenberry, Ch. II*, n. 2; see also *In re Ballay, Ch. I*, n. 7; *Baxstrom v. Herold*, 383 U.S. 107 (1966); *Specht v. Patterson, supra* n. 19; *Humphrey v. Cady, Ch. II*, n. 7; see Justice Douglas' concurrence in *McNeil v. Director, Paxtuxent Institution*, 407 U.S. 245, 257 (1972) *Suzuki v. Yuen*, ——— F. Supp. ———, 46 U.S.L.W. 2181 (D. Ha. Sept. 26, 1977).

59. *Miranda v. Arizona*, 384 U.S. 436 (1966).

60. *Lessard v. Schmidt, Finken v. Roop, Suzuki v. Quisenberry, Ch. II*, n. 2; *Memmel v. Mundy, supra* n. 19.

61. *Finken v. Roop, Ch. II*, n. 2; but see in same note, *Lessard v. Schmidt, Hawks v. Lazaro*. See also, *Lee v. County Court*, 27 N.Y.2d 432, 318 N.Y.S.2d 705 (1971).

62. *Supra* n. 39.

63. *Lessard v. Schmidt, Lynch v. Baxley, Doremus v. Farrell, Suzuki v. Quisenberry, Finken v. Roop, Ch. II*, n. 2.

64. *Hawks v. Lazaro, Bartley v. Kremens, Stamus v. Leonhard, Ch. II*, n. 2.

65. Rev. Code Wash. 71.05.250.

66. For example, *Lessard v. Schmidt, Lynch v. Baxley, Ch. II*, n. 2.

67. *Lessard v. Schmidt, In re Levias, Lynch v. Baxley, Hawks v. Lazaro, Doremus v. Farrell, Suzuki v. Quisenberry, Stamus v. Leonhard, Ch. II*, n. 2; see also *In re Ballay, Ch. I*, n. 7, and *United States ex rel. Stachulak v. Coughlin*, 520 F.2d 931 (7th Cir., 1975).

68. *Lessard v. Schmidt, In re Levias, Suzuki v. Quisenberry, Ch. II*, n. 2; *In re Ballay, Ch. I*, n. 7; *Stachulak v. Coughlin, supra* n. 67.

69. *Lynch v. Baxley, Hawks v. Lazaro, Bartley v. Kremens, Doremus v. Farrell, Stamus v. Leonhard, Finken v. Roop, Ch. II*, n. 2.

70. *In re Levias, Ch. II*, n. 2.

71. See *In re Ballay, Ch. I*, n. 7.

72. *Ibid.*

73. *Lynch v. Baxley, Suzuki v. Quisenberry, Doremus v. Farrell, Ch. II*, n. 2.

74. *McKiever v. Pennsylvania*, 403 U.S. 528 (1971).

75. *Lessard v. Schmidt, Lynch v. Baxley, Bell v. Wayne County Hosp., In re Quesnell, Suzuki v. Quisenberry, Ch. II*, n. 2; see also *Humphrey v. Cady, Ch. II*, n. 7; *Baxstrom v. Herold, supra* n. 58; *Gomez v. Miller*, 337 F. Supp. 386 (S.D.N.Y. 1971), *aff'd*, 412 U.S. 914 (1972); *Memmel v. Mundy, supra* n. 19.

76. Rev. Code Wash. 71.05.310; N.Y. Ment. Hygiene Law § 31.35.
77. *Humphrey v. Cady, Ch. II*, n. 7, p. 509.
78. *Johnson v. Zerbst*, 304 U.S. 458 (1938); and cases cited in Ennis and Friedman, *Ch. I*, n. 6, Vol. III, p. 1199.
79. *Pate v. Robinson*, 383 U.S. 375 (1966); see also *Covey v. Town of Somers*, 351 U.S. 141 (1956).
80. See, for example, *In re Quesnell, Ch. II*, n. 2.
81. *Lynch v. Baxley, Kendall v. True, Doremus v. Farrell, In re Quesnell, Finken v. Roop, Ch. II*, n. 2; see also *Anderson v. Solomon*, 315 F. Supp. 1192, 1194 (D. Md 1970); *Heryford v. Parker, supra* n. 19; *Fuller v. Mullinax*, 269 S.W. 2d 72 (Mo. 1954); and *Memmel v. Mundy, supra* n. 19.
82. *Lessard v. Schmidt, Ch. II*, n. 2, p. 1091; Hawks v. Lazaro, *Ch. II*, n. 2, p. 125; but see *Coll v. Hyland, Ch. II*, n. 2.
83. See Kittrie *Ch. I*, n. 18, p. 403.
84. *Lessard v. Schmidt, Lynch v. Baxley, Hawks v. Lazaro, Suzuki v. Quisenberry, Ch. II*, n. 2.
85. Appeal rights are specifically guaranteed in *Hawks v. Lazaro, Lynch v. Baxley, Suzuki v. Quisenberry, Ch. II*, n. 2; see also *Memmel v. Mundy, supra* n. 19.

IV

"Voluntary" Hospitalization

Who are the "voluntary" patients in mental hospitals?

Statistics for mental hospitalization in the United States for 1972 show that so-called voluntary patients outnumber involuntarily committed persons.[1] In Europe, the percentage of "voluntaries" compared with involuntary patients is even higher than in this country.[2] This is a new phenomenon; traditionally, almost all patients were involuntarily committed.[3]

In our opinion, a great many "voluntary" patients are really involuntary patients, and for that reason we have used quotation marks around the word *voluntary*.[4] It is unrealistic to describe them as true voluntary patients for three reasons. First, most of them do not want to be mental patients. They are in the hospital because they have no place else to live, or because of substantial pressure from courts, friends, or family. Second, most "voluntary" patients have almost no understanding of what it means to be a voluntary patient, or of their rights as a voluntary patient. And third, "voluntary" patients are not, in most hospitals, treated any differently from involuntary patients.

First, some people sign into mental hospitals in order to avoid criminal charges. By accepting "voluntary" status they can bargain for dismissal of the charges. Others are convicted, and as a condition of probation or parole agree to sign in as "voluntary" patients rather than be sent to prison. Children in the custody of their parents are committed to "voluntary" status by their parents, even though they protest (see discussion below). Guardians frequently commit an "incompetent" ward as a voluntary patient, even though the ward protests. This happens more often in jurisdictions where involuntary commitment procedures are protective but guardianship procedures are lax.[5] Still others choose "voluntary" status to avoid what they are told is the less advantageous status of "involuntarily committed mental patient." Many involuntarily committed patients "convert" to "voluntary" status after hospitalization. A great many patients who are called "voluntary" patients would more accurately be described as "nonprotesting" patients. They usually have no other place to live, so they accept hospitalization even though they do not want it. Many old people in mental hospitals are in this category. And finally, there are some, apparently a very few, who without threat or coercion simply choose hospitalization,[6] usually because family, friends, or mental health workers have convinced them that hospitalization will help them.

The category of "voluntary" patient includes all these different groups primarily because the mental health system attempts to avoid the appearance of coercion whenever possible. Mental health professionals believe treatment will be more effective if patients can be convinced they are voluntarily seeking it, even when they are not.[7] Also, to the extent that outsiders believe treatment is voluntary, there will be less criticism or scrutiny. Hospital personnel would rather be thought of as caring for voluntary patients than for involuntary patients. By expanding the category of "voluntary" to include many patients who are actually involuntary, fewer hearings are necessary and the process of justifying commitment can be avoided.

Second, few people who choose voluntary status know what they are getting into when they "sign in." Often the outside pressures cause them to minimize or rationalize the profound loss of liberty they are about to accept. Even more often, they simply have no idea and are not told about the conditions they will live under or the rights they will forfeit during their daily life in the hospital. Prospective patients rarely see the ward where they will live or meet the staff or patients with whom they will live before they accept voluntary status. Very few have any idea how they will react to whatever treatments are provided.

Recent studies have shown that most "voluntary" patients have no real comprehension of what it means to be a voluntary patient. In one study, only 8 of 100 "voluntary" patients were rated fully informed concerning the terms of their admission.[8] In another, of 40 "voluntary" patients interviewed between one and three days after admission, 2 denied signing the voluntary admission form, 24 did not remember signing the form, and 13 seriously distorted or could not recall the content of the form.[9] In effect, 39 of the 40 "voluntary" patients had no concept of their status or rights.

In Chapter VI, we will talk about the concept of "informed consent." In general, the law is beginning to require "informed consent" before certain psychiatric treatments can be used. Because the decision to accept voluntary status is, in practical effect, a consent to those treatments, that decision, too, should require informed consent. If it did, there would be very few "voluntary" patients.

Third, the day-to-day life of "voluntary" patients is indistinguishable from the day-to-day life of involuntary patients. They live on the same wards, eat the same food, wear the same clothes, and see the same staff. "Voluntary" patients are now so common that they are no longer considered a special class entitled to special care. Quite the contrary, *involuntary* patients often get more attention because of their protests and the need to prepare reports about them for courts; "voluntaries" languish as a result of their passiveness and the absence of any outside pressure.[10] "Voluntary" patients are also denied many of the legal protections, including precommitment hearing procedures and postcommitment periodic reviews, that are available to involuntary patients. These procedures focus attention on patients who would otherwise be lost in the typical large-hospital routine.

The label "voluntary" has been loosely and indiscriminately applied, without regard for reality. A similar gap between promise and reality—between the promise of treatment and the reality of custodial care—prompted federal judges to examine the rights of involuntary patients. The gap between the "voluntary" label and reality may prompt increased judicial attention to the rights of "voluntary" patients.[11]

What rights to release do "voluntary" patients have?

Surprisingly, very few. Most people, including most "voluntary" patients, assume that because the patients chose hospitalization, if they do not like it, they can leave at any time. But that assumption is far from the truth.

Most states prohibit voluntary patients from leaving when they request release. This is done in several ways. The statute either sets a time (two, five, ten, or even thirty days) after the request for release during which the hospital may continue to detain the patient in order to decide whether to file *involuntary* commitment proceedings,[12] or requires voluntary patients to agree at the outset to remain a specified period, such as four months.[13] Another method of preventing release on request is to require written formal requests. Many mental patients are not told the request must be in writing, and give up after an oral request is not honored.[14] Further, few states require notice to "voluntary" patients that they even have a right to request release.

Often requests to leave are used as evidence to support involuntary commitment proceedings. The psychiatrist may testify, for example, that "the patient cannot understand his need for treatment as evidenced by his request to leave." Also, psychiatrists and other hospital personnel often simply ignore "voluntary" patients who request release. They say such requests are "irrational," even though they honored the patient's request for admission. That was "rational."

Many voluntary patients cannot, as a practical matter, request release. Some would go to prison if they were released. Others, among them the aged, would have no place to live if they were released. In some states, "incompetent" patients whose guardians have "voluntarily" hospitalized them, and children whose parents have "voluntarily" hospitalized them, may not legally request release. If they do, no one will listen. Their release is dependent on the wishes of the hospital staff and the people who hospitalized them.

Added to these restraints on the release of "voluntary" patients are two other practical realities of mental hospitalization. First, during any period of "voluntary" hospitalization the hospital will have gathered information on ward charts and records. If release is requested "A.M.A."

(against medical advice), this often extensive information may be used as evidence for involuntary commitment. Few "voluntary" patients are aware that their daily routine and treatment may be used as evidence against them. It is very difficult to defend against psychiatric testimony that has been gathered over a long time. Second, "voluntary" patients often resist hospitalization less vehemently than involuntaries, even though they do not want to be in the hospital and would leave if they had an alternative. Resistance to hospitalization often delays the paralyzing effects of "institutionalization," which eventually destroys the desire or ability to live in the community. Once a patient is truly "institutionalized"—satisfied with and dependent on the structured, secure daily routine of a hospital ward—in all likelihood he will never be released.[15] If "voluntaries" are lulled into nonresistance, and neither the hospital nor outsiders push for release, it is likely that "institutionalization" will guarantee confinement for life.

For this reason, we believe no one should be *permitted* to be a "voluntary" patient for longer than two months without judicial authorization of continued hospitalization, after careful exploration and explanation of less restrictive alternatives (see Chapter III). At the very least, there should be a formal mechanism for periodically reviewing the propriety of continued "voluntary" hospitalization, and "voluntary" patients should be required to "sign in" again at regular intervals.[16]

Some states use a third kind of admission procedure that is much closer to what the average citizen assumes voluntary status to be. "Informal admission," as it is called, gives the mental patient just as much freedom as a general patient in a regular hospital.[17] The patient may come and go as he pleases. Unfortunately, this procedure is rarely used.[18] If it were available to more patients, it would do much to reduce the stigma of mental hospitalization.

Very few courts have ruled on any aspect of "voluntary" status. One case, however, is important. It ruled that a "voluntary" patient whose release on request could be prevented should be given review and release rights that were at least equal to the review and release rights of involuntary patients.[19] That court also ruled that "volun-

94

tary" patients have a right to a lawyer in the hospital equal to the right to counsel for involuntary patients. The court reasoned that the somewhat artificial label "voluntary" should not deprive a patient who is dissatisfied with hospitalization of any rights that involuntary patients have.

What rights do minors have when they are "voluntarily" hospitalized by their parents?

A large group of "voluntary" patients is comprised of young people who have been "voluntarily" hospitalized by their parents, without ever appearing before a court. This frequently happens when minors run away, take drugs, adopt a "hippie" lifestyle, or simply do not obey. Parents hospitalize many young people who are not mentally disordered, who cannot benefit from treatment, or who do not require confinement in a mental hospital in order to receive the services they do need.

Not long ago minors had few legal rights. The law did not recognize protest or consent by a young person; only the parent's word and signature had legal effect. Recently this situation has changed.[20] Many current commitment laws recognize both the consent and protest of young people who are 13 or older when their "voluntary" hospitalization is at issue.[21] And four federal courts have recently ruled that minors have a constitutional right to procedural due process, including judicial hearings, wh n their parents seek to hospitalize them "voluntarily."[22] One of those cases is now being considered by the United States Supreme Court and may be decided by early 1978.[23] The decision in that case should tell us a good deal more, not only about the rights of minors, but also about the rights of other "voluntary" mental patients, and the procedural guarantees the Court will require before "voluntary" admission to a mental institution.

"Minor voluntary" cases require courts to decide difficult questions of the "proper resolution of possible competing interests of parents, children, and the state."[24] Resolution of those questions requires courts to balance two competing interests to which the Supreme Court has afforded constitutional protection in the past—the right of parents and guardians to control the upbringing of their children, and the right of children to due process when their liberty is threatened by state action.

In our opinion, children 12 or older should have the same right to resist hospitalization, under the same standards and procedures, as adults. We also believe that any child who is old enough to protest hospitalization should have a right to judicial review, though perhaps under different standards and procedures. And whether children protest or not, the hospital should be required at frequent and regular intervals to document the propriety of continued hospitalization for each child.

Finally, hospitalized children should be treated as normally as possible. In particular, they should not be deprived of a public education during hospitalization.

NOTES

1. Stone, *Ch. I*, n. 13, p. 44.
2. World Health Organization, *Hospitalization of Mental Patients* (1955).
3. *Ibid.*
4. See Gilboy and Schmidt, "'Voluntary' Hospitalization of the Mentally Ill," 66 *Nw. U. L. Rev.* 429 (1971); Kittrie, *Ch. I*, n. 18; Szasz, "Voluntary Mental Hospitalization: An Unacknowledged Practice of Medical Fraud," 287 *N. Eng. J. Med.* 277 (1972).
5. For example, California, see Wexler, *Ch. II*, n. 36, p. 676, fn. 17. ("Conservatorships" are used to avoid strict commitment requirements.)
6. Gilboy, *supra* n. 4.
7. See concurring opinion of Burger, C.J., *O'Connor v. Donaldson, Ch. II*, n. 13; Katz, *Ch. I*, n. 6.
8. Olin and Olin, "Informed Consent in Voluntary Mental Hospital Admissions," 132 *Am. J. Psychiat.* 938 (1975).
9. Palmer and Wohl, "Voluntary Admission Forms: Does the Patient Know What He's Signing?" 23 *Hosp. & Comm. Psychiat.* 250 (1972).
10. Gilboy, *supra* n. 4.
11. Taken from Ennis, "Legal Rights of the Voluntary Patient," *J. Natl. Assoc. Private Psychiat. Hosp.*, pp. 4-5 (Summer 1976).
12. Kentucky Rev. Stat. §202.015 (3); N.H. Rev. Stat. Ann. §135:22; Rev. Code Wash. 71.05.050.

13. See, for example, now repealed Mont. Rev. Code §38.406.
14. See, Mont. Rev. Code §38.1303 (3).
15. *Ch. I*, nn. 6 and 7.
16. N.Y. Ment. Hyg. L. §31.25; see also *In re Buttonow*, 23 N.Y.2d 38, 244 N.E.2d 677 (1968).
17. N.Y. Ment. Hyg. L. §31.15.
18. Gilboy *supra* n. 4.
19. *In re Buttonow, supra* n. 16.
20. Ellis, "Volunteering Children: Parental Commitment of Minors to Mental Institutions," 62 *Calif. L. Rev.* 840 (1974).
21. For example, Rev. Code Wash. 72.23.070; Del Code Ann. §5123 (a) (c) (Supp. 1970).
22. *Welsch v. Likins, Ch. III*, n. 3; *Saville v. Treadway*, 404 F. Supp. 430 (M.D. Tenn. 1974); *J.L. et al. v. Parham, Ch. III*, n. 3; *Bartley v. Kremens, Ch. II*, n. 2.
23. *J. L. v. Parham, supra* n. 22.
24. *Wisconsin v. Yoder*, 406 U.S. 205, 231 (1972).

V

Mental Patients In The
Criminal Process

Until now, we have been discussing the rights of people
who have been neither accused nor convicted of crimes.
But there is another group that makes up a sizable portion of the population of mental institutions.[1] They are
people who have been accused, acquitted, or convicted of
crime, and who are said to be mentally disordered. This
group is sometimes referred to as "mad and bad."[2] Society's unwillingness to allocate resources to institutions for
the mentally disordered, and strong feelings about persons
who are accused of criminal acts, have led to lengthy,
overzealous, and sometimes brutal attempts to cure aber-
rant behavior of members of this group.[3]

Sometimes criminal defendants are confined with civilly
committed persons.[4] More often they are segregated in
high-security facilities that, for convenience, we will call
"prison mental hospitals." Sometimes those facilities are
staffed and operated by the state department of mental
hygiene, but usually they are under the state department
of correction. Thus patients in prison mental hospitals are
likely to encounter "guards" and other staff members who
are accustomed to dealing with criminals. Patients who
"misbehave" are likely to be subjected to the kinds of discipline usually used on prisoners, not patients. In some
cases, patients in prison mental hospitals have been subjected to extremely severe forms of discipline, which are
usually called "aversive conditioning." For example, at the
Vacaville facility in California, anectine, which halts

breathing, was used on mentally disordered prisoners who were told to cease certain behaviors as they choked for air.[5] Anectine is called the death drug because it simulates asphyxiation. At the Iowa State Mental Facility, apomorphine, which induces at least a half-hour of continuous vomiting and stomach spasms, was used as a disciplinary method on mentally disordered patients.[6] Straitjackets, spread-eagle bonds, and beatings are also used.[7] Electroshock was and may still be used not as treatment but solely as punishment.[8] Psychosurgery has been used for "aggressive" personalities.[9] And long-term, indefinite "strip-cell isolation" in a barren room, with few if any personal items, is common in almost every prison mental hospital. Several courts have recognized that conditions in prison mental hospitals are substantially worse than conditions in civil mental hospitals.[10]

Despite resort to these "therapies," no one has demonstrated an effective treatment for the types of mental disorders many psychiatrists say are associated with dangerous or criminal behavior.[11] So-called sociopathic personalities, probably the most common diagnosis for persons who commit criminal acts, are apparently not treatable.[12] Furthermore, it is impossible to predict whether people said to be either psychotic or sociopathic will commit dangerous acts.[13] One study that examined ex-prisoners whom psychiatrists had predicted were "dangerous" showed that 99 percent of those predictions were wrong, and that psychiatrists had needlessly confined almost 1,000 people to prison mental hospitals. In fact, there was evidence that ex-prisoners transferred from prison mental hospitals to civil mental hospitals fared better and caused fewer problems than did the regular civil patients.[14]

Because the conditions in prison mental hospitals are so severe and the treatments so harsh, several cases involving this type of confinement have reached the courts. All but one of the mental health cases decided by the Supreme Court in the last ten years have involved criminal or quasi-criminal defendants. In this chapter, we will discuss the various categories of mental patients in the criminal process and their emerging legal rights.

How are persons who are "incompetent to stand trial" committed?

The American criminal justice system requires that defendants in criminal cases actively participate in their defense. Defendants must therefore be able to understand the charges against them and the consequences of guilt, and be able to assist their lawyer in preparing a defense.[15] If a defendant is not able to understand the charges or to assist counsel, he is said to be incompetent to stand trial. In 1966, and again in 1975, the Supreme Court ruled that convicting a defendant who is incompetent to stand trial is a denial of due process.[16]

Almost every defendant who is thought to be mentally disordered is sent to a mental hospital for an evaluation of his competence to stand trial. Evaluations, which may last up to three months,[17] are initiated merely on the basis of a criminal charge and *any* evidence that the defendant is mentally disordered. Defense counsel, prosecutors, and judges can all request competency evaluations. Thus, usually without a hearing or any chance to contest the commitment for evaluation, or any chance to show that evaluation could take place in a local facility or by outpatient visits, the defendant is committed to a mental hospital for up to three months. It is so easy to commit defendants for evaluation that there are many unnecessary and inappropriate commitments. Actually, very few people committed for evaluation are subsequently found incompetent to stand trial. For example, in Massachusetts, 95 percent of all defendants committed for evaluation are returned after evaluation as competent to stand trial.[18]

Even though most competency evaluations take a psychiatrist less than one hour, defendants are often hospitalized and treated for the full evaluation period. During that time defendants will be asked about the alleged crime, although no warnings about self-incrimination are given; they may be evaluated as to insanity at the time of the alleged offense (see discussion below); they will probably be treated as if they had already been found guilty of the alleged crime; and they will be denied the right to be free on bail available to other criminal defendants.

The evaluation consists of a mental status examination. If a mental disorder is diagnosed, the hospital may recommend to the court a longer commitment for treatment of the condition. This does not mean, however, that the person is incompetent. Actually, a defendant can be severely mentally disordered and still be legally competent to stand trial.[19] This is an important point, which mental health professionals often ignore. In fact, "most psychiatrists" incorrectly assume that anyone who is mentally disordered is automatically incompetent to stand trial.[20] The presence of a mental disorder may be relevant, but it is certainly not conclusive.[21] Mental health professionals are beginning to recognize that the real issues in competency evaluation are essentially legal issues.[22] In order to evaluate whether the defendant understands the nature of the charges against him and is able to assist counsel in preparing a defense, mental health professionals need to know a great deal more about criminal proceedings than most of them do know.[23] And they *cannot* know as much about the defendant's competence to stand trial in a particular case as the defendant's attorney. For example, many defendants are found incompetent because they will not be able to testify coherently, or withstand the stress of a prolonged trial. Even if that is so, it may be irrelevant. Only the defendant and his lawyer know whether it will be necessary for the defendant to testify, a decision that often changes during trial. Similarly, very few defendants actually stand trial. About 90 percent simply plead guilty to the charge or to a reduced charge. In that event, the defendant's ability to withstand the stress of a prolonged trial would be irrelevant. The only relevant issue would be the defendant's capacity to understand the nature and consequences of a guilty plea. Again, only the defendant and his lawyer know whether the defendant will plead guilty or stand trial, and that decision often changes during pretrial proceedings.[24]

Furthermore, even if a defendant is unable to give his lawyer any information about the alleged crime or about an alibi, the lawyer may be able to get that information from co-defendants, witnesses, or other sources. If so, the defendant's inability to assist counsel may be irrelevant.

In our opinion, mental health professionals have little or no expertise in deciding the legal and practical questions that are relevant to a defendant's competence to stand trial or to plead guilty. Those questions should be decided by the defendant's lawyer, by an independent lawyer, or by the court.

If after evaluation the hospital recommends a finding of incompetency, an indefinite competency commitment usually follows, often without any judicial hearing. If the defendant or the prosecutor do not affirmatively contest the incompetency recommendation, most courts will simply sign an incompetency commitment order based on the recommendation.

After commitment, indefinite treatment begins. Very often incompetent defendants are either mentally retarded or have permanent mental disorders. These defendants are confined until it is definitely established that their mental condition will not improve. However, even though permanent disorders are usually obvious from the moment the defendant enters the hospital, retarded and permanently disordered persons make up a large proportion of all persons held as incompetent to stand trial.

Those who might improve enough to be returned to court to stand trial are treated. One new method, more innovative than most, is to "practice being a defendant" in a mock trial. Patients are rated on videotape performances for their demeanor, their responses, and their ability to control their behavior.

Many defendants who have been committed as incompetent and who are later returned for trial simply plead guilty. The total time they spend in institutions before a finding of guilt, however, may equal or exceed the time they would have served if convicted.[25]

For these and related reasons, it is becoming increasingly clear that incompetence to stand trial procedures, though ostensibly for the defendant's benefit, can also be used to the defendant's detriment.[26] The gap between purpose and reality is especially troubling when the defendant *wants* to stand trial to prove his innocence, but is considered by others to be incompetent.

Prosecutors often use incompetency commitments to get the defendant off the street, without opportunity for bail, and without the necessity for a time-consuming criminal trial.[27] And appointed defense lawyers often consent to incompetency commitments, especially when the prescribed fee will be inadequate to cover the expenses of a long criminal trial.[28]

What rights do allegedly incompetent defendants have?

Commitment for evaluation of competence is a deprivation of liberty and of the right to bail. Accordingly, we believe that no defendant should be committed over his objection unless there has been a judicial hearing to establish probable cause to doubt the defendant's competence. Furthermore, because the defendant's incompetence is irrelevant if there will be no criminal trial, we believe no defendant should be committed over his objection unless there has been an indictment or a preliminary hearing that shows probable cause for believing the defendant committed the alleged crime. Similarly, the current standard for commitment for evaluation is too vague and should be made more specific.

If the court find probable cause to evaluate the defendant's competence to stand trial, that evaluation should be conducted in the least restrictive setting, preferably on an outpatient basis, if the defendant is otherwise entitled to bail.[29] If not, the maximum period allowed for hospital evaluation should be no more than one week.

If after evaluation and subsequent court hearing the defendant is found incompetent, that finding should suspend criminal proceedings *against* the defendant, but not *by* the defendant. Lawyers for incompetent defendants should be *required* to make whatever pretrial motions can be made without the assistance of their clients, or with whatever limited assistance the client can provide (motions to suppress, to dismiss because of a statute of limitations, etc.).[30]

Incompetent defendants should not be hospitalized for treatment of their incompetence if they are otherwise entitled to bail and if treatment on an outpatient basis or in a less restrictive alternative would suffice. In our opinion, incompetent defendants should be hospitalized only if a court determines, after a hearing, that there is a "substantial probability" the defendant will attain competence to stand trial within the foreseeable future and, if so, that the intended hospital is staffed and equipped to provide the appropriate treatment and services. There is substantial support for this position.

In *Jackson v. Indiana*,[31] a unanimous Supreme Court ruled as follows:

> At the least due process requires that the *nature and duration* of commitment bear some reasonable relation to *the purpose* for which the individual is committed.

> We hold, consequently, that a person charged by a State with a criminal offense who is committed solely on account of his incapacity to proceed to trial cannot be held more than the reasonable period of time necessary to determine whether there is a *substantial probability that he will attain that capacity in the foreseeable future*. If it is determined that this is not the case, then the State must either institute the customary civil commitment proceeding that would be required to commit indefinitely any other citizen, or release the defendant. Furthermore, even if it is determined that the defendant probably *soon* will be able to stand trial, his continued commitment must be justified by *progress* toward that goal.

That holding was based upon the Court's belief that the only constitutionally acceptable "purpose" for pretrial commitment under criminal auspices—the "rationale for pretrial commitment"—is "that care or treatment will aid the accused in attaining competency."[32]

By repeated references throughout its opinion the Court made it clear that a finding of incompetence to stand trial does not, by itself, justify commitment under criminal auspices. There must be, in addition, a finding of "substantial probability," not just possibility, that the incompetent defendant "will attain" competency "in the foreseeable future."[33] Thus, in discussing the facts of the *Jackson* case, the Court noted that a physician had testified that Jackson's "prognosis appears rather dim," that "the evidence established little likelihood of improvement in [Jackson's] condition," and that "the record clearly establishes that the

104

chances of Jackson's ever meeting the competency standards ... are at best minimal, if not nonexistent.[34]

In essence, the Court ruled that a defendant may be committed under criminal auspices only if he is both incompetent and treatable. In order to make the latter finding, courts would require evidence on two separate though related questions: is the defendant himself amenable to treatment, and if so, is the hospital to which he will be committed staffed and equipped to provide the appropriate treatment and services?

Although *Jackson v. Indiana* did not expressly require a hearing on this second question, the necessity for such a hearing is certainly implicit in the decision, and may well be constitutionally required. The Court's insistence that "the nature . . . of commitment bear some reasonable relation to the purpose for which the individual is committed"[35] strongly implies the necessity for an inquiry into the "nature" of the treatment and services available at the intended facility. If the intended facility were equipped to provide only maximum security custodial care, there would be "no 'reasonable relation' . . . between so harsh a confinement and the purpose sought to be achieved."[36] Similarly, the Court's observation that there "are substantial doubts about whether the rationale for pretrial commitment—that care or treatment will aid the accused in attaining competency—is empirically valid given the state of most of our mental institutions" strongly implies the necessity—and certainly the propriety—of an inquiry into the nature of the particular institution to which the defendant will be committed.

It thus seems clear that a judicial inquiry into the nature of the services available at the intended facility is appropriate, and probably constitutionally required. The only remaining question is whether such an inquiry should be conducted before the individual is committed or after. We believe there are compelling reasons for conducting the inquiry prior to commitment. First, since the defendant will in any event be entitled to question the constitutional adequacy of his treatment immediately after commitment,[37] considerations of judicial economy favor resolution of that issue prior to commitment by the court that is already fully acquainted with the defendant's case and condition.

Second, given the fact, as the Supreme Court noted, that the availability of adequate treatment in "most of our mental institutions" cannot be assumed,[38] the mere finding that a defendant is treatable, without the additional finding that the intended hospital is, in fact, equipped to treat, would not satisfy *Jackson*'s requirement of "substantial probability" that the defendant will regain competence. Third, we believe that incompetent defendants have a constitutional right to be committed, if at all, to the least restrictive facility that is adequate to meet their needs, and inquiry into the "nature" of the intended facility may therefore be constitutionally required for this purpose, even apart from *Jackson*. It is now clear that the constitutional doctrine of the least restrictive alternative is applicable in mental commitment proceedings (see Chapter III).

Courts are beginning to recognize the wisdom of inquiry into the nature of the intended facility *before* commitment. Thus, in *Lynch v. Baxley*,[39] a three-judge federal court ruled, on constitutional grounds, that *before* a mentally ill person can be civilly committed to a civil mental hospital, the fact finder (judge or jury) must ascertain "the existence and availability of a treatment program for the illness suffered by the person whose commitment is sought" in order to support a precommitment finding that "there is treatment available for the illness diagnosed." We believe the same precommitment inquiry should be made before incompetence to stand trial commitments.

We also believe that if an incompetent defendant has been hospitalized and treated for six months and has not regained competence to stand trial, he should be released from the prison mental hospital and committed, if at all, to a civil hospital, under civil standards and procedures. If he does not meet the civil standards for commitment, he should simply be released. That is essentially what the Court required in *Jackson v. Indiana*, without specifying a time limit. Other courts have established maximum hospitalization periods ranging from six months to a year and a half.[40]

If the court determines that an incompetent defendant is not treatable, either before hospitalization or six months after hospitalization, the court should either dismiss the criminal charges or proceed with the trial. Although it is often said that "the conviction of an accused person while he is legally incompetent violates due process"[41] the Supreme Court has suggested that there might be circumstances in which the criminal trial of a permanently incompetent defendant could be permitted.

In *Jackson v. Indiana*,[42] a unanimous Court observed that "both courts and commentators have noted the desirability of permitting some proceedings to go forward despite the defendant's incompetency."[43] The Court then noted, with apparent approval, that "some States have statutory provisions permitting pre-trial motions to be made or even allowing the incompetent defendant a trial at which to establish his innocence, without permitting a conviction."[44] In those states, the trial is permitted, subject to "the qualification that a guilty verdict be set aside and the case retried after the defendant has become fully competent."[45]

As the Court in *Jackson* noted, many commentators have urged that consideration be given to trying defendants who are permanently incompetent.[46] Furthermore, in our view, refusal to try a permanently incompetent defendant who has expressed a desire to be tried would raise substantial constitutional questions under the Equal Protection Clauses of the state and federal constitutions. Incompetent defendants are functionally indistinguishable from defendants who are fully competent to stand trial except that they suffer from permanent amnesia concerning the facts of the incident involved and therefore cannot discuss the incident with counsel. Courts have uniformly held that amnesia concerning the incident does not, by itself, make it unfair or unconstitutional to bring a defendant to trial.[47] In those cases, the courts have held that the trial court should conduct an inquiry to determine whether the defendant can conceivably receive a fair trial; and after trial, if convicted, whether the defendant did in fact receive a fair trial. Specific criteria are set forth by which to measure the fairness of the trial, and special rules are to be applied at the trial to ensure fairness.

It seems clear to us that in *some* circumstances, it would not be unfair or unconstitutional to try a defendant who has been found to be permanently incompetent. And it would follow that it would not be unfair or unconstitutional to try a defendant whose competence is questionable, but who has not actually been declared incompetent, reserving decision on the incompetence question until the trial is completed. In many cases, this alternative disposition—reserving judgment on incompetence—would enable the court to make more accurate and more detailed findings about the defendant's actual trial competence than could possibly be made by pretrial prediction. Even before trial, ordinarily it should be possible to determine whether the defendant understands the nature of the charges and of criminal procedures. But it is much more difficult, before trial, to determine whether the defendant is able to assist counsel in preparing and presenting a defense. The extent to which the defendant follows the trial testimony, makes suggestions for cross-examination, or testifies himself may be determinative.

In close cases, courts should seriously consider reserving decision on the defendant's competency to stand trial until after the trial is completed. If the defendant is acquitted or the charges are dismissed, further inquiry would be unnecessary. If the defendant is found guilty, the court could examine the "best evidence" of the defendant's ability to stand trial, his actual conduct during the trial. (The court might wish to ask a forensic psychiatrist or a defense attorney to observe the defendant during the proceedings.) If after a postconviction hearing the court found the defendant to have been incompetent during the trial, it could set aside the verdict. The United States Supreme Court has noted, citing authorities, that reserving decision on a defendant's competence until the trial is completed is not only permissible, but a procedure that "may have advantages."[48]

Involuntary treatment of incompetent defendants, we should note, raises special problems. Under the influence of hospital-administered drugs, defendants may reveal information that will incriminate them in their later trials. And electroconvulsive therapy may destroy all memory of the alleged crime, or of an otherwise valid alibi.[49] Incompetent defendants should therefore have at least the same rights to refuse treatments as civilly committed patients (see Chaper VI).

What happens to defendants who are found not guilty by reason of insanity?

Although mental health professionals often confuse the two, incompetence to stand trial and the insanity defense are different. Incompetence refers to the defendant's mental condition at the time of trial; the insanity defense is concerned with the defendant's mental condition at the time of the alleged crime. Although the insanity defense is worded differently in different states,[50] and there is controversy about which wording is proper, the core concept is the same throughout the country: no one may be punished for a criminal act if he was not mentally responsible for the act. "Criminal intent" is an important element of all serious crimes. Defendants who commit criminal acts will be "acquitted by reason of insanity" if they were not mentally responsible at the time of the crime.

The insanity defense, and acquittals by reason of insanity, have received far more attention than incompetence to stand trial. But very few defendants ever raise an insanity defense, and even fewer are acquitted by reason of insanity.[51] Because the consequence of a successful insanity defense is likely to be long-term confinement in a prison mental hospital,[52] the defense is usually raised only in cases involving very serious crimes, where the likely consequences of criminal conviction are even more severe than the consequences of a successful insanity defense. For every defendant acquitted by reason of insanity, there are over 100 defendants hospitalized because of incompetence to stand trial.[53]

It is possible to plead not guilty, and at the same time to plead not guilty by reason of insanity. But in most jurisdictions, the same jury will consider both defenses. The defendant is then in the difficult position of saying to the same jury, "I did not commit the crime, but if I did, I was not mentally responsible for my actions." After the jury hears the state's evidence of guilt, it will be reluctant to "acquit," even by reason of insanity.

If the jury does acquit by reason of insanity, in some jurisdictions the same jury will then decide whether to commit the defendant to a mental hospital. In other jurisdictions, commitment to a hospital, at least for a period of evaluation, follows automatically upon acquittal by reason of insanity.

What are the rights of defendants who plead not guilty by reason of insanity?

Some jurisdictions use different juries to consider the defendant's plea of not guilty and his plea of not guilty by reason of insanity.[54] This is a sensible procedure, and may even be required by the Due Process and Equal Protection Clauses, though to date no court has so ruled.[55]

If the defendant is acquitted by reason of insanity, there is somewhat stronger support for requiring a new hearing, before a new jury or judge, to decide whether he should be committed to a hospital.[56] The defendant may well have been insane at the time of the crime, but not mentally disordered or dangerous at the time of the acquittal by reason of insanity. It may prejudice the defendant's chance to be released if he is deprived of a separate hearing on those issues.

Theoretically, determinations about the present and future dangerousness of insanity-acquitted defendants should be made using the same standards and procedures that would be used for an ordinary civil commitment. Several courts have relied on Supreme Court rulings[57] to hold that insanity-acquitted defendants have a right to a civil commitment hearing, with all the rights of persons facing civil commitment, soon after insanity acquittal.[58]

Finally, we should note that several authorities have argued forcefully that the insanity defense should be abolished.[59]

How are convicted prisoners committed to mental institutions?

Many persons who are convicted and sent to prison are thereafter found to be mentally disordered and transferred to prison mental hospitals. Sometimes "troublemakers" or "politically active" prisoners are transferred to prison mental hospitals.[60] There are insufficient mental health resources throughout the American prison system for mentally disordered prisoners who want psychiatric help.[61] On the other hand, many prisoners are forced to accept psychiatric treatment they do not want. Often prisoners resist transfer to prison mental hospitals because they correctly fear that their chances for parole will be diminished if psychiatrists report to a parole board that they have mental disorders. And in many jurisdictions, prisoners transferred to prison mental hospitals lose "good time" credits toward early release under the strange theory that mentally disordered persons are not responsible for their behavior, and therefore should not be able to earn credit for their good behavior.

On the other hand, some prisoners seek psychiatric help and transfer to prison mental hospitals. Favorable psychiatric reports greatly increase chances for release. And living conditions in some prison mental hospitals are better than in some prisons. Thus some prisoners resist transfer back to prison.

Traditionally, the transfer of prisoners between prisons and prison mental hospitals was an administrative decision. Wardens and hospital superintendents had full discretion to change the residence of prisoners.

What rights do convicted prisoners have to contest transfers between prisons and prison mental hospitals?

Many states have statutes that guarantee "treatment" for mentally disordered prisoners. But few state statutes specifically authorize prisoners to contest transfers between prison and prison mental hospitals. Courts, however, have ruled on constitutional grounds that prisoners have a right to contest such transfers under procedures designed to ensure fair decisions.[62]

The cases that protect prisoners from arbitrary transfers[63] rely partially on a Supreme Court decision, *Baxstrom v. Herold*,[64] which held that a convicted prisoner whose sentence had expired should be given protections of the regular civil commitment procedures before transfer to a mental hospital. Lower courts have extended that ruling to protect prisoners whose sentences have not expired.[65]

Courts have also ruled that prisoners should not lose "good time" and similar benefits just because they were transferred.[66] Much of this case law is based on the judicial recognition that conditions in prison mental hospitals are in many ways even more severe than conditions in prisons. One court listed the stark examples of how a prison mental hospital was worse than a prison and relied on the differences to require due process procedure.[67] A few courts have ruled that prisoners have a right not to be transferred arbitrarily from a prison mental hospital back to prison.[68]

The continued validity of these decisions may be affected by a very recent Supreme Court case[69] in which the Court ruled that, absent *statutory* standards for transfer, prisoners can be transferred *between prisons* based solely on administrative decisions. Whether that decision will be applied to transfers between prisons and prison mental hospitals is not clear. Courts may continue to rule that prisoners can contest transfer to prison mental hospitals on the ground that the severe conditions in such hospitals are an additional and substantial deprivation of liberty, warranting procedural safeguards. And courts may continue to rule that prisoners can contest transfers from prison mental hospitals to prisons on the ground that once "treatment" has been given, it cannot arbitrarily be withdrawn.

How do so-called sexual psychopaths and defective delinquents get committed to prison mental hospitals?

Two other categories of persons are committed to prison mental hospitals.[70] "Sexual psychopaths," people who are said to be a danger because of a predisposition to commit sexual offenses, are committed for indeterminate periods under special laws that exist in most states. They are committed for "treatment" designed to rehabilitate them. A few states, notably Maryland and Vermont,[71] have laws that authorize commitment of persons called "defective delinquents," who are said to need confinement and "treatment" because of a persistent propensity to crime that renders them dangerous. The common ground for the definitions of both "sexual psychopath" and "defective delinquent" is some undefined mental condition that prevents the individual from restraining an urge to commit crimes.

For both groups a persistent tendency to offend seems to be the main criteria for commitment; however, these are not "habitual criminal" proceedings, which require a predetermined number of felony (or misdemeanor) convictions, and lead to long but specified prison sentences. Many first- or second-time sexual offenders are committed under these special laws. Quite often the underlying offense did not cause physical injury, and many misdemeanor offenders are found in these programs. Several "exposing" incidents, or one or two minor incidents involving children, may be sufficient.[72]

Studies indicate that only 5 percent of sex offenders are assaultive or truly dangerous.[73] Almost all are minor offenders whose acts of voyeurism, consensual homosexuality, and exhibitionism may be offensive, but are physically harmless.[74] Comparatively few sex offenders repeat their offenses.[75] And it is extremely difficult to predict whether a particular offender will or will not commit a physically dangerous act in the future (see Chapter I).

The procedures for commitment of sexual psychopaths and defective delinquents are quite similar. Usually the procedures begin only after conviction for the underlying criminal offense, though in some jurisdictions the commitment occurs in lieu of criminal conviction.[76] Before or soon after conviction the defendant is sent to a program for evaluation. There, without counsel, warnings, or protection of any sort, he is evaluated over a period of several weeks. In ways that vary from program to program, someone forms an opinion of whether the defendant is an "appropriate candidate." Because the commitment standards are vague, it is difficult to tell what distinguishes persons who are recommended for commitment from those who are not.

If commitment is recommended, a hearing is held. The hearing is separate from the criminal proceeding, and is usually called a "civil" proceeding. This means the defendant does not receive the procedural protections he would receive in a criminal proceeding, even though the consequences—indeterminate commitment and the stigma of the label "sexual psychopath" or "defective delinquent"—may be more severe than the consequences of conviction on the underlying criminal charge.

If committed, the individual is more likely to be subjected to particularly intrusive forms of treatment, including aversive behavior modification and even psychosurgery,[77] than are ordinary mental patients. This is so even though most mental health professionals now agree there is no special treatment for such persons.[78] In fact, psychiatric treatments are likely to be even less effective for such persons than for ordinary mental patients.[79] (see Chapter I).

What rights do sexual psychopaths and defective delinquents have to resist commitment?

In our opinion, there are no legitimate reasons to treat sexual psychopaths and defective delinquents as special categories, using special standards and procedures.[80] But so long as they are treated differently, it will be important to understand the law applicable to their special categories.

In 1940, the Supreme Court upheld the constitutionality of a sexual psychopath law that, in our opinion, was excessively vague.[81] Since then, the Court has required more substantial *procedural* protections for commitment under sexual psychopath and defective delinquent laws, but it has not substantially narrowed or clarified the *standards* for commitment.[82] Most lower courts have maintained that distinction.[83]

The Supreme Court cases require procedural protections that are substantially equivalent to the procedures used in ordinary civil commitments.[84] Lower courts have required the right to counsel, jury trials, greater proof than a mere preponderance of the evidence, and other rights consistent with a fair hearing.[85]

Courts have not yet expressly recognized a right not to incriminate oneself during the evaluation procedures under these laws, but Justice Douglas' dissenting opinion in *Murel v. Baltimore City Criminal Court*[86] states the arguments for such a right. In a companion case to *Murel*, the Supreme Court recognized the right of a person who refused to speak during the evaluation process not to be confined for longer than his prison sentence would have been.[87]

The California Supreme Court has limited these special laws more than any other court. In two far-reaching opinions,[88] it has guaranteed strict procedures and has limited commitment to the length of the criminal sentence. These cases are the best reasoned and most informed of any of the recent rulings on psychopath commitments. Nevertheless, even they do not sufficiently acknowledge the fundamental problem in such commitments, which many experts have recognized[89]: there is no justification for creating these special categories of offenders.

NOTES

1. Stone, *Ch. I*, n. 13, p. 44.
2. See Morris, "Psychiatry and the Dangerous Criminal," 41 *S. Cal. L. Rev.* 514 (1968).
3. See, for examples, *Mackey v. Procunier*, 477 F.2d 877 (9th Cir. 1973); *Knecht v. Gillman*, 488 F.2d 1136 (8th Cir. 1973); *Morgan v. State*, 319 N.Y.S.2d 151 (Ct. Cl. 1970); Flint, "31 Ex-Employees at Ohio Hospital Appear in Court," *The New York Times*, Nov. 27, 1971 (Lima State Hospital); Arens, *The Insanity Defense* (1974); Wexler and Scoville, *Ch. III*, n. 23; Ennis, *Ch. I*, n. 20; *United States ex rel. Schuster v. Herold*, 524 F.2d 153 (2nd Cir. 1976); and 410 F.2d 1071 (2nd Cir. 1969), *cert. den.*, 396 U.S. 847 (1969); "Disposition of the Insane After Acquittal—The Long Road From Commitment to Release," 59 *J. Crim L.C. & P.S.* 583; Burt, "Of Mad Dogs and Scientists: The Perils of the 'Criminally Insane'," 123 *U. Pa. L. Rev.* 258 (1974); Morris, *supra* n. 2; *Clonce v. Richardson*, 379 F. Supp. 338 (W.D. Mo. 1974); Opton, "Psychiatric Violence Against Prisoners: When Therapy is Punishment," 45 *Miss. L.J.* 605 (1974); Note, "Conditioning and Other Technologies Used to 'Treat?' 'Rehabilitate?' 'Demolish?' Prisoners and Mental Patients," 45 *S. Cal. L. Rev.* 616 (1972) (hereafter cited as S. Cal. Note); *Kaimowitz v. Mich. Dept. of Mental Hygiene*, 2 Pris. L. Rptr. 433 (No. 73—19454-AW Cir. Ct. Wayne County, July 10, 1973), and Vol. I, *Mental Disability Law Reporter*, p. 147 (Am. Bar Association Commission on the Mentally Disabled, Sept.-Oct., 1976).
4. See, for example, *Donaldson v. O'Connor*, 493 F.2d 507 (5th Cir. 1974), *vacated and remanded*, 422 U.S. 563 (1975).
5. *Mackey v. Procunier*, S. Cal. Note, *supra* n. 3.
6. *Knecht v. Gillman*, *supra* n. 3.
7. *Morgan v. State*, *supra* n. 3.
8. Flint, *supra* n. 3.
9. *Kaimowitz v. Michigan Dept. of Mental Hygiene*, *supra* n. 3.
10. *Baxstrom v. Herold*, *Ch. III*, n. 58; *U.S. ex rel. Von Wolfersdorf v. Johnston*, 317 F. Supp. 66 (S.D.N.Y. 1970); *In re Kesselbrenner*, 350 N.Y.S.2d 889 (Ct. App. 1973); *Neely v. Hogan*, 310 N.Y.S.2d 63 (Sup. Ct. N.Y.Co. 1970); *U.S. ex rel. Schuster v. Herold*, *supra* n. 3.
11. S. Cal. Note, *supra* n. 3.

12. *Stone, Ch. I*, n. 13, p. 36.
13. *Ch. I*, nn. 13-15.
14. Steadman and Keveles, "Community Adjustment and Criminal Activity of the *Baxstrom* Patients: 1966-1970," 129 *Am. J. Psychiat.* 304 (1972).
15. *Dusky v. United States*, 362 U.S. 402 (1960); *Wieter v. Settle*, 193 F. Supp. 318, (W.D. Mo. 1961).
16. *Drope v. Missouri, Ch. I*, n. 16; *Pate v. Robinson, Ch. III*, n. 79; see also *Dusky v. United States, supra* n. 15.
17. Settle and Oppegard, "The Pre-Trial Examination of Federal Defendants," 35 *F.R.D.* 475 (1964).
18. McGarry, "Competence to Stand Trial and Mental Illness," *Crime and Delinquency Issues*, N.I.M.H. (1972).
19. *Adams v. United States*, 297 F. Supp. 596 (S.D.N.Y. 1969), and transcript of hearing reproduced in Brooks, *Ch. II*, n. 11, pp. 337-49. *Lyles v. United States*, 254 F.2d 725 (D.C. Cir. 1957), *cert. den.*, 356 U.S. 961 (1958); *Swisher v. United States*, 237 F. Supp. 921 (W.D. Mo. 1965), *aff'd*, 354 F.2d 472 (8th Cir. 1966); *Feguer v. United States*, 302 F.2d 214 (8th Cir. 1962), *cert. den.*, 371 U.S. 872 (1962); see also *People v. Valentino*, 356 N.Y.S.2d 962, 963 fn. 1 (Nassau Cty. Ct. 1974).
20. Stone, *Ch. I*, n. 13, pp. 202-03.
21. *Supra* n. 19.
22. *Competency to Stand Trial and Mental Illness*, Laboratory of Communty Psychiatry, Harvard Medical School [NAMH, DHEW Pub. No. (ADM) 74-103 (1974)]; *People v. Valentino, supra* n. 19; *Misuse of Psychiatry in the Criminal Courts: Competency to Stand Trial*, Group for the Advancement of Psychiatry (1974); Stone, *Ch. I*, n. 13, Ch. 12.
23. Leifer, "The Competence of Psychiatrists to Assist in the Determination of Incompetency: A Skeptical Inquiry into the Courtroom Function of Psychiatrists," 14 *Syr. L. Rev.* 564 (1963).
24. But see *Sieling v. Eyman* 487 F.2d 211 (9th Cir. 1973); and *People v. Heral*, 342 N.E.2d 34 (Ill. 1976).
25. McGarry, *supra* n. 18; Steadman and Braft, "Effects of Incompetency on Subsequent Criminal Processing: Implications for Due Process," 23 *Cath. U. L. Rev.* 754 (1974); See also Steadman, "Incompetency to Stand Trial: The Easy Way In," in *Crime and Delinquency: Dimensions of Deviance* (1973).
26. Ennis, *Ch. I*, n. 20, Chs. 1-3; Stone, *Ch. I*, n. 13, Ch. 12; Janis, "Incompetency Commitment: The Need for Procedural Safeguards and a Proposed Statutory Scheme," 23 *Cath. U. L. Rev.* 720 (1974).

27. Leavy, "The Mentally Ill Criminal Defendant," 9 *Crim. L. Bull.* 197 (1973); Stone, *Ch. I*, n. 13, Ch. 12.

28. See Charnoff and Schaffer, "Defending the Mentally Ill: Ethical Quicksand," 10 *Am. Crim. L. Rev.* 505 (1972).

29. Bail is guaranteed in *Martin v. Strayborn*, 342 N.E.2d 5, 1976); see also *United States v. Gorobetz*, 156 F. Supp. 808 (D. N.J. 1957).

30. *Jackson v. Indiana, Ch. II*, n. 1, p. 741 and fn. 20; *Neely v. Hogan*, *supra* n. 10; N.Y. Crim. Pro. Law §730.60 (4); Rev. Code Wash. 10.77.090(4); *People ex rel. Meyers v. Briggs*. 263 N.E.2d 109 (Ill. 1970); Foote, "A Comment on Pre-Trial Commitment of Criminal Defendants," 108 *U. Pa. L. Rev.* 832 (1960); Model Penal Code §4.06 (alt. subsec. 3 & 4, 1962); *Hale v. Superior Ct.* 539 P.2d 817 (Cal. Sup. Ct. 1975).

31. *Jackson v. Indiana, Ch. II*, n. 1. This language from *Jackson* was quoted and followed in *In re Kesselbrenner*, n. 10, *supra*. (Emphasis added.)

32. *Jackson v. Indiana, Ch. II*, n. 1, p. 735.

33. *Ibid.*, p. 738.

34. *Ibid.*, pp. 719, 723, 725, and 727.

35. *Ibid.*, p. 738.

36. *In re Kesselbrenner*, *supra* n. 10, p. 892.

37. See, for example, *O'Connor v. Donaldson, Ch. II*, n. 13, p. 574, fn. 10; *United States v. Walk.*, 335 F. Supp. 705 (N.D. Calif. 1971); *United States v. Pardue*, 354 F. Supp. 1377, 1382 (D. Conn. 1973); *Nason v. Superintendent of Bridgewater State Hosp.*, 233 N.E.2d 908, 913-14 (Mass. 1968); *Maatalah v. Warden, Nevada State Prison*, 470 P.2d 122 (Nev. 1970).

38. See also *Ch. I*, nn. 6 and 7.

39. *Lynch v. Baxley, Ch. II*, n. 2, p. 391.

40. *State ex rel. Walker v. Jenkins*, 203 S.E.2d 353 (W. Va. 1974); *State ex rel. Matalik v. Schubert*, 204 N.W.2d 13 (Wisc. 1973); see reading list in Brooks *Ch. I*, n. 8, p. 588; *In re David*, 505 P.2d 1018 (Cal. 1973); for example, Rev. Code Wash. 10.77.09.

41. *Pate v. Robinson Ch. III*, n. 79, p. 378.

42. *Ch. II*, n. 1.

43. *Jackson v. Indiana, Ch. II*, n. 1, p. 740, cites *People ex rel. Meyer v. Briggs*, *supra* n. 30. In the *Briggs* case, the Illinois Supreme Court held that a defendant who was permanently incompetent "should be given an opportunity to obtain a trial to determine whether or not he is guilty as charged or should be released." Released because the evidence was insufficient, the defendant, still incompetent, was later re-

arrested, tried and convicted. *People v. Lang*, No. 76-2564 (Cook County Crim. Ct. 1971).

44. *Ibid.*, p. 740.

45. *Jackson v. Indiana, Ch. II*, n. 1, p. 241 (citations omitted).

46. Burt and Morris, "A Proposal for the Abolition of the Incompetency Plea," 40 *U. Chi. L. Rev.* 66, 77 (Fall, 1972); for example, Mass. Gen. Laws Ann., Ch. 123 §17 (1972).

47. *Wilson v. United States*, 391 F.2d 460 (D.C. Cir. 1968); *People v. Francabandera*, 354 NYS2d 609 (Ct. App. 1974); *People v. Soto*, 327 NYS2d 669 (Nassau Cty. Ct. 1972); *People v. Pisco*, 330 NYS2d. 542 (Dutch. Cty. Ct., 1972).

48. *Drope v. Missouri, Ch. I*, n. 16, p. 182.

49. Stone, *Ch. I*, n. 13, pp. 213-15.

50. See, Brooks, *Ch. II*, n. 11, Chs. 4 and 5; Arens, *supra* n. 3; Goldstein, *The Insanity Defense* (1967); Wales, *Ch. I*, n. 17; Stone, *Ch. I*, n. 13, Ch. 13.

51. *Supra* n. 50.

52. Pugh, "Insanity Defense in Operation: A Practicing Psychiatrist's Views on *Durham* and *Brawner*," *Wash. U. L. Q.* 87 (1973); Morris, *supra* n. 2; and authorities *supra* n. 50.

53. Cooke, Johnson, and Pagamy, "Factors Affecting Referral to Determine Competency to Stand Trial," 130 *Am J. Psychiat.* 870 (1973).

54. *United States v. Robertson*, 507 F.2d 1148 (D.C. Cir. 1974); *Harper v. United States*, 350 F.2d 1000 (D.C. Cir. 1965).

55. See *Whalen v. Bower*, —— F. Supp. —— (No. 73-76 Phx., D. Ariz., April 26, 1973).

56. *Ibid.*; see also, *People v. Lally*, 277 N.Y.S.2d 654 (N.Y. 1966); *Bolton v. Harris*, 395 F.2d 642 (D.C. Cir. 1968); *State v. Clemons*, 515 P.2d 324 (Ariz. 1973); *Wilson v. State*, 287 N.E.2d 875 (Ind. 1972); *State ex rel. Rovach v. Schubert*, 219 N.W.2d 341 (Wisc. 1974); *People v. McQuillin*, 221 N.W.2d 569 (Mich. 1973); *State v. Krol*, 344 A.2d 289 (N.J. 1974).

57. *Baxstrom v. Herold, Ch. III*, n. 58; *Jackson v. Indiana, Ch. II*, n. 1.

58. See cases cited *supra* n. 56.

59. Wooten, *Crime and Criminal Laws* (1963), Chs. 2 and 3; Goldstein and Katz, "Abolish the Insanity Defense—Why Not?" 72 *Yale L. J.* 853 (1963); Morris, *supra* n. 2; Wentraub, "Criminal Responsibility: Psychiatry Alone Cannot Determine It," 49 *A.B.A.J.* 1075 (1963); Szasz, *Law, Liberty, and Psychiatry* (1963).

60. See, for example, *Schuster v. Herold*, *supra* n. 3.

61. *Attica: The Official Report* (1972), 70-71; Fink and Martin,

"Psychiatry and the Crisis in the Prison System," 27 *Am. J. Psychother.* 579 (1973).

62. *Chesney v. Adams*, 377 F. Supp. 887 (D. Conn. 1974); *Matthews v. Hardy*, 420 F.2d 607 (D.C. Cir. 1969), *cert. den.*, 90 S. Ct. 1231 (1970); *Souder v. McGuire*, 516 F.2d 820 (3rd Cir. 1975); *Burchette v. Bower*, 355 F. Supp. 1278 (D. Ariz. 1973); *Davy v. Sullivan*, 354 F. Supp. 1320 (M.D. Ala. 1973); *Romero v. Schauer*, 386 F. Supp. 851 (D. Colo. 1974); *U.S. ex rel. Souder v. Watson*, 413 F. Supp. 711 (M.D. Pa. 1976); *Schuster v. Herold, supra* n. 3.

63. *Schuster v. Herold, supra* n. 3; *Chesney v. Adams, Mathews v. Hardy, Souder v. McGuire, Souder v. Watson, supra* n. 62.

64. *Baxstrom v. Herold, Ch. III,* n. 58.

65. *Souder v. Watson, supra* n. 62; *Schuster v. Herold, supra* n. 3; *Gomez v. Miller, Ch. III,* n. 75.

66. See, for example, *People ex rel. Bram v. Herold*, 329 N.Y.S.2d 574 (Ct. App. 1972); *People ex rel. Slofsky v. Agnew*, 326 N.Y.S.2d 477 (Sup. Ct. Clinton Co. 1971).

67. *Schuster v. Herold, supra* n. 3.

68. *Burchette v. Bower, Davy v. Sullivan, Romero v. Schauer, supra* n. 62.

69. *Montayne v. Haymes*, 427 U.S. 236 (1976). See also *Meachum v. Fano*, 427 U.S. 215 (1976); but see *Liles v. Ward*, 424 F.Supp. 675 (S.D. N.Y., 1976), in which a federal district court distinguished *Montayne* and *Meachum* in a case involving transfer from a prison to a prison hospital.

70. See, generally, Kittrie, *Ch. I,* n. 18, pp. 191-92; Stone, *Ch. I,* n. 13, Ch. 11.

71. Md. Code Ann. Art. 31B; Vt. Stat. Ann. 18, §8501 *et seq.* (1968).

72. See *People v. Feagly*, 535 P.2d 373, 121 Cal. Rptr. 509 Cal. (1975); Stone, *Ch. I,* n. 13, p. 185.

73. Braekel and Rock, *The Mentally Disabled and the Law* (1971), p. 349.

74. Department of Mental Hygiene, *California Sexual Deviation Research* (1953), 15; Report of the New Jersey Commission on Sexual Offenders (1950), 13-14; Sutherland, "Sexual Psychopath Laws," 40 *J. Crim. L.C. & P.S.* 534-48 (1950); Ellis and Brancore, *The Psychology of the Sex Offenders* (1956), 32-33.

75. Tappan, "Sentences for Sex Criminals," 42 *J. Crim. L.C. & P.S.* 332 (1951); Note, "The Plight of the Sexual Psychopath: A Legislative Blunder and Judicial Acquiescence," 41 *Notre Dame Lwr.* 527 (1966).

76. Alabama, Florida, Iowa, Illinois, Indiana, Missouri, Washington, and District of Columbia.

77. *Kaimowitz v. Mich. Dept. of Ment. Hyg., supra* n. 3.
78. Comment, "The Validity of the Segregation of the Sexual Psychopath Under the Law," 26 *Ohio St. L.J.* 640, 653 (1965); Noyes and Kolb, *Modern Clinical Psychiatry* (1963), 470.
79. Wilkins, *Putting Treatment on Trial*, S. Hastings Center Report (Feb. 1975); Stone, *Ch. I*, n. 13, p. 185; see *People v. Feagly, supra* n. 72, Comment, *supra* n. 78.
80. Kozol *et al.*, "The Criminally Dangerous Sex Offender," 275 *N. Eng. J. Med.* 79, 80 (1966).
81. *Minnesota ex rel. Pearson v. Probate Ct.*, 309 U.S. 270 (1940).
82. *Specht v. Patterson, Ch. III*, n. 19; *Humphrey v. Cady, Ch. II*, n. 7; *McNeil v. Director, Ch. III*, n. 58; *Murel v. Baltimore City Criminal Court*, 407 U.S. 355 (1972).
83. *People v. Feagly, supra* n. 72; *Stachulak v. Coughlin, Ch. III*, n. 67; *Davy v. Sullivan, supra* n. 62; *People v. Burnick, Ch. I*, n. 16; *Tippet v. Maryland, Ch. I*, n. 16; *Sarzen v. Gaughen, Ch. I*, n. 16; *Dower v. Director*, 396 F. Supp. 1070 (D. Md. 1975).
84. See cases cited *supra* n. 82.
85. See cases cited *supra* n. 83.
86. *Murel v. Baltimore City Crim. Ct., supra* n. 82.
87. *McNeil v. Director, Ch. III*, n. 58.
88. *People v. Feagly, supra* n. 72; *People v. Burnick, Ch. I*, n. 16.
89. See Stone, *Ch. I*, n. 13, pp. 179-93.

VI

Rights In The Institution

What is life in a mental hospital like?

Life in a mental hospital is very different from life on the outside. People who have never been mental patients cannot easily understand how substantial the differences are. Some of the differences have been described.[1] Of course, the conditions and the experiences patients are likely to encounter will vary from institution to institution. But every institution substantially limits the freedom its patients would otherwise have to manage their lives. Sometimes limitations are intentionally imposed by hospital staff either as punishment or as therapy. More often limitations on personal freedom are imposed for the convenience of staff and for the more efficient operation of the institution. For example, because it is easier for institutions and more convenient for staff to distribute clean clothing if all patients wear uniform clothing, many hospitals prohibit patients from wearing their own clothes. The result is that all patients wear the same color, style, and quality of loose-fitting clothing.

Alone, this limitation on personal freedom might not seem significant. But it is only one of hundreds or perhaps thousands of similar limitations that, collectively, make life in a mental hospital vastly different from life on the outside. In many mental hospitals, patients cannot leave their wards, buildings, or the hospital grounds. They cannot eat what they want. They cannot sleep late, get up early, work at a job they choose, watch what they want on TV, associate with friends, communicate freely with persons outside the hospital, go to movies or listen to records of their choice, spend time alone with husbands, wives, boyfriends, or girlfriends, or play musical instruments. They cannot hike, swim, play tennis or golf, take their children to a zoo, spend money, or read what they want. In some institutions, patients cannot even practice their religious beliefs. Mental patients have virtually no privacy. They are usually forced to share their living and sleeping quarters with others; they cannot spend time alone or find a haven away from the noise and confusion of the ward.

In addition to these limitations on activities others take for granted, mental patients are subject to special practices. These include forced medication and "treatment," seclusion in small bare rooms, physical restraints such as straitjackets, gags, or straps, chemical restraints, transfer to more restrictive wards, and involuntary work assignments.

One court described aspects of life in a mental hospital as follows:

> . . . [T]he dormitories are barn-like structures with no privacy for the patients. For most patients there is not even space provided which he can think of as his own. The toilets in restrooms seldom have partitions between them. These are dehumanizing factors which degenerate the patient's self-esteem. Also contributing to the poor psychological environment are the shoddy wearing apparel furnished to patients, the non-therapeutic work assigned to patients (mostly compulsory, uncompensated house-keeping chores), and the degrading and humiliating admission procedure which creates in the patients an impression of the hospital as a prison or as a crazy house.[2]

During the trial of *O'Connor v. Donaldson*,[3] Kenneth Donaldson, a civilly committed mental patient, described the conditions on his ward as follows:

Q. Now, in the buildings you lived in in Department A, were those buildings locked?

A. Yes sir.

Q. Were the wards you lived on locked?

A. Yes.

Q. Were there metal enclosures on the windows?

A. Yes, padlocks on each window.

Q. Approximately how many beds were there in the rooms where you slept?

A. Some sixty beds.

Q. How close together were they?

A. Some of the beds were touching, the sides were touching, and others there was room enough to put a straight chair if we had a chair.

Q. Did you have chairs in the dormitory areas?

A. There wasn't a chair in the room I was in.

Q. All right, was there an outside exercise yard for your department?

A. Yes, there was a space outside the building, a good-sized space enclosed with a cyclone fence topped with barbwire.

Q. Did you go out to that exercise yard?

A. I went out from time to time when the other patients went out.

Q. Was there ever a period of time when you did not go out to the exercise yard?

A. Yes, there was one period in particular when nobody went out for two years.

Q. Now Mr. Donaldson, you were civilly committed. You had not been charged with any crime, is that right?

A. That is right.

Q. Were there criminal patients on your ward?

A. There were criminal patients on the ward.

Q. Approximately what percent of the population on your ward were criminals?

A. Looking back, roughly, I would say a third. I do not know the figures for the whole department.

Q. Let's talk just about your ward.

A. Okay. I would say about a third in the wards I was in.

Q. Now, did you sleep in the same rooms as the criminal patients?

A. Yes.

Q. Did you get up at the same time?

A. Yes.

Q. Did you eat the same food?

A. Yes.

Q. In the same dining room?

A. Yes.

Q. Did you wear the same clothes?

A. Yes. The entire operation of the wards I was on was geared to the criminal patients.

Q. Let me ask you, were you treated any differently from the criminal patients?

A. I was treated worse than the criminal patients.

Q. In what sense were you treated worse?

A. The criminal patients got the attention of the doctors. Generally a doctor makes a report to the court every month.

Q. For the criminal?

A. On the criminal patients, and that would be a pretty heavy case load. It didn't give them time to see the ones who weren't criminal patients.

Q. Was there a place on the ward you had access to for keeping personal possessions?

A. No, not at that time.

Q. What did you do with your personal possessions?

A. I kept mine in a cedar box under the mattress of my bed.

Q. Was there a place in the wards where you could get some privacy?

A. No, not any time in all of the years I was locked up.

Q. Were you able to get a good night's sleep?

A. No.

Q. Why not?

A. On all of the wards there was the same mixture of patients. There were some patients who had fits during the night. There were some patients who would torment other patients, screaming and hollering, and the fear, always the fear you have in your mind, I suppose, when you go to

125

sleep that maybe somebody will jump on you during the night. They never did, but you think about those things. It was a lunatic asylum.

The patient's life on the ward is also regulated by extensive, though usually unwritten, rules that are made and enforced, for the most part, not by professional staff but by nonprofessional staff. "Everyone knows the rules," most staff will say. But rarely are the rules posted or distributed to patients, and because they are not in writing, they vary from day to day, ward to ward, and employee to employee.[4]

When patients are accused of breaking these unwritten rules they may be punished, sometimes severely. Usually decisions about punishment are made by nonprofessional staff. Very few hospitals have standards or procedures for reviewing those staff decisions. Hearings are nonexistent. Complaints about punishment are rarely heeded because they are so common. In fact, many staff consider complaints to be symptoms of mental disorder. And because punishments are imposed immediately, patients have no opportunity to contact advocates, lawyers, family, or friends for assistance. Finally, because the punishment process is so haphazard, innocent patients are frequently punished.

Not only punishment decisions, but almost all decisions affecting life on the ward are made by nonprofessional staff. It could not be otherwise. Nonprofessional staff work on the wards three shifts a day seven days a week. Professional staff usually work in offices off the ward one shift a day, five days a week. Consequently, because nonprofessional staff have substantially more contact with patients than do professional staff, they control the patients' lives.

Although nonprofessional staff have greater power than professional staff, their primary responsibility is orderly and efficient operation of the hospital, not treatment, and it is that objective that guides the exercise of their power.

Professional staff necessarily rely on the observations and opinions of nonprofessional staff in planning treatment programs and in determining whether and when patients should be released. Ward staff will write in their records that the patient "lacked insight" or was "hostile," "aggressive," "violent," "depressed," "out of contact," "withdrawn," "apathetic," or "uncooperative." Favorable comments about behavior will not be entered until a patient has gained ward staff's favor. Patients soon learn that unless they please ward staff, the reports on which professional staff rely will not be favorable.

In short, everything about the patient's life depends upon pleasing the nonprofessional staff, and that requires the patient to behave in ways that make it easy for the staff to operate the hospital. Docile behavior, conforming to the routine, and following orders are therefore the prerequisites for greater privileges and, ultimately, release.

What rights do involuntarily hospitalized patients have to periodic review and release?

The first question most involuntarily hospitalized mental patients ask is "How do I get out?" In the past, most commitments to mental hospitals were indefinite. Release depended entirely on the discretion of the hospital administrator, who depended on treatment personnel, who depended on ward staff. Periodic administrative or judicial review of the necessity for continued hospitalization was rare.

There is a great deal of discussion, and very little case law, on the subject of periodic review.[4a] The basic point is quite simple. An individual's mental condition, or his social situation, often changes, and no one should continue to be confined when the reasons for confinement no longer exist. As Mr. Chief Justice Burger said in his concurring opinion in *O'Connor v. Donaldson*: "Commitment must be justified on the basis of a legitimate state interest, and the reasons for committing a particular individual must be established in an appropriate proceeding. Equally important, confinement must cease when those reasons no longer exist."[5]

Accordingly, there should be periodic review of the propriety of continued confinement. That much is clear. But two important points are not clear: (1) Who should conduct the review? The patient's doctor? Another doctor on the hospital staff? A lawyer? A judge? (2) How often should the review be conducted? Every week? Every month? Every six months? In our view, hospital personnel other than the patient's treatment team should conduct at least monthly reviews, including interviews with the patient. And a judge should review the propriety of continued confinement at least every six months, and should order the patient's release unless the hospital at that time establishes, under the same standards and procedures required for an initial hospitalization, that continued hospitalization is necessary and legally justified.

In most states, there are several ways civilly committed mental patients can be released.[6] By far the most common is administrative discharge. But allowing hospital personnel *sole* discretion over discharge is neither desirable nor constitutional. Even if the initial reasons for commitment continue, if a less restrictive alternative has become available, continued confinement in a mental hospital is unjustifiable.

We believe that periodic *judicial* review is constitutionally required. No court has so ruled, but the requirement is implicit in the Supreme Court's unanimous opinion in *O'Connor v. Donaldson*:

> Nor is it enough that Donaldson's original confinement was founded upon a constitutionally adequate basis, if in fact it was, because even if his involuntary confinement was initially permissible, it could not constitutionally continue after that basis no longer existed.[7]

The Supreme Court has thus ruled that both the initial confinement and continued confinement must satisfy *constitutional* requirements. Of course, *Donaldson* could mean only that hospital personnel must periodically review the constitutionality of continued confinement. But courts, not hospital personnel, have the final authority to determine whether the initial confinement was constitutional, and there is no persuasive reason why courts should not have the same final authority to determine whether continued confinement is constitutional. It seems clear, therefore, that periodic judicial review will at least be available on request when the patient alleges that he no longer meets constitutional standards for confinement. The only open question is whether periodic *judicial* review is constitutionally required even absent patient request. We believe it should be.

Some states, by statute, now require periodic judicial review.[8] Time periods between reviews vary from three months to a year. Some states have adopted an even more protective review procedure that requires the state to prove more to justify continued confinement than it had to prove to justify initial confinement. In California, for example, people who are dangerous to self may be committed for that reason for a maximum of 31 days. Thereafter, continued confinement would require an additional finding of danger to others or of "grave disability." Persons said to be gravely disabled may be committed for that reason for a maximum of 107 days.[9]

Most states have stricter release procedures and standards for persons committed under authority of the criminal law than for civilly committed persons. For example, "criminal" patients are rarely administratively discharged without court authorization. In our opinion, persons confined to mental hospitals under the criminal law should have substantially the same release and review rights as persons confined under the civil law. In four decisions of the United States Supreme Court[10] and in several lower court decisions,[11] the courts have held that persons confined to mental hospitals under criminal or quasicriminal authority should have substantially the same procedural protections as persons confined under civil law. The principle expressed in those cases is that neither criminal charges nor criminal conviction is a sufficient reason for varying the standards and procedures for determining the presence or absence of mental disorder (see Chapter V). In our opinion, those cases require that release and review procedures for this class of persons be substantially equivalent to release and review procedures for civilly committed persons.

Courts have recognized at least one exception to the general principle of equal standards and procedures for civil and criminal confinement; that is, after persons have been acquitted of crime by reason of insanity they may be committed to a mental hospital, at least for a short period of time, under standards and procedures less strict than civil procedures.[12] In addition, although this point has not been definitively resolved, a similar exception might allow short commitments for observation or treatment of persons thought to be incompetent to stand trial and observation of persons thought to be sexual psychopaths or defective delinquents. We believe such exceptions would not be justified for the reasons discussed in Chapter V. In any case, it seems clear that prolonged confinement of this class of persons will require standards and procedures substantially equivalent to civil standards and procedures.

One final word about release. Many states authorize mental hospitals to give "gate money," suitable clothing, and transportation to patients they release.[13] Very often patients do not know they have these rights when they leave, and they do not ask. Hospitals should post notice of these rights.

Is there a maximum period of time beyond which mental patients cannot be involuntarily confined?

In general, the criminal law establishes maximum periods of confinement for criminal offenses. Mental patients, however, are usually confined for indefinite periods, or are confined for definite periods that can repeatedly be renewed.[14] The mental health system would be a very different and more humane system if hospitals were allowed only a limited and nonrenewable period of time within which to treat or cure involuntarily confined patients. In our view, even if civil commitment continues to be permitted, no one should be involuntarily confined to a mental hospital for more than six months. This view is shared by many mental health professionals and organizations, including the American Psychological Association and the American Orthopsychiatric Association.[15]

It now seems beyond dispute that prolonged hospitalization is antitherapeutic and creates disabilities and problems as serious as, or more serious than, those that led to hospitalization. Prolonged hospitalization actually harms patients. Studies have shown that after a period of time the negative effects of "institutionalization" outweigh any therapeutic benefit to the patient of continued treatment. In fact, after a period of time the staff spends most of its energy attempting to "treat" the effects of institutionalization.[16]

Although no court has yet ruled on this issue, three Supreme Court decisions support the principle of a maximum duration for involuntary hospitalization.

In *Jackson v. Indiana,*[17] the Supreme Court held that "at the least, due process requires that the nature and *duration* of commitment bear some reasonable relation to the purpose for which the individual was committed" (emphasis added).

In *Jackson,* the Court prohibited the indefinite confinement of an incompetent defendant, and ruled that incompetent persons could be confined because of incompetence only for a limited and reasonable period of time.[18] Shortly thereafter, in *McNeil,*[19] the Supreme Court extended the principle of time limits on confinement established in *Jackson* and ruled that "just as that principle limits the permissible length of a commitment on account of incompetence to stand trial, so it also limits the permissible length of a commitment 'for observation.'" Thereafter, in *O'Connor v. Donaldson,*[20] the Supreme Court relied upon both *Jackson* and *McNeil* in ruling that a civil commitment "could not constitutionally continue" after "the basis" for the commitment no longer existed.

The due process principle of a maximum permissible period of confinement was applied in *Jackson* to confinement for incompetence to stand trial and in *McNeil* to confinement for observation. *Jackson* and *McNeil* were both unanimous decisions, and it therefore seems likely that at least a majority of the Court would apply the same time limitation to confinement for treatment. In *Donaldson,* the Court unanimously ruled that a nondangerous person committed for treatment could not be confined when he was no longer receiving treatment. It follows that a person committed for treatment cannot be confined after that point in time when continued confinement becomes harmful and antitherapeutic. That point seems to be about six months, or less.[21] After that time, involuntary patients should either be released, treated on a voluntary basis, or confined under the authority of the criminal law.

A. THE RIGHT TO REFUSE TREATMENT

Nonetheless, one of the few areas of agreement

among behavioral specialists is that uncooperative patients cannot benefit from therapy and that the first step in effective treatment is acknowledgement by the patient that he is suffering from an abnormal condition.[22]

May mental patients refuse treatment?

One of the major differences between life in a mental hospital and life on the outside is the extent to which treatments can be forced upon patients without their consent. With rare exceptions, persons outside mental hospitals, including patients in general hospitals, can refuse every form of treatment, and their right to refuse is protected by both criminal and civil laws.[23] This protection stems from the general legal principle that any unwanted bodily intrusion or physical contact is considered an assault. In mental hospitals, however, these general rules are ignored.

Almost all mental patients are forced to swallow drugs or receive them by injection. Many are shocked with electricity, and a few are subjected to operations, including operations on their brains. "It is widely *assumed* that the commitment of a person to a mental hospital, voluntary or involuntary, confers on the hospital administrators the authority to 'treat' him in whatever manner they deem appropriate."[24]

There is very little statutory or case law authority to support that assumption. Every state expressly authorizes, by statute, involuntary commitment, but very few states expressly authorize involuntary treatment. Even without express authority, however, most people in the mental health system assume that they have the right to force treatment. Only recently have mental patients begun to contest this assumption. There are only a few judicial rulings that discuss this issue. They recognize that mental patients have greater rights to refuse treatments than has been assumed.

We will discuss several legal bases of a right to refuse treatment.[25] But the primary reason most mental patients should have a right to refuse treatment is very simple: most mental patients have not been found legally incompetent by a court after a proper judicial hearing; therefore, they should have the same right as anyone else to pick and choose the treatments they will accept. In fact, the trend in mental health statutes is to preserve competence to make all decisions except decisions about commitment itself; commitment is not the equivalent of a finding of incompetence.[26]

As we discussed in Chapter II, some states permit commitment solely because a person "needs treatment." Some also require that the person be unable to "rationally choose whether to accept treatment." As we said in Chapter II, many courts have found standards such as these to be unconstitutional. In our opinion, when a mental patient is committed, unless there has been a separate incompetency proceeding that meets due process requirements, and unless it has been specifically found that the person cannot "rationally" decide to accept or refuse the specific therapy offered, the patient should retain the right to decide whether to be treated.[27] Nevertheless, although in almost every jurisdiction there is no express statutory or other legal authority to *force* treatment on committed persons,[28] forced treatment occurs every day in every state.

Privacy and personal autonomy. An important basis of a right to refuse treatment is the constitutional right to privacy and personal autonomy:

The makers of our Constitution undertook to secure conditions favorable to the pursuit of happiness. They recognized the significance of man's spiritual nature, of his feelings and of his intellect. They knew that only a part of the pain, pleasure and satisfactions of life are to be found in material things. They sought to protect Americans in their beliefs, their thoughts, their emotions and their sensations. They conferred, as against the government, the right to be let alone—the most comprehensive of rights and the right most valued by civilized men. To protect that right, every unjustifiable intrusion by the government upon the privacy of the individual, whatever the means employed, must be deemed a violation of the 4th Amendment.[29]

Several Supreme Court decisions have recognized a constitutional right to privacy and personal autonomy.[30] Recently, the Supreme Court ruled that this right protects even a minor's decision to accept or refuse the medical procedure of abortion.[31]

These principles are directly applicable to the constant intrusions that take place in mental hospitals,[32] and one court has relied upon the constitutional right of privacy and personal autonomy to protect a mental patient from psychosurgery:

> Intrusion into one's intellect, when one is involuntarily detained and subject to the control of institutional authorities, is an intrusion into one's constitutionally protected right of privacy. If one is not protected in his thoughts, behavior, personality and identity, then the right of privacy becomes meaningless.[33]

First Amendment rights. Courts have relied on the First Amendment to protect mental patients from treatments that interfere with their thought processes or their religious beliefs. Thoughts, feelings, and mental sensations are constitutionally protected by the First Amendment.[34] Two courts have relied specifically on the First Amendment to protect mental patients from psychosurgery and from behavior modification through drugs.[35] Another court ruled that a Christian Scientist mental patient could refuse tranquilizing drugs for religious reasons.[36]

Cruel and unusual punishment. The Eighth Amendment's ban on cruel and unusual punishment protects a mental patient's right to refuse certain forms of treatment. Therapies such as psychosurgery, behavior modification, electro-shock, and drugs may be so excessive as to "shock the conscience" and may violate the Eighth Amendment. For example, courts have recognized that the use of drugs for control[37] or for aversive conditioning[38] violates the Eighth Amendment, even though the intention of those administering the drugs was to treat, not punish.

Due process. One court ruled that a prison behavior

modification program was unconstitutional because the patient was not given adequate procedural protections prior to placement in the program.[39]

Least restrictive alternative. Another basis for a right to refuse treatment is the general rule that even when the state is otherwise permitted to interfere with the "fundamental personal liberties" we have just discussed, it may only do so in the least intrusive manner.[40] Thus the constitutional right to the least restrictive alternative requires the least intrusive treatment in the hospital, just as it requires the least restrictive conditions of confinement (see Chapter III). In other words, even if patients do not have a right to refuse all forms of treatment, they may nevertheless be able to refuse more intrusive forms of treatment unless less intrusive forms of treatment have been tried and found ineffective.

This means that when two or more therapies are possible, the patient should be able to choose among them. For example, both antidepressant medication and electroconvulsive therapy are commonly used to treat depression. Under the principle of the least restrictive alternative, the patient should be allowed to choose which form of therapy he prefers. Similarly, many patients would prefer seclusion or physical restraint rather than restraint or control by chemical medications. That choice should be respected.

What is the relationship between consent and the right to refuse treatment?

The concept of consent is closely related to the concept of a right to refuse treatment. Even if patients have a right to refuse treatment, if they consent to treatment, they have, in effect, waived their right to refuse. It is therefore important to understand what consent means.

Consent is a very complicated issue and is itself the subject of several books and articles.[41] In this answer, we will only mention the more important aspects of consent.

Because consent has such substantial consequences, including waiver of constitutional rights, courts have established principles for determining whether consent is valid. The fact that the patient has said "I consent" is not enough. Generally, in order for a consent to be valid, (1) it must be based on adequate knowledge and information, (2) it must be given by a person who has the legal capacity to consent, and (3) it must be voluntarily given.[42]

(1.) One of the most rapidly developing doctrines in mental health law is the doctrine of *informed* consent, which requires that the patient be given specific and adequate information about the proposed treatment procedure, including the way it is administered, its probability of success or failure, its risks and side effects, alternative treatment procedures, and the probable consequences of not receiving the treatment.[43]

Under the doctrine of informed consent, it is the duty of the mental health professional to provide the necessary information whether the patient requests it or not. The precise information that must be given will depend on the nature, severity, and consequences of the proposed treatment. In the next answer, we will briefly discuss the legal requirements for consent to particular treatments.

(2.) Conveying the relevant information is pointless if the patient lacks the capacity to understand. Most mental patients have the capacity to understand the kinds of information we discussed in paragraph 1. But some do not.

Some patients have been found by a court to be "mentally incompetent," which means they lack the legal capacity to make certain decisions about their lives. Other patients, though not yet adjudicated incompetent, nevertheless are, in fact, unable to understand the information given them. If there is reasonable doubt about a patient's capacity to understand, the mental health professional should request a court to decide whether the patient has the capacity to consent. If so, the patient's consent may be accepted. If not, the mental health professional will have to obtain the "substitute consent" of a court-appointed guardian or direct judicial authorization for the proposed treatment.[44] In addition, before giving "substitute consent," guardians should obtain judicial authorization to consent to the specific treatment (see Chapter IV).

(3.) Even if the necessary information has been conveyed and the patient has the capacity to understand it, the patient's consent will not be valid unless it is voluntarily given. Several courts have held that the coercive nature of mental hospitals makes it impossible for patients to give voluntary consent.[45] For example, a promise of release or transfer to a better ward contingent upon consent to treatment may influence the patient so much that the consent should not be considered voluntary.

In our view, in order to ensure that consent is truly voluntary, the patient should be given the right to revoke consent at any time, without penalty.[46]

Finally, some forms of treatment are so experimental, hazardous, or intrusive that courts will not permit involuntarily confined patients or substitute decision makers to consent to them.[47]

What have courts said about consent to, or refusal of, specific treatments?

Courts examine the validity of a consent to psychosurgery or sterilization differently from consent to less intrusive treatments. The validity of a particular consent or refusal will depend upon the nature of the treatment, the patient's interests, and the state's interests.

Psychosurgery is probably the most intrusive psychiatric therapy. Its effects are nonreversible and it usually profoundly alters personality and thought processes. There are several different methods of psychosurgery, including lobotomy and brain stimulation. At least one state prohibits it.[48] One state court has ruled that because psychosurgery is such a drastic procedure, an involuntarily confined mental patient will not be permitted to consent to it.[49]

Psychosurgery has generated a vast amount of legal and ethical discussion.[50] We believe it is beyond dispute that psychosurgery requires consent, and that even patients who have been found mentally ill and committed by court order can still refuse psychosurgery. Even if consent is given, it should be carefully examined and declared valid by a court before the psychosurgery is performed.[51]

Experimental treatments on mental patients. These treatments are nearly as controversial as psychosurgery. It is difficult to obtain informed consent to experimental treatments because their risks, side effects, and benefits are unknown. Most authorities agree that because of the peculiar problems of obtaining informed and voluntary consent to experimental treatments, those treatments should be subject to additional restrictions. In addition to the patient's voluntary consent, we believe experimental treatments should be subject to the following restrictions.[52] First, experimental treatments should not be used on involuntarily confined persons unless, because of their special problems, they are the only persons who might benefit from the treatment if successful. Second, there should be a strong expectation of benefit to the individual subjects of the experiment, and that benefit must clearly outweigh all expected risks to them. Third, the experiment must be conducted humanely. Fourth, corrective or follow-up care must be guaranteed. And fifth, the subjects of the experiment must be told that they have the right to terminate the experiment at any time without penalty. We believe that unless these requirements are met, patients should not be subjected to experimental treatments even if they consent. There are additional problems with experimental treatment of incompetent patients. If it is ever to be permitted, it should at least require the review and approval of a special committee appointed for that purpose, as one court has held.[53]

Sterilization is not a treatment, but it is still occasionally used on mental patients, and more often on the retarded. It is usually nonreversible and directly affects the fundamental right to have children.[54] Cases have permitted sterilization with the consent of a competent person after complete due process procedures.[55] Some of these cases forbid sterilization of minors and incompetents.[56] Thus the right to refuse sterilization is respected, and consent, even when given, is closely analyzed before it is declared valid.

Electroshock. ECT treatment is still quite commonly used in many hospitals and is one of the most controversial therapies.[57] In many mental hospitals, however, it is not used at all. There is considerable debate about its success in general. Some authorities believe that ECT helps a majority of the patients on whom it is used. Others believe that it helps few patients. But even if shock therapy helps a substantial percentage of the patients on whom it is used, there is very little evidence that psychiatrists can predict whether ECT will benefit an individual patient. No one really understands how ECT works when it does. The procedure is simple: Powerful jolts of electric current are used to shock the brain. Unconsciousness and at least one violent convulsion follow. Afterward, memory of up to several weeks prior to the treatment is lost, sometimes forever. Occasionally the convulsions cause broken bones, particularly when muscle-relaxing medications are not administered. Usually the long-lasting effects are not so profound as the effects of psychosurgery. But many patients view electroshock as torture. The experience and the disorientation that follow it are, at least, unpleasant. Nevertheless, in most states shock therapy is routinely administered without the consent of the patient. If anyone consents, it is often a parent or relative who participated in the hospitalization of the patient.

At least two courts have recognized the right of mental patients to be fully informed before they consent to ECT.[58]

At least one court has ruled that patients who have not been found incompetent by a court retain the right to refuse shock treatment.[59] Several states regulate by statute the use of shock treatment, and at least one requires a hearing before ECT treatment.[60] Some state statutes expressly require the consent of a competent patient,[61] but all allow substituted consent for "incompetents."[62] One federal court ruled that electroshock could not be administered without the patient's express consent after consultation with counsel.[63]

Behavior modification includes a very broad range of behavior-change techniques. Examples are token economies on wards of hospitals—where behaviors earn or lose tokens that buy essential needs as well as privileges[64]—and anectine therapy—in which a drug that simulates loss of breathing ability is administered as part of a behavior-change program.[65] Other examples include isolation of prisoners in bare cells with privileges added only when their behavior is acceptable,[66] and shots of apomorphine, which causes vomiting, as punishment for unacceptable behavior.[67]

Some forms of behavior modification are much more severe than others. The less severe forms usually do not require consent. Mental patients are placed on token economy wards, for example, without their consent. Involuntary placement on such a ward may not be constitutional if the token economy program inhibits the exercise of specific constitutional rights such as communication, privacy, or association, or if it withholds basic necessities such as food, clothing, or shelter from patients who do not conform their behavior to the program's requirements. More intrusive behavior modification programs almost certainly require the patient's consent, or substituted consent under due process standards and procedures.[68]

Drug therapy is by far the most common treatment in mental hospitals. It is the least expensive and, according to one study, the treatment that leads to the earliest release.[69]

On the other hand, there is evidence that the most commonly used drugs, phenothiazines, may in the long run be antitherapeutic for a substantial percentage of mental patients. A recent study showed that a group of hospitalized mental patients who received drugs seemed to do better while in the hospital and were released sooner than a matched control group of hospitalized mental patients who received no drugs. But the study showed that after release the group that had received no drugs adjusted much better to life in the community and had fewer subsequent rehospitalizations than did the group that had been given drugs.[70] This study should trouble mental health professionals because it provides evidence that even if drugs do help patients adjust to life in the hospital, as many mental health professionals believe, they may inhibit the patient's adjustment to life in the community.

There are additional reasons why it might be reasonable for patients to refuse drugs. Most drugs used in mental hospitals have serious side effects after prolonged use. The most common drugs, the phenothiazines, can cause permanent and irreversible damage to brain cells, a condition called "tardive dyskinesia." The symptoms include uncontrollable rhythmic lip, tongue, facial, and hand movements, deterioration of posture, and inability to speak normally (see Appendix B). Short-term reversible effects include muscle spasms, skin color changes and rashes, loss of sexual drive, dizziness, drowsiness, weight gain, enlargement of the breasts, dry mouth, blurred vision, depression, and lowered body temperature (see Appendix B). One major problem with these drugs is that the normal temporary effects are often similar to the permanent effects of tardive dyskinesia, so that patients may not know they have developed tardive dyskinesia until the drugs are discontinued. For this and similar reasons, many mental health professionals recommend regular "drug holidays," during which patients are taken off drugs entirely for specified periods.

Despite the dangerous and uncomfortable side effects of most drugs used in mental hospitals, almost every hospitalized mental patient is on a drug regimen. In many hospitals, drugs are drastically misused and overused[71] to "quiet things down" and to "control" patients. Drugs are often a substitute for staff, programs, or decent living conditions. They are used as an effective method for suppressing complaints. Sometimes they are used as punishment.

Generally, mental hospitals neither inform patients about the risks and benefits of drugs nor respect a patient's refusal to take drugs. Drugs are routinely forced on objecting patients by "shooting" them with a needle while they are physically restrained. Some patients struggle; others learn resistance is in vain. Much of the physical abuse of patients in hospitals occurs during these incidents.

Of course the law protects "normal" patients from unwanted drugs. Everyone but mental patients can refuse any drug he does not want, and doctors have a duty to inform "general" patients of the likely effects of drugs before they consent to drug therapy.[72] Several courts have recognized a similar right for mental patients in many situations. One court said, "[C]ertainly absent an emergency, unconsented to medical treatment is a tort" when it ruled that forced drugging may violate at least four constitutional rights.[73]

Several courts have forbidden drugging for control, or as a substitute for understaffing and lack of programs.[74] One court specifically recognized a right to refuse drugs before a commitment hearing.[75] And two other courts have recognized a right not to be drugged excessively if participation at the commitment hearing would be affected.[76] One statute permits refusal of drugs during the 24-hour period before the initial commitment hearing.[77]

In short, courts and legislatures are just beginning to

recognize a patient's right to refuse drugs. As the side effects of drugs become more widely known, it is likely that the right to refuse medication will be substantially expanded.

Psychotherapy is the most common nonorganic therapy.[78] It presents few problems about the right to refuse treatment because it essentially depends on consensual participation. On the other hand, requiring the attendance of patients at individual or group psychotherapy sessions may raise the issue of a right to refuse participation if punishments follow refusal.

B. THE RIGHT TO BE PROTECTED FROM RESTRAINTS, LOSS OF PRIVILEGES, AND PUNISHMENTS

What rights do mental patients have to be protected from restraints, loss of privileges, and punishments?

The scope of a right to be protected from restraints, loss of privileges, or other punishments the hospital believes are necessary to maintain order and safety is largely undetermined.[79] As with so many other issues in mental hospitals, the undefined line between "treatment" and control of patients makes the problem difficult. For example, drugs are routinely used for both treatment and control of the same patient at the same time.[80]

Hospital staff almost always attempt to justify restraints, seclusion, denial of privileges, or other restrictions as necessary for "treatment." Each of these restrictions may abridge specific constitutional rights. Seclusion, physical restraints, straps, cuffs, and straitjackets inhibit movement and personal freedom, and abridge the right to religious worship, association with other patients, and communication with the outside. Chemical restraints also interfere with the right to think and speak.[81] Some of the "privileges" patients commonly lose include grounds privileges, telephone use, and the right to be with members of the opposite sex. In fact, when patients first arrive at hospitals they are often placed on locked wards and automatically denied ground privileges, telephone access, the opportunity to associate with the opposite sex, the opportunity to go to church. After a period of evaluation and good behavior (often including adequate performance at a job in the hospital), certain privileges are allowed. When a patient is involved in a dispute, refuses medication, breaks any of the special ward rules, or does not "progress" sufficiently, privileges are withdrawn or delayed.[82]

Seclusion and loss of privileges are usually entirely within the discretion of ward staff. In practice, ward staff often make the decision to administer or increase drug dosages and to place patients in restraints, although doctors often review these measures after they are imposed.

As we mentioned earlier in this chapter, few hospitals have standard written policies that regulate ward staff discretion. Different shifts of staff react differently to similar rule violations. Patients have little or no notice of the rules they will be punished for violating. And there are no due process procedures to allow wrongfully punished patients to challenge arbitrary decisions.

Courts are beginning to face some of these issues. One federal court found that certain rights were absolute, and that no "treatment" reason could justify their denial[83]: the right to send and receive sealed mail to and from attorneys, doctors, mental health professionals, and public officials; the right to physical exercise; the right to be outdoors; the right to religious worship; the right to interact with the opposite sex; and the right not to be forced to perform labor for maintenance of the hospital. The same court permitted denial of other rights when the denial was related to treatment, but limited the authority of hospital staff to restrain or seclude patients. It required that a professional staff member make such decisions, and required frequent and regular professional review of the patient's condition.[84] The court also prohibited the use of drugs for control or punishment, or as a substitute for a therapeutic program.[85]

Other courts have ruled that due process rights are violated when a patient is transferred from an open ward to a locked ward without an opportunity for notice, a hearing, and other procedural rights.[86]

Several courts have required that hospital decisions conform to the doctrine of the least restrictive alternative[87] (see Chapter III). This doctrine can be a powerful tool for challenging the necessity for particular punishments and restrictions.

C. THE RIGHT TO TREATMENT

Do involuntarily confined mental patients have a right to treatment?

One of the most widely discussed, and most commonly misunderstood, of the rights of mental patients is the so-called right to treatment. Several lower courts have ruled that involuntarily confined mental patients have a right to treatment.[88] And the decision of the Supreme Court in *O'Connor v. Donaldson*[89] gives substantial, though indirect, support to that view. The actual holding in *O'Connor v. Donaldson* is important, but, as the plaintiff had urged, quite narrow. The Court unanimously held that "a finding of 'mental illness' alone [we believe that means without an additional finding of "dangerousness"] cannot justify a State's locking a person up against his will and keeping him indefinitely in simple custodial confinement [we believe that means confinement without treatment]."[90] That holding is repeated, in slightly different wording, three paragraphs later: "In short, a State cannot constitutionally confine without more [again, we believe that means without more than custodial care] a nondangerous individual who is capable of surviving safely in freedom by himself or with the help of willing and responsible family members or friends."[91]

Because the holding is phrased negatively—it specifies what the state *cannot* do rather than what it must do—many people have questioned whether it does establish a constitutional right to psychiatric treatment. That question is based upon a misunderstanding of the legal theory underlying the so-called right to treatment.

Most people, and certainly most mental health professionals, think of the phrase "right to treatment" as describing an affirmative and unconditional right to receive a certain level of psychiatric service. In fact, the Constitution provides little support for such a right, and the Supreme Court in *O'Connor v. Donaldson* was not even asked to declare such a right. Rather, the plaintiff only asked the Supreme Court to rule that nondangerous involuntary patients have a conditional right either to receive a certain level of psychiatric services, or else to be restored to liberty. More precisely, the plaintiff asked the Court to rule that nondangerous patients have a constitutional right to liberty that can be abridged, if at all, only if they receive treatment. And that, in effect, is precisely what the Court ruled.

The words "right to treatment" nowhere appear in the United States Constitution. There is no specific or explicit constitutional "right to treatment." The "right to treatment" is really only a shorthand phrase, and a somewhat misleading one at that, for describing the legal requirements that can arguably be implied, or derived from, several explicit constitutional rights. The principal constitutional rights that have been relied upon as the foundation for a right to treatment are the Due Process Clause of the Fourteenth Amendment, which includes both procedural due process and substantive due process; the Equal Protection Clause of the Fourteenth Amendment; and the Cruel and Unusual Punishment Clause of the Eighth Amendment. Those explicit constitutional rights, like most of the provisions of the Bill of Rights, share one common feature. They are essentially rights against state involvement.[92] Accordingly, it follows, in a very general sense, that rights derived from those explicit constitutional rights will be triggered only when the explicit rights are themselves triggered—that is, only when the state is in some manner "denying" persons liberty, or is in some manner inflicting "cruel and unusual punishment."

There has been very little thoughtful analysis of the various legal foundations for a right to treatment,[93] or of the possibility that the nature and scope of a right to treatment derived from one constitutional provision might be different from the nature and scope of a right to treatment derived from a different constitutional provision. This section, however, is not the occasion for such an analysis.

The legal theory used in *O'Connor v. Donaldson* is called substantive due process. The theory is actually quite straightforward: all persons have an explicit constitutional right to liberty. The Due Process Clause places substantive limitations on deprivations of liberty. That is, even if the procedures resulting in deprivation of liberty are fair, the state can deprive persons of liberty under those procedures only if the state has a substantial and legitimate interest in doing so. For example, the state does not have a substantial and legitimate interest in confining people because they have red hair. Thus, even if a state were to give all persons "charged" with having red hair all the usual procedural rights, including a free lawyer and jury trial, the state still could not confine people who were found, under those procedures, to have red hair because that would violate the substantive limitations on state power imposed by the Due Process Clause.

In *O'Connor v. Donaldson,* the Court ruled that states do not have a sufficiently substantial and legitimate interest in confining nondangerous persons for the purpose of providing custodial care to justify the deprivation of liberty. States may or may not have a sufficiently substantial interest in confining nondangerous persons for the purpose of providing treatment to justify the deprivation of liberty. We do not think they do, but the Supreme Court did not answer that question. But let us assume for the moment, as we do not, that confinement for the purpose of treatment is a sufficiently substantial and legitimate state interest to justify deprivation of liberty. Even if that were so, traditional due process theory would still require a court to determine whether the ostensible state interest has a foundation in fact. In short, if the state interest that justifies deprivation of liberty is treatment, then, absent treatment, the justification disappears, and the individual is entitled to restoration of his constitutional right to liberty.

Accordingly, instead of talking about an affirmative and unconditional right to treatment, it would be more accurate to talk about a conditional right either to be treated, or else restored to liberty. And in order to preserve the individual's equally important right to *refuse* treatment, it would be more accurate still to talk about a right to the *opportunity* to receive treatment, or else to the restoration of liberty.

The *Donaldson* decision left undecided several very important questions. The Court expressly ruled, for example, that there was "no reason now to decide whether mentally ill persons dangerous to themselves or to others have a right to treatment upon compulsory confinement by the state, or whether the state may compulsorily confine a non-dangerous mentally ill individual for the purpose of treatment."[94]

Patients and mental health professionals are obviously concerned about how these and other open issues will be resolved in the future. We do not know. But we do know the positions we and other lawyers will be urging in future litigation, and they are positions we are reasonably confident the courts will adopt.

1. *Treatment of dangerous patients.* Our position will be that even persons who are dangerous to themselves or others (as defined below) have a constitutional right to the opportunity for treatment (as defined below), or else to release from civil confinement. Several lower courts have adopted this position.[95]

2. *Hospitalization of the nondangerous mentally ill.* Our position will be that civil confinement of a nondangerous person is not constitutionally permissible even if that person is given adequate treatment. The *Donaldson* opinion strongly suggests that the Supreme Court would agree with this position, and Mr. Chief Justice Burger's concurring opinion suggests that he would favor this position: "Nor can I accept the theory that a State may lawfully confine an individual thought to need treatment and justify that deprivation of liberty solely by providing some treatment. Our concepts of due process would not tolerate such a 'tradeoff.' "[96]

3. *The definition of custodial care.* The *Donaldson* opinion requires something "more" than custodial care, but does not define custodial care. In our opinion, if a hospital merely provides clothing, shelter, a "structured environment," routine medical care, occasional or even daily psychiatric medication, infrequent or purely administrative contacts with mental health professionals, or occasional "group therapy," that should be considered a "custodial" facility within the meaning of *Donaldson*. If a mental health professional refuses to release a nondangerous person confined under those conditions, that should be considered a violation of *Donaldson*. We expect there will be considerable litigation on this point, but we are reasonably

confident our position will prevail. *Donaldson* was, after all, a unanimous opinion. The Court obviously felt strongly that custodial care is not enough, and we do not believe that a maintenance regime will satisfy the Court.

In other words, token efforts at "treatment" will not justify confinement in what is, essentially, a nontreatment environment. It therefore becomes important to adopt at least a rough working definition of what is meant by "treatment."

4. *The definition of treatment.* The Court did not define treatment. It did rule, however, that courts *can* get involved in the business of determining whether treatment is provided, whether it is "adequate," and "how much or what kind of treatment would suffice."[97] Moreover, the opinion strongly suggests that the Court is prepared to rule in future cases that a hospital environment will not be considered a treatment environment unless each patient is cared for under a "program" that is individually "designed" to "alleviate or cure his supposed illness."[98]

The general consensus among lower courts has been that "treatment" refers to a level of services that gives the patient a reasonable opportunity to cure or improve his mental condition, and that is provided pursuant to a comprehensive written plan that is tailored to meet specified long- and short-range objectives for that individual patient, using specified methods and services. The absence of such a plan should be a *prima facie* indication that only custodial care is being provided. Hospitals claiming to provide treatment should have the burden of proving that, in addition to individualized treatment plans, they provide a humane physical and psychological environment and qualified staff adequate to implement the individualized treatment plans. Several courts have already adopted this three-point definition of treatment.[99]

Even more important questions will have to be decided in future cases. If patients do have a right to treatment or release, it is surely arguable that they have a right to *effective* treatment.[100] That is, if treatment does not offer a reasonable opportunity for cure or improvement, it does not justify deprivation of liberty. Accordingly, it is likely that mental health professionals will soon be called upon to prove, to the satisfaction of judges, that psychiatric treatment actually works. Given restrictions on human experimentation, it may be difficult to provide such proof. As we noted earlier, mental health professionals can say that patients seem to improve after receiving certain medications, but they cannot say that patients improve because of the medications unless they have studied a control group of similar and similarly situated patients who did not receive medication (see Chapter I).

Even if certain treatments can be shown to be effective for certain classes of patients, mental health professionals may be required to prove that they can predict, with reasonable accuracy, whether those forms of treatment will benefit an individual member of that class. For example, a recent study by the research department at Langley Porter Neuropsychiatric Institute[101] concludes that "there is a subgroup of schizophrenics who do well or better long term without the routine or continuous use of antipsychotic medication. This finding underlines the need for more selective utilization of antipsychotic medication." Unfortunately, the authors could not identify factors for predicting which patients would benefit from phenothiazines and which would not. That is troublesome because in the sample they studied it was found that patients "treated with placebos in contrast to those treated with chlorpromazine while hospitalized showed significantly greater long-term clinical improvement, less pathology at followup, fewer rehospitalizations and better overall functioning in the community between one and three years after discharge."

If that study is accurate, it suggests that antipsychotic medication, the most common form of "treatment" in public mental hospitals, may be antitherapeutic in the long run for a substantial but not easily identifiable subgroup of acute schizophrenic patients. For those patients, a right to treatment would mean a right *not* to be treated with antipsychotic medication.

There are, of course, several different methods for evaluating the effectiveness of treatment.[102] The three most common forms of evaluation could be called (a) precondition, (b) process, and (c) outcome.

a. Courts could determine whether the hospital provides the minimum preconditions for treatment. One teacher, without books, pencils, paper, or blackboard, could not possibly "teach" 5,000 pupils to read or write. Similarly, without a decent physical environment and equipment, and without adequate numbers of appropriately trained staff, mental hospitals could not possibly "treat" patients. This "precondition" approach to evaluating treatment in mental hospitals is the method most often used by courts. The advantage of this method is that it can be used to force substantial improvements in the hospital environment and personnel.

b. Or courts could look at the "process" of treatment. Does each patient have an individually tailored treatment plan? Is it regularly reviewed and revised? Is a designated mental health professional responsible for the treatment of each patient? And so on. Several courts have used this method of evaluating treatment. And many courts have combined the precondition and process methods. The major problem with both these methods is that neither guarantees the treatment will actually work.

c. The third method, the "outcome" method, directly measures whether the patient was cured or improved. To date, courts have paid little attention to the outcome method, but we expect increased judicial reliance on this method in future cases.

In addition, we expect two other judicial responses to the problem of measuring the effectiveness of treatment. First, courts may begin to require proof *during the commitment hearing* that "there is treatment available for the illness diagnosed," as one court has already done.[103] That is, *before* involuntary hospitalization, the hospital will have to prove that it has the staff and facilities necessary to provide a "treatment program for the illness suffered by the person whose commitment is sought."[104] That requirement would put mental health professionals in the unusual but entirely appropriate position of opposing hospitalization in individual cases because of the unavailability of treatment.

Second, courts could simply establish a rule-of-thumb presumption that if a patient has not recovered or improved within a given period of time, that would be *prima facie* evidence that the patient is not treatable or that the hospital has not provided treatment that gives the reasonable opportunity for cure or improvement discussed earlier in this chapter. In either event, the patient would probably be entitled to release. That is, instead of attempting to measure the efficacy of treatment in individual cases, courts could simply limit the maximum permissible period of involuntary confinement for the purpose of treatment. As we noted earlier, the Supreme Court has already ruled that the Due Process Clause prohibits the indefinite confinement of persons as mentally incompetent to stand trial on criminal charges, and prohibits the indefinite confinement of persons committed for observation to determine whether they suffer from a mental disorder.[105] As the Court unanimously ruled in one of those cases, "due process requires that the nature and *duration* of commitment bear some reasonable relation to the purpose for which the individual is committed."[106] Given the Supreme Court's imposition of due process deadlines on commitment because of incompetence to stand trial and on commitment for observation, it seems fair to conclude that the Court would be willing to impose a due process deadline on commitment for treatment.

For these and other reasons, the American Psychological Association, the American Orthopsychiatric Association, and the American Civil Liberties Union have recommended that courts "put a time limit on involuntary commitment . . . there is no logic in the continued confinement of persons when treatment demonstrably can no longer succeed . . . durational limitations take into account the debilitating effects of long-term institutionalization, and provide a built-in mechanism for guaranteeing that the patient is released from an institution at a point before the beneficial effects of his hospitalization are clearly outweighed by its detrimental effects."[107]

It seems to us only a matter of time before courts impose absolute and nonrenewable time limits on the permissible period of involuntary hospitalization for the purpose of treatment.[108] At the expiration of such periods, involuntary patients would have to be released or converted to true voluntary status.

5. *The definition of "dangerous."* In *Donaldson*, the Court did not define what it meant by "dangerous." It did think it relevant that there was no evidence of a dangerous

"act" and no "evidence" that Donaldson had been "suicidal" or "likely" to inflict "injury" upon himself.[109] And the Court noted that a person would be, at least "literally," dangerous to self "if for physical or other reasons he is helpless to avoid the hazards of freedom either through his own efforts or with the aid of willing family members or friends." The Court contrasted dangerous persons with "harmless" persons, and apparently assumed that constitutionally, a person could not be considered dangerous to self merely because that person's "living standard" in the "community" was inferior to the "comforts" of a custodial institution.[110] Thus we cannot be sure where the Court will draw the line on "dangerous to self," but we can be reasonably confident that people who can "survive" (a word used three times by the Court) in the community, cannot be considered dangerous to themselves, even if their standard of living—food, clothing, and shelter—is lower than that they would receive in a custodial facility. The important point here is that the Court has clearly rejected a "welfare" standard in favor of a "survival" standard. Thus, although it may be thought to be in a person's welfare or best interests to sleep in a hospital bed and eat warm food rather than to sleep on a park bench and eat from a can, persons who sleep on benches and eat from cans cannot, without more evidence, be considered dangerous to self within the meaning of *Donaldson*.

Despite these uncertainties, we believe a finding of danger to self or others will require proof, based upon *evidence* of a recent overt act, threat, or attempt, that it is probable the prospective patient would inflict substantial *physical* injury upon himself or others in the immediate future unless hospitalized. As we noted earlier, several courts and legislatures have already adopted that definition or its substantial equivalent.[111] This is essentially the standard urged by the American Psychological Association, the American Orthopsychiatric Association, and the American Civil Liberties Union.[112]

In summary, it seems probable to us that courts will eventually rule that both dangerous and nondangerous patients have a constitutional right either to receive effective treatment or to be released from involuntary confinement.

Whether "voluntary" patients will have a similar right is less clear.

Do "voluntary" mental patients have a right to treatment?

In some states, voluntary patients have a statutory right to treatment. But they probably do not have a constitutional right to treatment. As we noted in the preceding answer, the "right to treatment" is a conditional right that is triggered by deprivation of some other specific constitutional right—usually the right to liberty. Since "voluntary" patients are presumably entitled to release upon request, and thus have not been "deprived" of their right to liberty, the legal theory that supports a right to treatment probably does not apply to them. Of course, many "voluntary" patients are really confined involuntarily (see Chapter IV), and therefore they should have the same rights—including a right to treatment or release—as involuntary patients.

Although truly voluntary patients probably do not have a constitutional right to treatment (services that give them a reasonable opportunity to get better), they may well have a constitutional right to be protected from harm (services that at least prevent them from getting worse). This theory has been applied in one case, a case involving mentally retarded residents of a state institution.[113] The court ruled that once the state had accepted custody of the residents—even voluntary residents—it had a constitutional duty to provide whatever services were required, including affirmative services that are indistinguishable from "treatment" services, and to prevent preventable intellectual, emotional, social, and physical harm and deterioration.

As we noted earlier in this chapter, prolonged hospitalization causes similar harm and deterioration to most mental patients, and it is therefore fair to conclude that voluntary mental patients may have a constitutional right to receive whatever services are necessary to protect them from harm.

Do mental patients have a right to communicate with people outside the mental hospital?

Usually hospitals restrict the communication rights of mental patients when they are first committed. Mail, telephone, and visitation rights are often withdrawn or granted as part of the privilege system of discipline rather than as part of a treatment plan.

The right to communicate and associate are protected by the First Amendment. The right to speak with a lawyer is protected by the Sixth Amendment. Therefore, even if there is a legitimate reason for abridging those rights, as with other fundamental rights there should be a compelling reason to abridge them, and all less restrictive ways of achieving the legitimate objective without abridging those rights should first have been tried.

A mere claim that the patient's "treatment" requires abridgment of those rights should not be sufficient. The patient should be able to contest such abridgments in court, at which time the hospital should have to prove the necessity for the abridgment.

There is growing recognition that mental patients have rights to communicate and to have visits from lawyers, public officials, and outside mental health professionals.[114] Some states and courts have recognized the right of mental patients to have full access to the press, friends, and other people by mail or telephone.[115] In one recent case a federal court ruled that patients in a Wisconsin hospital who contacted local reporters and were punished as a result had a right not to have their mail censored, and had a right to a due process hearing before the hospital took punitive measures against them.[116]

What privacy rights do hospitalized mental patients have?

Usually, patients do not have private places to store letters, books, toothbrushes, photographs, and other private possessions. They rarely have a place to go where they can be alone, or out of earshot from ward noise and activity. They usually are forced to sleep in a crowded dormitory. Furthermore, most mental hospitals subject patients to unannounced searches of their belongings and then display or read private and personal letters and writings.[117] Several courts have recognized the importance of privacy in connection with right-to-treatment lawsuits. As one federal court put it, "patients have a right to privacy and dignity."[118] And at least two courts have restricted researchers from viewing mental patients or their records without the consent of the individual patients.[119]

Do hospitalized mental patients have a right to spend or control the disposition of their money or other assets?

Many patients have sources of income that continue after hospitalization. These include Social Security, veterans' benefits, other disability benefits, tax refunds, and proceeds from investments or trusts. Some mental patients are paid for work they do in the hospital.

Most statutes and court decisions now recognize that there is a substantial difference between "mental illness" and "mental incompetence."[120] Outside the hospital, persons who have been found "mentally ill" but not "mentally incompetent" can still manage their own business affairs and control the disposition of their assets. But in some states, persons hospitalized because of "mental illness" are treated as if they were "mentally incompetent." Many states appropriate any money the hospitalized patient receives. Some state laws expressly authorize hospital superintendents to confiscate all money in excess of a specified amount, and apply the excess to the cost of hospitalization. The balance is usually placed in an account the hospital keeps for patients. Usually hospitals allow patients to keep a few dollars, or draw small amounts from their hospital accounts, to purchase cigarettes and sweets.

The Social Security Administration permits mental hospitals to fill out simple forms that designate the superintendent of the hospital "payee" for Social Security payments owed the patient.[121] Payments meant for patients go to the superintendent, whose business office at the hospital deducts the cost of hospitalization, pays bills, and acts as trustee for the patient. The hospitalized patient thus loses control over his Social Security funds without any judicial hearing, notice, or finding that he is incompetent to handle funds.

Recently, several courts have invalidated these procedures on due process grounds,[122] ruling that states may not appropriate patients' assets for any purpose without notice and a hearing to determine whether the appropriation is justifiable. Several courts have invalidated these procedures on equal protection grounds, ruling that persons who have not been declared "incompetent" should not be treated as if they were incompetent just because they are or have been hospitalized.[123] One court ruled that the fact of confinement does not justify the appropriation of a patient's assets.[124]

Although hospitals claim that these summary or short-cut procedures are designed to protect and preserve the patient's assets, they are often used to deplete the patient's assets in order to reimburse the hospital for the costs of the patient's care and treatment (see next question). One court ruled that state hospitals should not be in a better position to collect alleged debts than other creditors, who must file lawsuits to collect unpaid debts, and therefore prohibited the use of the short-cut Social Security procedures to collect debts.[125]

Must involuntarily hospitalized patients pay the costs of their hospitalization?

Almost all states have statutes that require patients and/or their families to pay the costs of both voluntary and involuntary hospitalization.[126]

If the patient and his relatives are indigent, those costs are paid for by the state or county. But if they have any financial resources at all, some payment will be required. Generally, the mental health commissioner or hospital board determines the amount to be paid. Sometimes the amount is determined by the court during the commitment hearing. Some states have elaborate and complex procedures for the determination of liability which take up pages and pages of the statute. In other states the procedures can be described in a few sentences.

Because the practice of making patients pay for the cost of their involuntary hospitalization is so universal, and has been going on for so long, any legal challenge to its validity will probably fail initially. Nevertheless, it is important for patients to begin to resist paying for "treatment" involuntarily incurred.

Implied contract. The practice of compelling involuntary mental patients to pay the state for their maintenance and treatment is, in theory, difficult to justify. In most situations, financial liability requires a "contract" or express agreement to pay. One person agrees to buy what the other agrees to sell. In legal terms, this is called "a meeting of the minds." Without such an agreement, there is no "contract" and no liability to pay. Obviously, when a person is "treated" against his will, no *express* contract exists.

In some situations, however, the courts will find an *Implied* contract. For example, when a person goes into a restaurant and orders a meal, there is no express contract that he will pay for the meal, but there is an implied contract that he will pay. But when a patient is committed to a hospital against his will, an agreement to pay cannot even be implied because the facts do not indicate that the patient has silently agreed to pay.

Sometimes, however, a court rules that a contract will be implied as a matter of *law*, even though the facts do not indicate that the person has silently agreed to pay. This occurs when one party derives "unjust enrichment" from the other party. For example, Mr. Smith asks a construction company to build a house for him on plot A, but the construction company accidentally builds the house on the adjoining plot B, which is also owned by Mr. Smith. All the while, Mr. Smith is aware of the mistake the construction company is making, but remains silent. When the house is built, Mr. Smith refuses to pay, claiming that he only agreed to pay for a house built on plot A. In such a case, the law recognizes a contract implied in *law*, because otherwise, Mr. Smith would be unjustly enriched—he would get a free house.

Has an involuntary patient who refuses to pay been unjustly enriched? There are at least three arguments against such a proposition. First, if the patient has been enriched, he has not been "unjustly" enriched because, unlike Mr. Smith, he did not remain silent in order to get something for nothing. Second, one could argue that he has not been enriched at all. Most state hospitals are woefully understaffed and give meager or inadequate treatment. Even in states where "medical and psychiatric care and treatment" is a statutory right, the doctor-patient ratio is usually inadequate. Many studies show that hospitalized mental patients who recover do so despite their "treatment," and not because of it. And other studies indicate that as a general rule, the longer a patient remains in a state hospital, the less likely he is ever to leave. For many, commitment is *anti*therapeutic. And third, many state patients are forced to perform cost-saving labor for the hospital for no pay. Certainly those patients have already paid for the cost of their maintenance through their work.

Double taxation. There is another argument to be made against the financial liability of *all* state hospital patients. One of the primary justifications for the commitment of people to state hospitals is that the welfare of the community will best be served by removing the mentally ill from the community until they are no longer a danger or a burden. Since mental hospitals are set up for the benefit of the community, they are largely supported by taxes. For the mental patient and his relatives to pay taxes and also pay hospitalization charges amounts to double taxation. Few would argue that the parents of schoolchildren should pay for their children to attend public schools or that people whose houses catch fire should pay for the services of the fire department. Public schools, fire departments, and state hospitals exist largely for the benefit of the entire community and should be financed in the same manner.

Even if the patient has to pay for the costs of his involuntary hospitalization, he should be permitted to contest the *amount* he is supposed to pay. If part of his hospital bill is to pay the salaries of hospital psychiatrists, for example, he should be permitted to show that in *his* wing of the hospital there were no psychiatrists. And if part of his hospital bill is to cover the costs of recreation equipment or a crafts room, he should be permitted to show that he was kept in a locked ward and never had access to those facilities. In other words, the patient should not have to pay for something he did not get. Challenging the amount of a hospital bill is an indirect way of raising the right-to-treatment arguments discussed above.

Despite these arguments, only a few courts have ruled that involuntarily hospitalized patients or their families do not have to pay the costs of hospitalization.[127] One court for example, ruled that Connecticut could not charge jail inmates the costs of hospitalization when the state transferred them to mental hospitals, because other prisoners were not required to pay for similar services.[128]

What rights do hospitalized patients have to refuse to work, or to be paid for work?

Many state hospitals depend on patient labor to operate the hospital.[129] Patients work cleaning wards, washing dishes, and serving food. They work in the laundry, the boiler room, on hospital farms, and in hospital offices. Most patients are paid little or nothing for that labor.

The precise circumstances under which patients can refuse to work, or must be paid for work, are unclear. Most of the litigation in this area has been based on the Thirteenth Amendment to the United States Constitution, or on a federal statute called the Fair Labor Standards Act.[130]

The Thirteenth Amendment provides:

Neither slavery nor involuntary servitude, except as punishment for crime whereof the party shall have been duly convicted, shall exist within the United States. . . .

Some courts have ruled that the Thirteenth Amendment prohibits *all* forced labor in mental hospitals.[131] Other courts have ruled that the "involuntary servitude" language of the Thirteenth Amendment prohibits certain kinds of forced labor in mental hospitals, but not all kinds. Although the Thirteenth Amendment does not expressly authorize forced "therapeutic" labor, several courts have nevertheless ruled that hospitals *can* force patients to perform labor if the labor is "therapeutic."[132] Unfortunately, most courts have not defined what they mean by "therapeutic" labor, and hospitals usually claim that *all* labor is therapeutic, at least in the sense that it "gives patients something to do." The rule of thumb that seems to be developing is that patients cannot be forced to perform labor that involves the operation and maintenance of the hospital.[133]

Because the Thirteenth Amendment prohibits only involuntary labor, it does not prohibit even hospital-maintaining labor if the patient voluntarily consents to work. But as we noted earlier (Chapter IV,) it is often difficult to determine whether an involuntarily confined patient's consent is truly voluntary. There are enormous pressures on patients to work. If they work, they will be considered cooperative, and that may facilitate their release. If they do not work, their confinement may be prolonged.[134] Patients who do not work may be transferred to less pleasant wards, denied grounds privileges, and subjected to increased medication.[135]

In our opinion, the Thirteenth Amendment should be interpreted to prohibit all forced labor, whether "voluntary" or not, and labor performed by involuntary patients should be presumed to be involuntary unless they have been informed, in writing, that privileges and release will not be conditioned on their consent to work, and that they can stop working at any time.

The other approach used in this area has been statutory. In 1966, Congress amended the Fair Labor Standards Act to provide a minimum wage to "employees" of state mental hospitals.[136] Subsequently, a federal court ruled that working patients should be considered employees within the meaning of that statute, and were thus entitled to the minimum wage, whether the work they performed was therapeutic or not.[137] But even more recently, the Supreme Court declared that minimum wage statute to be unconstitutional, for reasons that have nothing to do with mental patients.[138] Essentially, the Court ruled that Congress cannot set minimum wages for state employees who perform traditional state functions (police, fire, hospitals, etc.), whether patients or not. Thus, unless there is a *state* statute that requires payment for labor (several states do have statutes requiring compensation for patient labor, and others have minimum wage or fair labor statutes that, arguably, might apply to working patients), patients will have to rely in future cases on their constitutional rights under the Thirteenth Amendment.

NOTES

1. See *Goffman, Ch. I*, n. 17; Ferleger, "Losing the Chains: In-Hospital Civil Liberties of Mental Patients," 13 *St. Cl. Lwr.* 447 (1973); Wexler & Scoville, *Ch. III*, n. 23; Rosenhan, *Ch. I*, n. 10; Deane, "The Reaction of A Non-Patient to a Stay on a Mental Hospital Ward," 24 *Psychiatry* 61 (1961); Barry, *Bellevue Is a State of Mind* (1971).

2. *Wyatt v. Stickney*, 334 F. Supp. 1341, 1343-44 (M.D. Ala. 1971).

3. *Donaldson v. O'Connor*, 493 F.2d 507 (5th Cir. 1975), *vacated,* 422 U.S. 563 (1975).

4. Ferleger, *supra* n. 1.

4a. See, for the most recent case, *Fasulo v. Arafeh,* ——— N.E. 2d ———, 46 U.S.L.W. 2168 (Conn. Sup. Ct. Sept. 20, 1977).

5. *O'Connor v. Donaldson, Ch. II,* n. 13, p. 580.

6. See, generally, Harvard Article, *Ch. I,* n. 14, pp. 1376-94 Brooks, *Ch. II,* n. 11, pp. 946-55.

7. See *O'Connor v. Donaldson, Ch. II,* n. 13, pp. 574-75.

8. See, for example, Rev. Code Wash. 71.05.320.

9. See Calif. Welf. Institns. Code, §§5200 *et seq.*

10. *Baxstrom v. Herold, Ch. III,* n. 58; *Specht v. Patterson, Ch. III, n.* 19; *Humphrey v. Cady, Ch. II,* n. 7; 44 *Jackson v. Indiana, Ch. II,* n. 1.

11. See cases cited in *Ch. V,* nn. 56 and 88.

12. *People v. Lally, Ch. V,* n. 56.

13. N.Y. Mental Hygiene Law §29.17.

14. This raises equal protection issues. If society does not have a sufficient interest to confine convicted criminals indefinitely, it does not have a sufficient interest to confine mental patients indefinitely.

15. See, generally, Ennis and Friedman, *Ch. I,* n. 6, p. 437.

16. *Ibid.*; Vol. I, pp. 437-50, 514-20, Vol. II, pp. 749-55. See also, n. 7, *supra.*

17. *Jackson v. Indiana, Ch. II,* n. 1.

18. Lower courts have specifically limited commitment periods. See cases cited in *Ch. V,* n. 40.

19. *McNeil v. Director, Ch. III,* n. 58.

20. *O'Connor v. Donaldson, Ch. II,* n. 13.

21. *Ennis and Friedman, Ch. I,* n. 6, and *supra* n. 16.

22. *O'Connor v. Donaldson, Ch. II,* n. 13, p. 579 (Burger, C.J., concurring).

23. See Harvard Article, *Ch. I,* n. 14, pp. 1194 and 1344 and fn. 10. Note, "Experimentation on Human Beings," 20 *Stan. L. Rev.* 99 (1967); *Schloendorff v. Society of N.Y. Hospital,* 105 N.E. 92 (N.Y. 1914); *Stack v. N.Y.N.H. and H.R.R.,* 58 N.E. 686 (Mass. 1900). Prosser, *Handbook On the Law Of Torts,* §18 (4th Ed. 1971).

24. Brooks, *Ch. II,* n. 11, p. 877 (emphasis added).

25. Schwartz, "In the Name of Treatment: Autonomy, Civil Commitment and the Right to Refuse Treatment," 50 *Notre Dame Lwr.* 808 (1975); Comment, "Advances in Mental Health: A Case for the Right to Refuse Treatment," 48 *Temp. L.Q.* 354 (1975).

26. Braekel and Rock, *Mentally Disabled and the Law* (1971), pp. 250-65; Alexander and Szasz, "From Contract to Status via Psychiatry," 13 *St. Cl. Lwr.* 537 (1973). See also authorities cited *infra* n. 120.

27. See *Winters v. Miller*, 446 F. 2d 65 (2nd Cir. 1971), *cert. den.*, 404 U.S. 985 (1971).

28. Harvard Article, *Ch. I*, n. 14, p. 1350.

29. *Olmstead v. United States, Ch. II*, n. 5 (Brandeis, J., dissenting).

30. *Roe v. Wade*, 410 U.S. 113 (1973); *Griswold v. Connecticut*, 381 U.S. 479 (1965); *Eisenstadt v. Baird*, 405 U.S. 438 (1972); see Warren and Brandeis, "The Right to Privacy," 4 *Harv. L. Rev.* 193 (1890); Westin, *Privacy and Freedom* (1968); Fried, "Privacy," 77 *Yale L.J.* 475 (1968); Pound, "Interests of Personality," 28 *Harv. L. Rev.* 343 (1915).

31. *Bellotti v. Baird*, 428 U.S. 132 (1976); *Danforth v. Planned Parenthood*, 428 U.S. 52 (1976).

32. Harvard Article, *Ch. I*, n. 14, p. 1195 and fn. 12, pp. 1344-58.

33. *Kaimowitz v. Michigan Dept. of Mental Hygiene, Ch. V*, n. 3.

34. *Abrams v. United States*, 250 U.S. 616 (1919); *Whitney v. California*, 274 U.S. 357 (1927); *Stanley v. Georgia*, 394 U.S. 557 (1969); Emerson, "Toward a General Theory of the First Amendment," 72 *Yale L. J.* 877 (1963); Kittrie, *Cr. I*, n. 18; "Legislating the Control of Behavior Control: Autonomy and the Coercive Use of Organic Therapies," 47 *S. Cal. L. Rev.* 237, 255-56 (1974).

35. *Kaimowitz v. Michigan Dept. of Mental Hygiene, Mackey v. Procunier, Ch. V*, n. 3.

36. *Winters v. Miller, supra* n. 27.

37. *Scott v. Plante*, 532 F.2d 939 (3rd Cir., Mar. 26, 1976); *Welsch v. Likins, Ch. IV*, n. 22; *Nelson v. Heyne*, 491 F.2d 352 (7th Cir. 1974); *cert. den.* 417 U.S. 976 (1974); *Morales v. Thurman, Ch. III*, n. 10; *U.S. ex rel. Wilson v. Coughlin*, 472 F.2d 100 (7th Cir. 1973).

38. *Knecht v. Gilman, Ch. V*, n. 3.

39. *Clonce v. Richardson, Ch. V*, n. 3.

40. See *Winters v. Miller, supra* n. 27.

41. Rada, "Informed Consent in the Care of Psychiatric Patients," 8 *J. Nat'l. Assoc. Private Psychiat. Hosp.* 9 (Summer, 1976); Note, *S. Cal. L. Rev., Ch. V*, n. 3; Wexler, *Ch. II*, n. 24; Ellis, "Volunteering Children: Parental Commitment of Minors to Mental Institutions," 62 *Cal. L. Rev.* 840 (1974); Andy, "The Deci-

sion Making Process in Psychosurgery," 13 *Duq. L. Rev.* 783 (1975); Vaux, "Look What They've Done to My Brain, Ma!: Ethical Issues in Brain and Behavior Control," 13 *Duq. L. Rev.* 907 (1975); Friedman, *Ch. I*, n. 5; Spoonhour, "Psychosurgery and Informed Consent," 26 *U. Fla. L. Rev.* 432 (1974); Zwerdling, "Informed Consent and the Mental Patient: California Recognizes a Mental Patient's Right to Refuse Psychosurgery and Shock Treatment," 15 *St. Cl. Lwr.* 725 (1975); Alexander & Szasz, *supra* n. 26; Note, "Informed Consent in Medical Malpractice," 55 *Cal. L. Rev.* 1396 (1967); Note, "Restructuring Informed Consent," 79 *Yale L. J.* 1533 (1970); Waltz and Scheuneman, "Informed Consent to Therapy," 64 *Nw. U. L. Rev.* 628 (1969).

42. Harvard Article, *Ch. I*, n. 14, p. 1351; *Kaimowitz v. Michigan Dept. of Mental Hygiene, Knecht v. Gillman, Ch. V*, n. 3.

43. Rada, *supra* n. 41.

44. See, for example, Rev. Code Wash: 71.05.370 (7).

45. *Kaimowitz v. Michigan Department of Mental Hygiene, Ch. V*, n. 3; see also *Knecht v. Gilman, Ch. V*, n. 3; *Friedman, Ch. I*, n. 5; Wexler, *Ch. II*, n. 24; Harvard Article, *Ch. I*, n. 14, pp. 1351-58.

46. See, for example, *Knecht v. Gilman, Ch. V*, n. 3.

47. *Kaimowitz v. Michigan Dept. of Mental Hygiene, Ch. V*, n. 3; see also *Relf v. Mathews*, 403 F. Supp. 1235 (D.D.C. 1975).

48. Rev. Code Wash. 71.05.370 (9).

49. *Kaimowitz v. Michigan Department of Mental Hygiene, Ch. V*, n. 3.

50. See, "Medical Experimentation: A Symposium on Behavior Control," 13 *Duq. L. Rev.* 673-936 (1975); "Symposium: Psychosurgery," 24 *Buff. U.L. Rev.* (1974); Spoonhour, *supra* n. 41; Gobert, "Psychosurgery, Conditioning and the Prisoner's Right to Refuse 'Rehabilitation' " 61 *Va. L. Rev.* 155 (1975); Zwerdling, *supra* n. 41; Schwartz, *supra* n. 25; Temple, "Comment," *supra* n. 25.

51. See *Wyatt v. Stickney*, 344 F. Supp. 373, 380 (M.D. Ala. 1972), *aff'd sub nom. Wyatt v. Aderholt*, 503 F. 2d 1305 (5th Cir. 1974).

52. See, generally, Katz, *Experimentation with Human Beings* (1972); and Pappworth, *Human Guinea Pigs* (1967).

53. *Wyatt v. Stickney*, *supra* n. 51, p. 380; see also Friedman, *Ch. I*, n. 5.

54. *Skinner v. Oklahoma*, 316 U.S. 535 (1942).

55. *Buck v. Bell*, 274 U.S. 200 (1927); *Relf v. Mathews*, 403 F. Supp. 1235 (D.D.C. 1975), and 372 F. Supp.

1196 (D.D.C. 1974); *Wyatt v. Aderholt,* 368 F. Supp. 1383 (M.D. Ala. 1974); *Wade v. Bethesda Hospital,* 356 F. Supp. 380 (S.D. Ohio 1973); But see *In re Moore,* 221 S.E. 2d 307 (S. Car. 1976).

56. *Relf v. Mathews* and *Wyatt v. Aderholt, supra* n. 55.

57. See Rouché, "Annals of Medicine: As Empty As Eve," *The New Yorker* 84 (Sept. 9, 1974); *Psychobiology of Convulsive Therapy* (Fink *et al.,* eds., 1974) 199; Electroconvulsive Therapy in Massachusetts: A Task Force Report," 3 *Mass J. Men. Health* 4 (1973); Kalinowski, "The Convulsive Therapies," *Treating Mental Illness* (Freedman and Kaplan, eds., 1972); Kalinowski and Hoch, *Shock Treatments, Psychosurgery and Other Somatic Treatments in Psychiatry* (1952); Miller, "Psychological Theories of E.C.T.: A Review," 113 *Brit, J. Psychiat.* 301 (1967).

58. *Mitchell v. Robinson,* 334 S.W. 2d 11 (Mo. 1960); *Wilson v. Lehman,* 379 S.W.2d 478 (Ky 1964).

59. *New York City Health and Hospitals Corp. v. Stein,* 335 N.Y.S. 2d 461 (Sup. Ct. N.Y. Co. 1972). See also *Price v. Sheppard,* 239 N.W. 2d 905 (Minn. 1976).

60. Rev. Code Wash. 71.05.370 (7); see also *Doe v. Younger,* 129 Cal. Reptr. 535 (Ct. Apps. 1976), and Calif. Welf. and Institns. Code §5325 (f-g).

61. See Harvard Article, *Ch. I,* n. 14, p. 1348.

62. *Ibid.,* pp. 1347-51.

63. *Wyatt v. Stickney, supra* n. 51, p. 380.

64. Wexler, "Token and Taboo: Behavior Modification, Token Economies and the Law," 61 *Calif. L. Rev.* 81 (1973).

65. *Mackey v. Procunier, Ch. V,* n. 3; see S. Cal. Note, *Ch. V,* n. 3.

66. *Clonce v. Richardson, Ch. V,* n. 3.

67. *Knecht v. Gillman, Ch. V,* n. 3.

68. See, generally, "Symposium: Viewpoints on Behavioral Issues in Closed Institutions," 17 *Ariz. L. Rev.* 1-143 (1975).

69. May, *Ch. I,* n. 6.

70. Rappaport, *Ch. I,* n. 6.

71. See *Report to the Congress: Controls on the Use of Psychotherapeutic Drugs and Improved Psychiatrist Staffing Are Needed in Veterans Administration Hospitals,* comptroller *General Report* (M.W.D.–75-47, 1975). See, generally, Silverman and Lee, *Pills, Profits and Politics* (1976).

72. Harvard Article and authorities cited in *Ch. I,* n. 14, pp. 1194-1201.

73. *Scott v. Plante, supra* n. 37; see also *Souder v. McGuire, Ch. V,* n. 62.

74. *Welsch v. Likins*, *Ch. IV*, n. 22; *Nelson v. Heyne*, *supra* n. 37; *Morales v. Turman*, *Ch. III*, n. 10.

75. *Bell v. Wayne County Hospital*, *Ch. II*, n. 2.

76. *Lessard v. Schmidt* and *Lynch v. Baxley*, *Ch. II*, n. 2.

77. Rev Code Wash. 71.05.240.

78. Note, *S. Cal. L. Rev.*, *Ch. V*, n. 3.

79. Harvard Article, *Ch. I*, n. 14, pp. 1358-65.

80. Ferleger, *supra* n. 1.

81. Shapiro, *supra* n. 34.

82. Ferleger, *supra* n. 1.

83. *Wyatt v. Stickney*, *supra* n. 51, p. 382.

84. *Ibid.*, p. 379; see also Ennis and Friedman, *Ch. I*, n. 6; Vol. II, pp. 761-66.

85. *Wyatt v. Stickney*, *supra* n. 51, p. 380.

86. *Williams v. Robinson*, 432 F. 2d 637 (D.C. Cir. 1970); *Jones v. Robinson*, 440 F. 2d 249 (D.C. Cir. 1971); *Brown v. Schubert*, 347 F. Supp. 1232 (E.D. Wisc. 1972).

87. *Covington v. Harris*, *Ch. III*, n. 3; *Wyatt v. Stickney*, *supra* n. 51. p. 379.

88. *Wyatt v. Stickney*, 325 F. Supp. 781, 344 F. Supp. 373, 344 F. Supp. 387 (M.D. Ala. 1972), *aff'd sub nom. Wyatt v. Aderholt*, 503 F. 2d 1305 (5th Cir. 1974); *Rouse v. Cameron*, 373 F. 2d 451 (D.C. Cir. 1966); *Welsch v. Likins*, 373 F. Supp. 487 (D. Minn. 1974), *partially vacated on other grounds*, 550 F.2d 1122 (8th Cir. 1977); *Davis v. Watkins*, 384 F. Supp. 1196 (N.D. Ohio, 1974); *In re Ballay*, 482 F. 2d 648, 659 (D.C. Cir 1973): *Kesselbrenner v. Anonymous*, 33 N.Y. 2d 161, 305 N.E. 2d 903 (N.Y. 1973); *Renelli v. Department of Mental Hygiene*, 340 N.Y.S. 2d 498 (Sup. Ct. Rich. Co. 1973); *Nelson v. Heyne*, 355 F. Supp. 451 (N.D. Ind. 1972), *aff'd*, 491 F. 2d 352 (7th Cir. 1974), *cert. den.*, 417 U.S. 976 (1974); *Inmates of Boys Training School v. Affleck*, 346 F. Supp. 1354 (D.R.I. 1972); *Morales v. Turman*, 364 F. Supp. 166 (E.D. Tex. 1973) *vacated on other grounds*, 535 F. 2d 864 (5th Cir. 1976); *reinstated* —— U.S. —— 97 S. Ct. 1189 (March 21, 1977); *Martarella v. Kelley*, 349 F. Supp. 575 (S.D.N.Y. 1972), *enforced*, 359 F. Supp. 478 (S.D.N.Y. 1973); *M. v. M.*, 336 N.Y.S. 2d 304 (Fam. Ct. 1970); *In re I.*, 316 N.Y.S. 2d 356 (Fam. Ct. 1970); *Stachulak v. Coughlin*, 364 F. Supp. 686 (N.D. Ill, 1973), *aff'd*, 520 F. 2d 931 (7th Cir. 1975); *Davy v. Sullivan*, 354 F. Supp. 1320 (M.D. Md. 1973); *Sas v. Maryland*, 334 F. 2d 506 (4th Cir. 1964), *cert. den.*, 407 U.S. 355 (1972); *In re Maddox*, 88 N.W.2d 470 (Mich. 1958); *Commonwealth v.*

Page, 159 N.E.2d 82 (Mass. 1959); *United States v. Walker,* 335 F. Supp. 705 (N.D. Cal. 1971); *U.S. v. Pardue,* 354 F. Supp. 1377 (D. Conn. 1973); *Nason v. Superintendent, Bridgewater State Hospital,* 233 N.E. 2d 908 (Mass. 1968); *Maatallah v. Warden, Nevada State Prison,* 470 P. 2d 122 (1970).

89. *O'Connor v. Donaldson, Ch. II,* n. 13.

90. *Ibid.,* p. 515. The Court used "confinement" and "custodial care," as interchangeable terms, and contrasted those conditions with what we would loosely call "treatment." "The evidence showed that Donaldson's confinement was a simple regime of enforced custodial care, not a program designed to alleviate or cure his supposed illness" (422 U.S. at p. 569).

91. *Ibid.,* p. 576.

92. The Fourteenth Amendment provides that states shall not "deprive" persons of "liberty" "without due process of law," and shall not "deny" to persons "the equal protection of the laws." The Eighth Amendment provides that "cruel and unusual punishment" "shall not" be "inflicted."

93. But see Birnbaum, "The Right to Treatment," 46 *A.B.A.J.* 499 (1960); Harvard Article, *Ch. I,* n. 14, pp. 1316-57; Note, "Rights of the Mentally Ill During Incarceration: the Developing Laws," 25 *U. Fla. L. Rev.* 494 (1973); Comment. *"Wyatt v. Stickney* and the Right of Civilly Committed Mental Patients to Adequate Treatment," 86 *Harv. L. Rev.* 1282 (1973); Robitscher, "Right to Psychiatric Treatment: A Social-Legal Approach to the Plight of the State Hospital Patient," 18 *Vill. L. Rev.* 11 (1972); Murdock, "Civil Rights of the Mentally Retarded: Some Critical Issues," 48 *Notre Dame Lwr.* 133 (1972); Chambers, *Ch. I,* n. 6; Goodman, "The Right to Treatment: The Responsibility of the Courts," 57 Geo. L.J. 680 (1969); Katz, *Ch. I,* n. 6; Note, "The Nascent Right to Treatment," 53 *Va. L. Rev.* 1134 (1967); Note, "Civil Restraint, Mental Illness and the Right to Treatment," 77 *Yale L.J.* 87 (1967); Drake, "Enforcing the Right to Treatment," 10 *Am. Crim. L. Rev.* 587 (1972); Schwitzgebel, *Ch. I,* n. 6.

94. *O'Connor v. Donaldson, Ch. II,* n. 13, p. 573.

95. E.g., *Lynch v. Baxley, Ch. II,* n. 2, p. 391; *Wyatt v. Stickney, supra* n. 88.

96. *O'Connor v. Donaldson, Ch. II,* n. 13, p. 589.

97. *Ibid.,* p. 574, fn. 10.

98. *Ibid.,* p. 569.

99. *Wyatt v. Stickney, supra* n. 88; *Welsh v. Likins, Ch. III,* n. 3; *Rouse v. Cameron, supra* n. 88. But in many cases, it will be possible to conclude that a facility is only a custodial facility without working through this analysis. For example, any hospital that is not accredited as a psychiatric facility by the Joint Commission on the Accreditation of Hospitals should be considered, by definition, a custodial facility. This does not mean, however, that accredited facilities should be presumed to be treatment facilities.
100. Schwitzgebel, *Ch. I,* n. 6.
101. Rappeport *et al., Ch. I,* n. 6.
102. See Schwitzgebel, *Ch. I,* n. 6.
103. *Lynch v. Baxley, Ch. II,* n. 2, p. 391.
104. *Ibid.*
105. *Jackson v. Indiana, Ch. II,* n. 1; *McNeil v. Director, Patuxent Institution, Ch. III,* n. 58.
106. *Jackson v. Indiana, Ch. II,* n. 1, p. 738.
107. See Ennis and Friedman, *Ch. I,* n. 6, Vol. I, pp. 437-50.
108. The organizations mentioned agreed that "if a patient is still involuntarily confined in a hospital after four months have elapsed, there is a strong likelihood that he is not receiving adequate treatment. . . . If a patient is still hospitalized involuntarily after six months, the overwhelming likelihood is that treatment has failed and there is no justification for continued involuntary confinement." *Ibid.,* p. 439.
109. *O'Connor v. Donaldson, Ch. II,* n. 13, p. 568.
110. *Ibid.,* p. 575.
111. See cases cited in *Ch. II,* n. 61, and New York Mental Hygiene Law §31.39; Rev. Code Wash. 71.05.020(3).
112. Ennis and Friedman, *Ch. I,* n. 6, Vol. I, pp. 241-253.
113. *NYSARC v. Rockefeller, Ch. III,* n. 10; see an important new case, *Harper v. Cserr,* 544 F.2d 1121 (1st Cir. 1976).
114. *Wyatt v. Stickney, supra* n. 51, pp. 379-80; *Stowers v. Ardmore Acres Hosp.,* 172 N.W. 2d 497 (Mich Ct. App. 1969).
115. Rev. Code Wash. 71.05.370; *Brown v. Schubert, supra* n. 86.
116. *Brown v. Schubert, supra* n. 86.
117. Ferleger, *supra* n. 1, pp. 465-69.
118. *Wyatt v. Stickney, supra* n. 51, p. 379.
119. *Commonwealth v. Wiseman,* 249 N.E. 2d 610, *cert. den.,* 398 U.S. 960 (1969); *State ex rel. Carroll v. Junker,* 482 P. 2d 775 (Wash. 1971); see, Brooks, *Ch. II,* n. 11, p. 825.
120. See, for example, Rev. Code Wash. 71.05.060; D.C. Code §21-564(a); see also *Protecting the Constitutional Rights*

of the Mentally Ill, Hearings—87th, *Ch. I*, n. 6; Allen, Ferster, and Wiehofen, *Mental Impairment and Legal Incompetency* (1968); Greenblatt, York and Brown, *From Custodial to Therapeutic Patient Care in Mental Hospitals*, (Russell Sage Foundation, 1955); Williams, "Money and the Therapeutic Process," 18 *Canada's Ment. Health* 1: 20 (1970); Cummings and Cummings, *Ego and Milieu* (1962); *Wyatt v. Stickney*, *supra* n. 51, p. 379; *Winters v. Miller*, *supra* n. 27, p. 68; *Logan v. Arafeh*, 346 F. Supp. 1265, 1269-70 (D. Conn., 1972), *aff'd sub nom, Briggs v. Arafeh*, 36 L. Ed. 2d 304 (1973); *McAuliffe v. Carlson*, 377 F. Supp. 896, 386 F. Supp 1245 (D. Conn. 1974), *rev'd on other grounds*, 520 F. 2d 1305 (2d Cir. 1975); "Position Statement on Civil Rights of Mental Patients," Nat'l. Assoc. for Mental Health 11/4/71, quoted in *Vecchione v. Wohlgemuth*, 377 F. Supp. 1361 (E.D. Pa. 1974); *cert. den. Vecchione v. Beal*, ——— U.S. ——— (No. 77-382, Nov. 7, 1977); Braekel and Rock, *Ch. I*, n. 6; see also Stone, *Ch. I*, n. 13, pp. 163-70; Brooks, *Ch. II*, n. 11, Part IV; Harvard Article, *Ch. I*, n. 14, pp. 1214-15 and fn. 81 and 82, and authorities cited therein.

121. 42 U.S.C. 405 (j).
122. *Dale v. Hahn*, 311 F. Supp. 1293 (S.D.N.Y.), *aff'd* 440 F.2d 633 (2nd Cir. 1971) and 486 F.2d 76 (2nd Cir. 1973); *Vecchione v. Wohlgemuth*, *supra* n. 120; *McAuliffe v. Carlson*, *supra* n. 120; *Brown v. Solomon*, ——— F. Supp. ——— (consent decree 73-625K, D. Md. 1973); *McConaghley v. New York*, 304 N.Y.S.2d 136 (N.Y. Civ. 1969).
123. *Dale v. Hahn*, *supra* n. 122; *Vecchione v. Wohlgemuth*, *supra* n. 120.
124. *McAuliffe v. Carlson*, *supra* n. 120.
125. *Brown v. Solomon*, *supra* n. 122.
126. See Brooks, *Ch. II*, n. 11, pp. 930-37; Harvard Article, *Ch. I*, pp. 1365-72.
127. *Department of Mental Hygiene v. Kirchner*, 388 P. 2d 720 (Cal. 1964); *Miller v. State*, 171 N.W.2d 3 (Mich Ct. App. 1969); *McAuliffe v. Carlson*, *supra* n. 120; *Dept of Mental Hygiene v. Hawley*, 379 P. 2d 22 (Cal. 1963).
128. *McAuliffe v. Carlson*, *supra* n. 120.
129. Friedman, "The Mentally Handicapped Citizen and Institutional Labor," 87 *Harv. L. Rev.* 567 (1974); see Ferleger, *supra* n. 1, pp. 477-83; Brooks, *Ch. II*, n. 11, pp. 937-44; Harvard Article, *Ch. I*, n. 14, pp. 1372-76; Stone, *Ch. I*, n. 13, pp. 109-17.

130. 29 U.S.C. §213.
131. *Tyler v. Harris*, 226 F. Supp. 852 (W.D. Mo. 1964); *Johnston v. Ciccone*, 260 F. Supp. 553 (W.D. Mo. 1966); see also *Henry v. Ciccone*, 315 F. Supp 889 (W.D. Mo. 1970); *Tyler v. Ciccone*, 299 F. Supp. 684 (W.D. Mo. 1969); *Parks v. Ciccone*, 281 F. Supp. 805 (W.D. Mo. 1968).
132. *Jobson v. Henne*, 355 F. 2d 129 (2nd Cir. 1966); but see *Wyatt v. Stickney*, *supra* n. 51, p. 381.
133. *Wyatt v. Stickney*, *supra* n. 51, p. 381.
134. Ferleger, *supra* n. 1, pp. 477-83.
135. Ennis, *Prisoners of Psychiatry* (1972), Ch. 7, "Learn to Labor and to Wait"; also Hearings—91st, *Ch. I*, n. 6, p. 340.
136. 29 U.S.C. 203 (o) (1) (s) (4), (1970).
137. *Souder v. Brennan*, 367 F. Supp. 808 (D.D.C. 1973).
138. *National League of Cities v. Usery*, 426 U.S. 833 (1976), *overruling Maryland v. Wirtz*, 392 U.S. 183 (1968). See also *Employees v. Missouri Public Health Dept.*, 411 U.S. 279 (1973).

VII

Rights In The Community

Up to this point we have been discussing the rights of persons during the commitment process and during hospitalization. We begin now a discussion of the rights of persons in the community. There is enormous discrimination in the community against persons who have been hospitalized, or even treated on an outpatient basis, for mental disorder. Many states have laws that prohibit ex-patients from voting, driving, holding office, serving on juries, or pursuing specific professions.[1] Cities, counties, and towns limit where ex-patients can live by zoning laws. Employers discriminate against ex-patients in hiring or promotion. The government routinely denies security clearances for ex-patients, thus foreclosing various job opportunities. Colleges and graduate schools deny admission to ex-patients. Many landlords will not rent to ex-patients.

Furthermore, all states have special laws under which people who have never been hospitalized, as well as those who have, may be found "mentally incompetent." Persons who have been found "incompetent" usually lose the legal right to enter into contracts, to sue or be sued, to marry or divorce, and to manage their assets and business affairs.

In terms of the number of people affected, the rights of people in the community is a more important area than the rights of people who are in hospitals or facing hospitalization.[2] Unfortunately, however, the rights of people in the community have received much less judicial and legislative attention.[3] That is beginning to change. Courts and legislatures are starting to pay serious attention to the rights of persons in the community. But the body of case law and statutory law in this area is still quite small, and there is very little that can be said with certainty about the rights of persons in the community. Accordingly, the conclusions and opinions we express in this chapter are necessarily more speculative than those we expressed in the preceding chapters. There do seem to be three general points, however, that serve as the basis for most of the developing law in this area.

First, a history of hospitalization or treatment for mental disorder in the *past* will not justify discrimination in the *present*. For example, even if schools can refuse to employ teachers who are mentally disordered, they must do so on the basis of evidence of present mental disorder. A mere history of mental disorder in the past will not suffice.

Second, even present mental disorder will not justify discrimination unless there is some rational connection between the disorder and denial of the job, benefit, or right involved. The fact that a person may believe he is a messenger from outer space is irrelevant if that belief does not interfere with his job performance. In fact, certain mental disorders may actually increase the effectiveness of job performance. "Obsessive-compulsive" personalities often make good employees in jobs where meticulous attention to detail is important. Persons whose mental condition makes it difficult to relate to others often make good employees in jobs where lack of contact with others would hinder the performance of "normal" employees.

Third, the doctrine of the least drastic alternative (see Chapter III) can be applied to lessen the extent of state interference in the lives of mentally disordered persons in the community. For example, if an individual is "incompetent" to manage a complicated investment portfolio, but not to manage a simple checking account, a committee might be appointed to manage the portfolio, but not the checking account.

With these general points in mind, we can turn to a discussion of emerging rights in the community.

What rights do ex-patients have to stay in the community?

Many ex-patients are returned to the community on "conditional" or "convalescent" status.[4] In order to be re-

171

leased from the hospital on that status, they must usually agree to continue taking medication, to visit mental health professionals on an outpatient basis, and so forth. If they violate those conditions, or if they are thought to be getting "sicker," their conditional status may be summarily revoked, and they may be hospitalized again, without ever appearing before a judge.

In a criminal law context, the Supreme Court has ruled that a convicted person's interest in maintaining parole status is similar to an unconvicted person's interest in liberty, and has therefore required at least rudimentary due process protections before parole status can be revoked.[5] The ex-patient's interest in continued conditional leave is even greater, and society's countervailing interest in reconfinement is less (the ex-patient has not been convicted of crime and has no unexpired punishment or sentence to serve). In our opinion, revocation of conditional leave should require essentially the same standards and procedures as would be required for an initial hospitalization (see Chapter III).[6] Furthermore, there should be a definite time limit on the permissible period of conditional status. After that time, the individual should be treated exactly like any other citizen.[7]

What rights do patients and ex-patients have to be protected from discrimination because of present or past mental disorder?

Some states now have statutes that expressly prohibit discrimination because of mental disorder in jobs, housing, and other areas.[8] Other states have laws that provide that hospitalization or a finding of "mental illness" shall not be considered the equivalent of a finding of "mental incompetence," or shall not, of itself, authorize the loss or abridgment of other civil rights.[9] And a federal statute, the Rehabilitation Act of 1973, prohibits discrimination because of mental disorder in jobs that receive federal funding.[10] The purpose of that statute is "to promote and expand employment opportunities in the public and private sector for handicapped individuals and to place such individuals in employment."[11] A "handicapped individual" is defined as any person who "has" or "has a record" of "physical or mental impairment which substantially limits

172

such person's functioning. . . ." The statute requires "an affirmative action program plan for the hiring, placement, and advancement of handicapped individuals" by all federal executive branch agencies and departments.[12] And it provides that "no otherwise qualified handicapped individual . . . shall, solely by reason of his handicap, be excluded from the participation in, be denied the benefits of, or be subjected to discrimination under any program or activity receiving Federal financial assistance."[13] Thus the federal statute prohibits discrimination even against persons who *are* "mentally handicapped" if they are "otherwise qualified."

In addition to these state and federal statutory arguments against discrimination, there are constitutional arguments that can be made. The principal constitutional theories that have been used to date are procedural due process and substantive due process, and they are often used together. Essentially, the argument is that if persons are to be discriminated against because of mental disorder, they should at least be given an opportunity to show that they are not disordered, or that their disorder would not interfere with their performance. For example, in one case,[14] a federal court held that a board of education, even when it had reason to suspect the present mental fitness of a teacher, could not discharge the teacher on psychiatric grounds unless the teacher first had the opportunity to challenge the need for dismissal at a due process hearing. That holding was reaffirmed in a subsequent case.[15]

Another court ruled that an applicant for a taxicab license could not be denied a license because of an allegation of "mental illness" without an opportunity for a hearing to contest that allegation, and suggested that *past* mental disorder would not be a sufficient basis for denial of the license.[16] Still another court ruled that an employee could not be denied a security clearance because of mental disorder without proof that the disorder would, in fact, interfere with his job performance or jeopardize security.[17] One court ruled that denial of a driver's license because of mental disorder would require procedural due process protections.[18]

Many of these cases are based on the growing recognition that *past* mental disorder is not a reliable basis for predicting future disorder, that persons who have sought treatment for mental disorder are not necessarily more disordered than persons who have not, and that mental health professionals are not particularly qualified to predict future school or job success or failure.[19]

Voting. Studies have shown that there is no significant difference between the voting patterns of hospitalized mental patients and those of the communities from which they come.[20] And courts are beginning to rule that mentally disordered persons may register and vote.[21]

Zoning. As increasing numbers of persons are being released from, or kept out of, hospitals, many communities have reacted by passing laws that make it difficult or impossible for such persons to live in those communities. This will be one of the major areas of litigation in the next few years. The Supreme Court's decision in *O'Connor v. Donaldson*[22] offers indirect but strong support for those who challenge such zoning restrictions. There, the Court unanimously said that the state could not "fence in" the harmless mentally disordered merely to save its citizens from "exposure to those whose ways are different . . . unattractive or socially eccentric. Mere public intolerance or animosity cannot constitutionally justify the deprivation of a person's physical liberty."[23] If the state cannot "fence in" the mentally disordered for those reasons, it should not be able to fence them out, either. Even before *Donaldson,* a federal court declared unconstitutional a local zoning ordinance that as a practical matter prohibited ex-patients from living in public hotels.[24] And in other cases,[25] courts have ruled that mentally disordered foster children in group homes should be considered natural children for zoning purposes. This is a rapidly developing area of the law, and new decisions will no doubt issue while this book is being printed.[26]

Education. Recently, several courts have ruled that every child has a right to a public education, regardless of the degree of mental, emotional, or physical handicap.[27] Under those decisions, children can be excluded from regular school programs only after it is determined at a hearing that they cannot benefit from regular instruction. If excluded from regular programs, children must be given special programs, including individual instruction where necessary. Most of those decisions are based on constitutional grounds, but one recent decision was based on the federal Rehabilitation Act of 1973[28] discussed at the beginning of this answer.

What rights do persons have in proceedings to declare them mentally incompetent to manage their assets or affairs?

In many ways, a finding of "mental incompetence" is a more substantial interference in an individual's life than a finding of "mental illness." In some states, for example, the "committee" (usually one person) or "guardian" of an "incompetent" person can place that person in a mental hospital without obtaining judicial authorization.[29] And in all states, committees and guardians are authorized to control and disburse the incompetent person's assets. As we noted, "incompetents" usually lose the right to vote, execute contracts, marry, divorce, and so forth. But despite the stigma and severe consequences that result from a finding of incompetence, the procedures that lead to such findings are even less protective than the procedures that lead to a finding of "mental illness" and commitment to a hospital. In many states, the person alleged to be incompetent does not even receive notice of the judicial hearing to declare him incompetent. He may not be permitted to attend the hearing or cross-examine those who say he is incompetent. He may not have or be assigned a lawyer. The hearings usually last only a few minutes. The rules of evidence are ignored. And frequently there is absolutely no evidence that the person has, in fact, squandered or wasted any of his assets.

Unfortunately, there is a relatively small amount of case law in this important area.[30] In our opinion, incompetency proceedings are sufficiently serious to require essentially the same procedural protections that would be applied in a civil commitment proceeding. Furthermore, we believe the doctrine of the least drastic alternative (Chapter III) should be applied in incompetency proceedings. Persons who are "incompetent" to manage only part of their affairs should not lose the right to manage other parts of their affairs. At least one state has provided for a form of limited control over a person's affairs called a "conservatorship" proceeding. Under that proceeding the conservator is given only those specific powers the court determines are absolutely necessary. In all other respects, the conservatee retains the same control over his affairs as any other citizen.[31]

What rights do patients or ex-patients have to prohibit disclosure of information about their hospitalization or treatment?

Although this is an extremely important question, and is the subject of a good deal of legal and professional literature,[32] there is a surprisingly small body of case law on the question. Most states have statutes that expressly provide that mental hospital records are confidential, but the statutes vary greatly in their coverage. Some statutes prohibit disclosure of the fact of hospitalization;[33] others only prohibit disclosure of information about the patient's diagnosis and treatment. Most statutes permit disclosure to other persons within the hospital or state mental health system, and many permit disclosure to private physicians, police, welfare officials, and insurance companies. Some even permit disclosure to prospective employers. Other statutes prohibit disclosure to almost everyone, unless the patient or ex-patient consents to disclosure.

In addition to these "confidentiality" statutes, most states have statutes that create a "doctor-patient privilege" (or in some states, a broader psychologist-patient, social worker-patient, or therapist-patient privilege) under which physicians, at the direction of their patients, must refuse to disclose information about the patient that was gathered for the purpose of treatment (information gathered for other purposes, such as evaluation for a court, usually can be disclosed). This "doctor-patient privilege" prohibits disclosure of protected information even when a court could otherwise order disclosure. In this sense, it is more protective than the "confidentiality" statutes, which usually provide for disclosure upon court order. These "privilege" statutes, however, also have exceptions. One recent decision, for example, ruled that a psychologist had a duty to disclose to the intended victim a patient's threat to injure another person.[34] We think that decision is wrong, particularly given the unreliability of predictions of dangerous behavior (see Chapter I), and will result in increased involuntary hospitalization and decreased client-therapist trust, without significantly enhancing the safety of others. In fact, we favor legislation that would exempt mental health professionals from civil or criminal liability for any act committed by a patient whom they release from, or refuse to commit to, a mental hospital.[35]

We believe information about hospitalization or treatment that is linked to individuals by name or other identifying information should not be disclosed to anyone without judicial approval, after a hearing at which the patient or ex-patient can oppose disclosure. Such information should not even be disclosed to the central office of the mental health system, to researchers, or to computers. Furthermore, states should by statute prohibit employers from asking whether a job applicant has ever been hospitalized or treated for mental disorder.

Closely related to these problems is the problem of *access* to information. Many patients and ex-patients want to examine their own records, but in most states they are not permitted to do so. One state mental hospital in Washington has for several years allowed all patients to examine their own records and has found that policy to be therapeutic.[36] But a federal court was not persuaded that an ex-patient had a *constitutional* right to examine her own records.[37]

We believe that patients and ex-patients should be able to examine their own records on demand, unless the hospital or therapist carries the burden of applying for, and thereafter receiving, judicial authorization to deny access to the records. In particular, we believe it is fundamentally unfair to permit prospective employers to require job applicants to consent to release of hospital or treatment records without permitting the applicant to examine the records he is asked to release so that he can correct, qualify, or supplement those records, or decide to withdraw the job application rather than consent to disclosure.

NOTES

1. See, for examples of statutory discrimination, Harvard Article, *Ch. I*, n. 14, pp. 1198-99; Deutscher and Green,

"Mental Health Is a Social Problem," 37 *Am. J. Ortho-psychiat.* 832 (1967).

2. Whatley, "Social Attitudes Towards Discharged Mental Patients," in *The Mental Patient: Studies in the Sociology of Deviance* (1968), p. 401.

3. The mentally disordered may be entitled to special legal protections: "Mental Illness: A Suspect Classification?" 83 *Yale L.J.* 1237 (May 1974); Harvard Article, *Ch. I,* n. 14, pp. 1229-30.

4. See Brooks, *Ch. II,* n. 11, pp. 943-951; *State v. Carter,* 316 A.2d 449 (N.J. 1974).

5. *Morrissey v. Brewer,* 408 U.S. 471 (1972).

6. *Government of the United States ex. rel. Shaban v. Essen,* 386 F. Supp. 1042 (E.D.N.Y. 1974); *Mersell v. Kremens,* ——— F. Supp. ——— (E.D. Pa., Aug. 25, 1975); Note, "Hearing Prior to Revocation of Mental Convalescent Status: A Comment on the Constitutional Imperatives," 49 *N.D.L. Rev.* 835 (1973).

7. See Brooks *Ch. II,* n. 11, p. 955.

8. See, for example, N.Y. Ment. Hyg. L. §15.01; N.Y. Exec. L. §296.

9. See, for example, Rev. Code Wash. 71.05.060, and *Ch. VI,* n. 120.

10. 29 U.S.C. §701, 791 and 794 (1973); see also 1973 U.S. Code Congressional and Administrative News, p. 2122.

11. 29 U.S.C. §701(8).

12. U.S.C. § 791(b).

13. U.S.C. § 794.

14. *Lombard v. Board of Education,* 502 F.2d 631 (2nd Cir. 1974).

15. *Newman v. Board of Education,* 508 F.2d 277 (2nd Cir. 1975); see also *Suarez v. Weaver,* 484 F.2d 678 (7th Cir. 1973); *Calo v. Paine,* 385 F. Supp. 1198 (D. Conn. 1974); *Bevan v. N.Y. State Teacher Retirement System,* 355 N.Y.S.2d 185 (App. Div. 3rd, 1974); *Groad v. Jansen,* 173 N.Y.S.2d 946 (1958).

16. *Freitag v. Carter,* 489 F.2d 1377 (7th Cir. 1973).

17. *Smith v. Schlesinger,* 513 F.2d 462 (D.C. Cir., 1975).

18. *Jones v. Penny* 387 F. Supp. 383 (M.D.N. Car. 1974).

19. See Ennis and Friedman, *Ch. I,* n. 6, Vol. I, pp. 77-100.

20. Klein and Grossman "Voting Patterns of Mental Patients in a Community State Hospital," 3 *Comm. Mental Health J.* 149 (1967); Wellner and Gaines, "Patient's Right to Vote," 21 *Hosp. Comm. Psychia.* 163 (1970).

21. *McGill v. Alton*, 523 F.2d 1051 (3rd Cir. 1975), and *McGill v. Alton*, ———— F. Supp. ———— (W.D. Pa., Jan. 26, 1976, No. 74-1164); *Boyd v. Board of Registrars*, 334 N.E.2d 629 (Mass 1975). See also Plotkin, "Too Crazy to Vote?" *Mental Health Law Project Summary of Activities*, Vol. II, No. 3, p. 1 (Fall, 1976, 1220 19th St. N.W., Wash. D.C. 20036).

22. *O'Connor v. Donaldson, Ch. II*, n. 13.

23. *Ibid.*, p. 575.

24. *Stoner v. Miller*, 377 F. Supp. 177 (E.D.N.Y. 1974).

25. *City of White Plains v. Ferraioli*, 34 N.Y.2d 300 (1974); *Little Neck Community Assoc. v. Working Organization for Retarded Children*, 383 N.Y.S.2d 364 (2nd Dept. 1976).

26. See, in general, Friedman, "Analysis of the Principal Issues and Strategies in Zoning Exclusion Cases," in Ennis and Friedman, *Ch. I*, n. 6, Vol II, pp. 1093-1105; see also *City of Los Angeles v. California Department of Health* (Cal. 1975); *State ex rel. Thelen v. City of Missoula*, 543 P.2d 173 (Mont. 1975); Minn. Stat. § 462.357, subdivisions 7-8; *Driscoll v. Goldberg*, (Case No. 72-Cl, 1248, 73 C.A., Ohio Ct. App. 7th D., 1974); *Anderson v. City of Shoreview* (No. 401575, D. Ct., Minn. 1975); *Gaining Community Acceptance: A Handbook for Community Residence Planners* (Westchester Community Service Council, 713 County Office Building. White Plains, N.Y. 10601); Hopperton, *Zoning for Community Homes* (Ohio State Univ. 1975).

27. See, generally, Wald, "The Right to Education," in Ennis and Friedman, *Ch. I*, n. 6, Vol. II, pp. 831-56; and see, in particular, *Mills v. Board of Education of District of Columbia*, 348 F. Supp. 866 (D.D.C. 1972); *Pennsylvania Association for Retarded Children v. Commonwealth of Pennsylvania*, 334 F. Supp. 1257 (E.D. Pa. 1971), and 343 F. Supp. 279 (E.D. Pa. 1972); *Fialkowski v. Shapp*, 405 F. Supp. 946 (E.D. Pa. 1975); *Frederick L. v. Thomas*, 408 F. Supp. 832 (E.D. Pa. 1976); *In re Suzanne E.*, 381 N.Y.S.2d 628 (Fam. Ct. Westchester Co. 1976). But see *San Antonio Independent School District v. Rodriguez*, 411 U.S. 1 (1973); and *Cuyahoga County Association For Retarded Children and Adults v. Essex*, 411 F. Supp. 46 (N.D. Ohio, 1976).

28. *Hairston v. Drosick*, 423 F. Supp. 180 (S.D. W.Va., 1976).

29. See Wexler, *Ch. II*, n. 24, p. 676 fn. 17.

30. See, in general, Allen, *et al., Ch. VI*, n. 120, fn. 417

and the authorities cited therein; and *Dale v. Hahn,* *Ch. VI,* n. 122.

31. Rev. Code Wash. 11.92 *et seq.*; 34-A McKinney's N.Y. Ment. Hyg. L. §§ 77.01-77.41.

32. Slovenko, "Psychotherapist-Patient Testimonial Privilege: A Picture of Misguided Hope," 23 *Cath. U. L. Rev.* 649 (1974) and authorities cited therein; Fleming and Maximov, "The Patient or His Victim: The Therapist's Dilemma," 62 *Calif. L. Rev.* 1025 (1974); see generally for a survey of recent literature, Brooks, *Ch. II,* n. 11, *Ch.* 20. And see, *State v. O'Neill,* 545 P.2d 97 (Ore. 1976).

33. See, for example, Rev. Code Wash. 71.05.390.

34. *Tarasoff v. Board of Regents of Univ. of Calif., Ch. I,* n. 16; Fleming, *supra* n. 32.

35. See, for example, Rev. Code Wash. 71.05.120.

36. Western State Hospital, Steilacoom, Wash.

37. *Gotkin v. Miller,* 514 F.2d 125 (2d Cir. 1975).

VIII

Lawyers And Mental Patients

What is the proper role of the lawyer?

We hope the information in this book will help mental patients help themselves. But whenever court proceedings are necessary, and in many other situations, patients will need the assistance of lawyers. There is now, for the first time, a fairly large and growing mental health bar. But it is still true that few lawyers have substantial experience representing mental patients. Most lawyers feel uncomfortable in this area. They have difficulty relating to mental patients; they are unduly awed by the "expertise" of mental health professionals, and they are not certain of their proper role. Should they vigorously oppose the involuntary hospitalization of a client whom they believe is seriously mentally disordered? Should they oppose shock therapy when the psychiatrist says it will help their client? And so on.

This chapter is written primarily for lawyers. Throughout the book we have made specific suggestions we believe will improve the quality of legal representation of mental patients. This chapter contains additional suggestions we hope lawyers will find useful.

Essentially, lawyers should have the same attitude toward a client who is a mental patient as they have toward any other client. They should remember that they are lawyers, not social workers, mental health professionals, or surrogate families. Their job is to provide legal advice and representation, not "treatment." Unfortunately, many lawyers are either afraid of mental patients, or they adopt a paternalistic, benevolent attitude toward them. Neither reaction is appropriate.

Lawyers frequently decide for themselves what is in their client's "best interests," often without consulting the client.[1] In our opinion, it is perfectly appropriate for a lawyer to attempt to persuade a client that a certain course of action would be in the client's interests, but if the client is not persuaded, it is the duty of the lawyer to represent the client's wishes, so long as they are not unethical or criminal.[2]

Many lawyers understand and even agree with this point, but they nevertheless feel "guilty" if they successfully oppose civil commitment when they believe their client "needs" to be hospitalized. We hope the information in this book about the antitherapeutic effects of hospitalization and the unreliability of psychiatric diagnoses will make such lawyers feel less guilty. But even if they feel guilty, lawyers should vigorously represent their client's wishes, just as they would represent the wishes of a criminal defendant whom they believe to be guilty. The mental health lawyer's rule of thumb should be that if his client is not sufficiently disordered or dangerous to be committed in the face of vigorous opposition, then he should not be committed at all. In our opinion, lawyers who do not represent their client's wishes usurp the function of the judge or jury and effectively deny the client his constitutional right to a fair trial.[3]

Lawyers who vigorously represent mental patients and respect their decisions usually play a unique role in the eyes of their clients; they act differently from family, friends, and doctors, all of whom simply want to "help." Mental patient clients usually perceive this difference. Often a relationship of trust develops between lawyers and mental patients. Because of that trust, the client may accept advice from the lawyer that he would not accept from others. For example, if a lawyer knows that a client is less likely to be committed if he is medicated during the commitment hearing because the client's physical appearance and actions may appear more stable than the impression he makes when he is not on drugs, it may be wise for the lawyer to attempt to influence his client to take the drugs. Although many patients may not want to take

182

drugs, they may decide to do so if they believe their chances for release will be improved (see Chapter III). Similarly, a lawyer might advise his client to postpone a request for a judicial hearing for a week or two so the case will be heard by a different, and more sympathetic, judge. In our opinion, these kinds of advice are quite proper. But because a trusted lawyer's advice will almost always be followed, the lawyer bears a heavy responsibility not to misuse that trust.

Actually, relationships of trust between mental patients and lawyers are not always easy to form. Many mental patients have had lawyers they could not trust, and patients, like most people, judge new lawyers from past experiences. The initial interview or meeting is almost always the critical point for establishing a close working relationship. The lawyer should advise the client that he will represent the client's wishes even if he disagrees with them, but that he will first try to persuade the client to change his mind if he believes the client is wrong.

The lawyer should allocate sufficient time for the first interview—at least 30 minutes and preferably longer. Often clients are understandably agitated or outraged by their predicament, and facts about the particular legal problem come out in a jumbled rush. It is helpful for the lawyer to assure the client, as he would any other, that he is going to get all the facts straight, no matter how long it takes. This will help the attorney-client relationship because it will distinguish the lawyer from ward staff, who rarely spend more than a few minutes with patients.[4]

After the initial rush of information from the client, pointed step-by-step questions about the problem will help to organize both his thoughts and the lawyer's. But questions should not be the only interview technique; listening to information the lawyer considers to be irrelevant to the legal issue, but which the client feels is important, is usually advisable. Sometimes this information becomes relevant later, and it almost always helps the lawyer understand his client better. Also, careful listening gives the client more confidence in the lawyer, especially if the lawyer carefully explains why certain information is not relevant to the particular legal problem he is trying to help solve.

If possible, the lawyer should read the client's hospital records even before the first interview. Often the hospital's version of events will conflict with the client's. If the lawyer gets an idea of what these conflicts are, how serious they are, and what explanations and corroborations his client has for his version, it is more likely that he and the client will be able to present the client's side of the story effectively. If hospital records are available at an early interview, the client's memory may be refreshed about particular incidents and his story may be more coherent. Also, hospital records may help to determine how drugged the client is at the interview, or was at the time of an incident, and they obviously provide some information about witnesses, times, places, and events.

In *every* case, lawyers should encourage the participation of their clients to the greatest extent possible. A copy of every letter and pleading should be sent to the client. The client should be kept up-to-date about all conversations with witnesses. If there is a *useful* task the client can perform to help his case, he should be asked to do it.

Preparation for judicial hearings should be careful and complete. If the client is to testify, he should know in advance every question he will be asked by his attorney. And the attorney should know the substance of the client's answers. The lawyer should also advise the client about the types of questions the opposing side will probably ask on cross-examination. Advice about the client's demeanor, dress, and speaking habits can be helpful. Telling the client what to expect in the courtroom, including the roles of the judge, court reporter, prosecutor, and witnesses, is essential.

What trial techniques can lawyers use to provide effective representation for mental patients?

Each case is different from the one before, and the attorney will have to adapt the suggestions contained in this section to the particular facts and circumstances of his case. For tactical reasons (unduly annoying an otherwise sympathetic judge, for example), it may be wise to forego many of the cross-examination techniques suggested here. It makes an enormous difference, for example, whether the opposing psychiatrist is unfamiliar with court proceedings or is an experienced forensic psychiatrist. Questions that will fluster the former may well be answered to the patient's detriment by the latter. So none of the suggestions in this section should be followed blindly.

One other warning: psychiatrists are not stupid. It is unlikely that any of the techniques suggested here will ever "trip up" an opposing psychiatrist or force him to admit he was mistaken. But if you are willing to spend the time, you should be able to lessen the impact of his testimony very substantially.

1. Invoke judicial proceedings whenever possible. Many cases can be resolved by negotiating with the hospital doctors. But it is amazing how starting judicial proceedings speeds up the negotiating process. In fact, the *mere filing* of a petition for a writ of habeas corpus is very often enough to prod the hospital into discharging the patient. Most doctors hate to testify in front of a judge (especially if they know the patient's lawyer will conduct a rigorous cross-examination), and they are even more afraid of appearing before a jury. So demand a trial, and a jury trial whenever possible (if the case actually goes to trial, you can drop your demand for a jury if you think a jury might be more likely to hospitalize than the judge).

2. Raise constitutional and statutory objections whenever possible. If only factual questions are raised in a hospitalization proceeding ("Is the prospective patient mentally ill?"; "Is he dangerous?"; and so forth), the hospital may well go ahead with the trial because if it loses, the only consequence will be that that particular patient is allowed to go free. But if you raise constitutional or statutory objections that, if successful, might result in the discharge of hundreds or thousands of other patients, the hospital will be less likely to run the risk of losing, and may simply release the patient. Almost *every* hospitalization proceeding raises substantial constitutional questions ("Does the privilege against self-incrimination apply?"; "Can the prospective patient be hospitalized if there are less drastic alternatives?"; and so forth), many of which have been discussed in this book. And many such proceedings raise important questions of statutory interpretation (for example, "What does danger to others mean?"). If those questions can legitimately be raised, raise them.

Even if the hospital still goes ahead with the trial, the judge may well rule in your client's favor on the *facts* so that he does not have to decide the thorny legal issues.

3. Use expert witnesses whenever possible. Judges are excessively deferential to "expert opinion" on psychiatric issues. So it is important, whenever possible, to bring in an expert of your own to testify that your client is not mentally ill or dangerous, or that even if he is, hospitalization is not necessary. A dispute between experts forces the judge to use his own common sense and to pay attention to your legal arguments. In some states, a so-called independent psychiatrist can be appointed, at state expense, but those psychiatrists are often appointed from a list of names suggested by the same hospital psychiatrists whose recommendation your client is opposing. Sometimes court appointed independent psychiatrists turn out to be staff members of state hospitals. Not surprisingly, this type of expert will usually agree with hospital psychiatrists. It is really damaging to have an "independent" psychiatrist testify against your client, so be very careful of such lists. If possible, you should submit your own list of psychiatrists to the judge and ask him to pick one or two as the court-appointed psychiatrist. That way, your chances of favorable testimony are immensely improved (see Chapter III).

4. Challenging the expertise of psychiatrists and psychologists. If you cannot round up expert witnesses for your side of the case, or if a so-called independent witness testifies against your client, you will then have to challenge the expertise of the opposing witnesses. Only "expert" witnesses are permitted to give "opinions." All other witnesses must restrict themselves to statements of "fact." Psychiatrists and, to a lesser extent, psychologists have uncritically been accorded expert status in every state. In fact, however, they do not meet any of the normal criteria of expertise. Specifically, their opinions are based not on facts or upon proven principles (as are the opinions of all other experts), but upon unproven theories (see Chapter I).

In other areas of expert testimony (ballistics, for example), it can be expected that if 100 experts analyze the same situation, more than 90 of them will reach the same opinion. But that is not true of psychiatrists and psychologists. Statistically, they can be expected to agree only about 54 percent of the time,[5] a rate of agreement only slightly better than the law of averages. And for specific diagnoses, the rate of agreement is even lower.

Disagreement is so common because the opinions of psychiatrists and psychologists are determined as much by their own personal biases and values as they are by any fixed body of psychiatric or psychological knowledge (see Chapter I).

It is fairly certain that opinions based on polygraph (lie detector) tests are accurate 75 percent of the time, but no court will accept as evidence the opinion of a lie detector operator, unless the person against whom the test is to be used has consented to its use. Why, then, should a court accept the opinions of psychiatrists or psychologists, which are far less reliable?[6]

Citations of hundreds of empirical studies to back up this point are available in a little known but excellent book by Jay Ziskin entitled *Coping with Psychiatric and Psychological Testimony.* This book is essential reading for any lawyer about to handle a mental commitment case.

Even if the judge does not exclude the opinion testimony of a psychiatrist or psychologist, in the process of challenging the expertise of the witness you should be able, at least, to lessen the force of his testimony. Ziskin points out, for example, that Professor Anastasi, author of *Psychological Testing,* which is one of the leading textbooks on the subject, has concluded that the Rorschach test has "little or no predictive or concurrent validity" and is, in effect, worthless as a clinical test.[7] Psychologists frequently base their opinions on Rorschach test results. By pointing out the unreliablity of such tests, you may persuade the judge to exclude any opinion based upon them. And even if he admits such opinions into evidence, they will obviously be less persuasive to him (or to a jury) than if the unreliability of Rorschach tests had not been emphasized.

Ziskin's book contains hundreds of similarly useful studies and once again we urge you to read it. He even has a chapter on suggested questions for challenging the expertise of psychiatrists and psychologists.

5. *Danger standard—challenging predictions of danger-*

ous behavior. A prediction of dangerous behavior is an "opinion," and under the ordinary rules of evidence, only a qualified "expert" can give opinion testimony; everyone else can testify only about "facts."

In the preceding section, we urged you to challenge the ability of psychiatrists and psychologists to make psychiatric diagnoses with an acceptable degree of certainty. Everything said there applies with even more force to psychiatric predictions of dangerous behavior. With rare exceptions, there is nothing in the education, training, or experience of psychiatrists that makes them any more qualified to predict dangerous behavior than police, or lawyers, or anyone else.[8] Thus, if hospitalization requires a prediction of dangerousness, it may be advisable to challenge the psychiatrist's qualifications to make that kind of prediction. The judge may overrule your objection, but at least you will have raised an appealable point of law, and you may succeed in flustering the psychiatrist, or, at least, in weakening his credibility.

Begin by asking if he took any courses in medical school or thereafter in the prediction of dangerous behavior. The answer will almost certainly be no. Then ask if he has published any books or articles on the subject—again, the answer will probably be no. If he claims that on the bases of his "expertise" he is able to make such predictions, ask him first if the accuracy of his clinical predictions has ever been empirically verified, and then ask if he is aware of the numerous studies that conclude, almost without exception, that psychiatrists cannot predict dangerous behavior. Be as specific as you can, quoting from the studies (see notes 6-15 in Chapter I), asking if he disagrees with those conclusions, and if so, to specify his *empirical* basis for disagreement. If you do all this skillfully, you may even persuade the psychiatrist to agree that prediction of dangerous behavior is a role thrust upon him by society, for which he does not feel particularly qualified. (Note: Your objection to the psychiatrist's opinion testimony can be linked up with your objection to the preponderance of the evidence test, discussed in Chapter III. Because the psychiatrist's ability to predict dangerous behavior is, at best, doubtful, the judge should at least require proof of danger "beyond a reasonable doubt" before hospitalizing a person based on such predictions.)

6. *Danger standard—questioning the expert.* Unless you are certain the answer will be favorable, *never* ask an opposing psychiatrist whether he believes your client is dangerous. Even if he does not believe your client is likely to be dangerous, he will probably say, "Well, I think he might possibly be dangerous in a stress situation," or something like that. You could then hammer away at the ambiguity of words like "might" or "possibly," or even "dangerous," but the damage would have been done.

If you must ask about dangerousness, avoid questions that permit generalized answers or opinions, and try to be as specific as possible, asking only yes-no questions. If the psychiatrist has already testified, in general terms, that he thinks your client is dangerous, the questioning on cross-examination might go as follows:

Q: Doctor, I suppose you have not personally seen Mr. X mutilate or physically injure himself, is that correct?

A: Well, yes, that is correct.

Q: And I suppose you have not personally seen him physically injure other persons, is that correct?

A: Yes, that is correct.

Q: Has he ever, in your presence, attempted or threatened to inflict substantial physical injury on himself or you or on a third person?

A: No.

Q: So putting aside for the moment whatever you may have heard about Mr. X from other sources, you do not have *personal* knowledge that he has ever committed, attempted, or threatened any physically injurious act, is that correct?

A: Yes, that is correct.

At this point, you will have the psychiatrist in a difficult position. He will next have to admit (a) that he does *not* believe your client is physically dangerous to himself or others, or (b) that he believes your client *is* physically dangerous to himself or others but his belief is not based on evidence of past dangerous conduct, or (c) that he believes your client *is* physically dangerous to himself or others but his belief is based on evidence of past dangerous conduct supplied by others.

If he answers (a), you can then argue that anything less than physical danger (i.e., public nuisance, writing annoying letters,) does not constitute "danger" within the meaning of the commitment statute and does not satisfy constitutional requirements. If he answers (b), you can then stress the astonishing inaccuracy of predictions of future dangerous behavior that are not based on evidence of past dangerous behavior (see Chapter I), and you can point out that your client has never done, in the past, what the psychiatrist claims he will do in the future. If he answers (c), you can then point out that the validity of the psychiatrist's opinion depends on the truth and accuracy of the evidence of past dangerous behavior supplied by others. Usually, those other persons will be laymen. Suppose, to take a common example, that the psychiatrist's opinion is based on a statement by the father of your client that your client threw a chair at him. The psychiatrist will have to admit the *possibility* that the father lied, or exaggerated, or even provoked the incident. If you ask the psychiatrist whether your client actually threw the chair through the air, or merely interposed it between himself and his father, he probably will not know. At the least, you should be able to weaken the impact of the "impartial expert's" opinion by showing that it is based in large part upon information supplied by nonexperts who are not at all impartial. At best, you may persuade the judge to disregard the expert's opinion, or to exclude it unless the persons who gave him the underlying information are made available for cross-examination.

7. *Beware of one-sided reports.* One of the most serious problems with hospital records and psychiatric reports is that they invariably emphasize the worst features of a patient, or prospective patient, saying little or nothing about his good features. Rarely do such reports convey a balanced view of the individual's strengths and weaknesses.

In one case, for example, the opposing psychiatrist submitted a report to the court that characterized the client as hostile and aggressive toward the psychiatrist. On cross-examination, he conceded that the "main thing" he remembered from the interview was that the client wanted to be, and was, friendly and helpful to other persons. But he had omitted those favorable impressions from his report. His report also emphasized, again and again, that the client thought the psychiatrist was going to "murder" him. Again, he omitted from his report, but admitted on cross-examination, that the client had explained during the interview that by "murder" he meant only that the psychiatrist was trying to deprive the client of his liberty, which, to him, was "as important as life itself."[9]

It is important to point out how one-sided psychiatric reports invariably are, both to show the judge that in many respects your client speaks and behaves quite normally, and to challenge the impartiality of the expert. If the psychiatrist has submitted a report of his evaluation, or if his testimony has been quite brief, you can ask how long he interviewed your client. If he says 10 or 15 minutes, you can stress the unreliability of such a short examination. If, as is more likely, he claims to have examined your client for an hour or so, you should then ask if his report or testimony "left out" any particularly unusual statement or conduct that occurred during the examination and that he would consider indicative of mental illness (or dangerousness). This question could backfire, but professional pride in the thoroughness of his work will probably prompt him to say no. Next, by pointing out that his report was only a paragraph or two long, or that his testimony consumed only five minutes, you should be able to force him to admit that his report (or testimony) does not mention *most* of what was said or done during the interview. Since he will already have admitted that he did not leave out any particularly bizarre incidents, you should then be able to force him to admit that *most* of what your client said or did was entirely normal or, at the least, not sufficiently unusual to warrant comment.

8. *Stress the unreliability of the clinical interview*. Numerous studies have shown that the results of psychiatric examinations depend as much, or more, on factors independent of the person being examined as they do on the statements or conduct of the person himself. The most important of the variable factors is, of course, the personality of the examiner. One examiner, by his attitude,

may provoke hostility that another examiner would not. Studies have shown that the sex, race, social class, and theoretical orientation (Freudian, Adlerian, Jungian, etc.) of the examiner have a definite and profound impact on his evaluation—so much so that, as Ziskin notes, "there is no way of knowing whether the 'anxiety' or 'hostility' or 'sexual preoccupation' or any other characteristic being attributed to the subject of an examination is in fact an attribute of the subject or whether it is, as the foregoing studies have shown, a reflection of an attribute of the examiner."[10] Other studies stress the critical importance of the time and place of the examination, and the purpose of the examination as told to, or perceived by, the subject. The point, of course, is that psychiatric examinations are not at all scientific. Psychiatrists find what they expect to find.

On cross-examination, the psychiatrist should be asked if he concedes that the variable factors discussed in this section could have affected his opinion. If he says no, challenge him with the studies cited by Ziskin and demand that he specify countervailing studies. If he says yes, then ask him first exactly how each variable could have affected his opinion, second, how he knows that, and third, what he did to compensate for the possible influence of those variables.

9. *Do not be personally antagonistic to the opposing psychiatrist.* Generally, it is a good idea to treat the opposing psychiatrist with courtesy and at least a minimum of respect. Sarcasm and personal attacks will usually anger the judge (many judges identify rather closely with psychiatrists) and will provoke even more damaging testimony from the psychiatrist. One useful approach is to treat the psychiatrist as an honest but overworked professional, forced by society to play a role he does not relish or feel particularly qualified to perform.

Occasionally, however, it may be necessary, or even advisable, to challenge the psychiatrist's personal competence or integrity. You can begin by asking if he is "board certified"—that is, whether he is certified as a psychiatrist by the American Board of Psychiatry and Neurology. Most psychiatrists are not. If you found out prior to trial that he is not a member of the American Psychiatric Association, you could then ask about that. Sometimes it is helpful to point out that the opposing psychiatrist is being paid for his testimony, particularly if the payment comes from the relative or other person who initiated the commitment proceeding.

But again, the general rule is to avoid personalized attacks on the opposing psychiatrist's competence or integrity, unless you have no alternative.

10. *Watch for medication changes.* Frequently, the court hearing is held *after* your client has already been hospitalized for some time. In those circumstances, find out the type and amount of medication your client has been receiving, and watch for changes. A patient who appears normal while under tranquilizing medication may appear excessively agitated and volatile if that medication is discontinued or reduced. A similar point can be made for an otherwise depressed or sluggish patient who is receiving antidepressant medication. On the other hand, there are many patients who appear relatively normal when they are receiving no medication, but who shuffle around like zombies and who become incoherent when receiving medication. It is distressingly common for doctors to begin, discontinue, or change the patient's medication shortly before a hearing so that the patient will appear before the judge at his worst. If the medication has, in fact, benefited your client or stabilized his appearance, and you have agreed with your client that he should continue to take medication for the hearing, the best procedure is to tell the doctor well before the hearing that you expect him to maintain that medication level through the hearing. If he does so, your client will make a good first impression on the judge, which is likely to persist even if the psychiatrist tells the judge that without medication your client would seem much worse. If the medication makes your client seem more "out of it" than he is, you should tell the doctor that you expect him to discontinue the medication well before the hearing.

But even if the doctor ignores your wishes and changes your client's medication so that he appears sicker to the judge than he otherwise might, you can at least point out to the judge that under proper medication, your client would have been in better condition. And you might even be able to persuade the judge that the psychiatrist is not as "impartial" as he claims to be by forcing him to admit (a) that he changed your client's medication shortly before trial and (b) that the change makes your client appear more disturbed than he would appear if he were receiving more (or less) medication.

What should lawyers know before undertaking right-to-treatment lawsuits?

Before undertaking right-to-treatment lawsuits, lawyers should, of course, be familiar with the law and the legal theories underlying such lawsuits (see Chapter VI). But they should know a great deal more than that. They should know, first, that many patients and ex-patients do not want or approve of such suits, either because they do not *want* treatment or because they are convinced that a right to treatment, once firmly established, will serve a legitimizing function in justifying involuntary hospitalization. These concerns are legitimate. On the other hand, conditions in most public mental hospitals are so inhumane, and providing humane conditions in an institutional setting would be so expensive, that right-to-treatment suits may be used as a tactical device for forcing the discharge of large numbers of inappropriately confined patients. And patients who are not discharged as a result of successful right-to-treatment suits will at least benefit from more humane conditions of confinement. In our opinion, lawyers who bring right-to-treatment suits should clearly focus the court's attention on this issue. They should urge the court to order the state to provide a meaningful *opportunity* for treatment, leaving to the patient the decision whether to exercise that opportunity. In other words, every right-to-treatment suit should be linked with a right-to-refuse-treatment suit[11] (see Chapter VI).

Lawyers should also know that properly prepared right-to-treatment suits are enormously expensive and time consuming. The litigation involving Willowbrook Developmental Center for the mentally retarded,[12] for example, required a substantial portion of the time of five to eight lawyers over a three-year period, and cost approximately $50,000 for transcripts of depositions, travel and lodging costs for expert witnesses, and other nonsalary expenses.

And implementation of a successful right-to-treatment suit is usually a frustrating, time-consuming, and expensive undertaking.[13]

In short, right-to-treatment suits should not be brought without careful planning, marshalling of resources, and clear and unequivocal examples of inhumane institutional conditions.[14]

Before undertaking right-to-treatment litigation, lawyers should visit the institution, establish contacts with sympathetic staff, and investigate at least the following areas:

1. Evaluate the daily lives of patients in the hospital. Where, how, and for how long or often do patients sleep, wash, eat, receive clean clothing, socialize, get outside, play, engage in athletics, watch TV, read newspapers and periodicals, see movies, work, receive therapy, receive drugs, visit outsiders, telephone, write letters, have privacy, interact with the opposite sex, use a library, receive medical care, receive dental care, and so forth. These activities should be analyzed in detail for the different classes of patients in the hospital.

2. Life on every ward, not just one or two, should be analyzed. Often patients on one ward live in vastly different conditions from patients on other wards. "Back ward" life is usually far worse than life on acute admission wards.

3. Find out normal capacities of wards and compare with actual population. Compare population with state fire and health codes.

4. Find out staff-patient ratios not only for the whole institution, but also for each shift on each ward. There is usually a substantial difference between the number of staff scheduled to be on duty, and the number actually on duty.

5. Determine disease and death rates. Often the incidences of disease and death are much higher in mental hospitals than for similar age groups in the community.[15]

6. Obtain statistics of average length of stay for patients in different patient categories, including involuntary, voluntary, criminal defendant, and children.

7. Determine if all patients have written and individualized treatment plans with specific short-term and long-term goals, and specified methods for reaching those goals.

Finally, compare gathered information with standards

for mental hospitals prescribed by the Joint Commission on the Accreditation of Hospitals and by the federal cases that have ordered implementation of specific standards.[16]

After obtaining this information, the lawyer should seriously consider alternatives other than litigation, including legislation, and should discuss his findings and the alternatives with administrative and legislative officials. Only if other realistic alternatives fail should the lawyer undertake right-to-treatment litigation.

NOTES

1. Schaffer, "Introduction," 13 *St. Cl. Lwr.*, 369, 376 (1973).
2. Cohen, *Ch. III*, n. 23.
3. See authorities cited in *Ch. III*, nn. 23 and 25, and *Memmel v. Mundy*, *Ch. III*, n. 19.
4. Rosenhan, *Ch. I*, n. 10.
5. Ziskin, *Ch. I*, n. 4.
6. Ennis and Litwack, *Ch. I*, n. 6.
7. Ziskin, *Ch. I*, n. 4, p. 166.
8. Ennis and Litwack, *Ch. I*, n. 4, fn. 6.
9. *United States v. Adams*, *Ch. V.*, n. 19, and testimony reproduced in Brooks, *Ch. II*, n. 11, pp. 337-48.
10. Ziskin, *Ch. I*, n. 4, p. 129.
11. See Schmidt, "Conclusion," *Ch. III*, n. 14.
12. *New York State Association for Retarded Children v. Rockefeller*, *Ch. III*, n. 10, and *New York State Association for Retarded Children v. Carey*, 393 F. Supp. 715 (E.D.N.Y. 1975).
13. Lottman, "Enforcement of Judicial Decrees: Now Comes the Hard Part," Vol. 1, No. 1, *Ment. Disab. L. Rep.* (ABA, July-August 1976), pp. 69-76.
14. Wald and Schwartz, "Trying a Juvenile Right to Treatment Suit: Pointers and Pitfalls for Plaintiffs;" Ennis and Friedman, *Ch. I*, n. 6, Vol. 3, pp. 1259-1312.
15. Dunham and Weinberg, *The Culture of State Mental Hospitals* (1960).
16. *Wyatt v. Stickney Ch. VI*, n. 88.

Appendix A

Statistical Information about the Mental Health System

Table 1. NUMBER OF TOTAL PATIENTS TREATED IN INPATIENT PSYCHIATRIC FACILITIES IN U.S., 1972*

Type of Facility	Resident Patients	Admissions	Total Inpatient Care Episodes
State and county mental hospitals	274,837	377,020	651,857
Private mental hospitals	12,098	110,733	122,831
VA psychiatric hospitals	36,854	171,562	208,416
General hospital psychiatric units	18,705	456,743	475,448
Resident treatment centers for emotionally disturbed children	17,100	12,010	29,110
Federally funded community mental health centers	7,018†	111,991	119,009
Other multiservice mental health facilities	1,223	37,473	38,696
All facilities	367,835	1,227,532	1,645,367‡

*Data calculated by Division of Biometry, National Institute for Mental Health, April 25, 1975.

†Average daily census.

‡1,645,367 × 80% = 1,316,293.60—ball-park figure of number of individuals treated at least once in inpatient psychiatric facilities, FY 1972 (takes into account duplicate admissions of same person).

Table 2. NUMBER OF TOTAL PATIENTS
TREATED IN INPATIENT PSYCHIATRIC
FACILITIES IN U.S., 1971*

Type of Facility	Resident Patients	Admissions†	Total Inpatient Care Episodes
State/county mental hospitals (NIMH Statistical Note #60, p. 5)	339,027	497,229	836,256
Private mental hospitals (NIMH Statistical Note #99, p. 9)	10,207	91,151	101,358
General hospital psychiatric units (NIMH Statistical Note #70, p. 9)	—	—	521,707‡
Federally funded community mental health centers (NIMH Statistical Note #95, p. 1)	6,195	—	6,195§
VA psychiatric hospitals (VA Chief of Biometrics, L. Mesard, 7/23/75)	47,000¶	109,000	156,000
Federal mental hospitals (St. Elizabeth's) (Margaret Connors, Biometrics, SEH, 7/16/75)	3,865	4,511	8,376
Total patients for all facilities	406,294	701,891	1,629,892

*Data calculated by Gail Marker, MSW, from information supplied by Division of Biometry, National Institute for Mental Health.

†Includes "first admissions," "readmissions," and "return from long-term leave" patients.

‡Figure is for "discharges," but NIMH Statistical Notes equate discharge with number of persons treated since turnover rate in these hospitals is very high (median stay is 11 days). (See NIMH Statistical Notes 70.)

§This is probably a low figure since no admission data are included. This figure was calculated on the basis of centers reporting an average census of 21 inpatients per center, and there were 295 centers.

¶Approximately 9,200 were designated "psychiatrically medically infirm" patients (treated primarily for medical disability).

Appendix B

Psychoactive Drugs

Introduction

Expatients (Project Release) and patient advocates (Institutional Legal Services Project) have recently begun to compile and disseminate information about the kinds of drugs commonly used in mental hospitals. The information in this appendix has been excerpted almost word for word from *Consumer's Guide to Psychiatric Medication* by David Briggs (Project Release, New York, N.Y., 1975) and *Ain't Nobody's Body But Your Own* by Carol Van Airsdale (Institutional Legal Services Project, Seattle, Washington, 1976). We have not independently checked the accuracy of the information contained in this appendix, but we have no reason to doubt its accuracy. We have been informed that the information in these two publications was taken from standard medical reference works, and was checked for accuracy by psychiatrists.

Psychoactive medications are divided into several categories. First there are the *major tranquilizers* or "antipsychotic" drugs. Thorazine and Mellaril are the best known in this group. The major tranquilizers sometimes can control the symptoms of a "psychosis" partially to significantly in many patients. Second, there are other drugs, such as the *antiparkinsonian* drugs for neuromuscular side effects, primarily those caused by the major tranquilizers. Artane is one of these drugs. Third, there is lithium carbonate, which is sometimes considered a major tranquilizer but is chemically different. It is used to attempt to control manic-depression. Fourth, there are the *antidepressants*, of which there are three subtypes: the *tricyclics*, the *ampheta-*

mines, and the *MAO inhibitors.* Fifth, there are the *anti-anxiety drugs* or *minor tranquilizers,* of which Librium and Valium are in general use. These drugs are used for "anxiety" and tension. And finally, there are the *sleeping pills,* or *sedatives,* with which most people are familiar.

It should be emphasized that psychiatric medication is not a cure, but a controlling agent like aspirin. In addition, no one can predict whether a given patient will respond to any particular drug or whether side effects will be a problem. The frequency and severity of these side effects vary with the individual.

If medication is prescribed, it should be a *part* of an *individualized treatment plan* for each person in the hospital. Also, most certification standards for hospitals providing involuntary treatment require that a person be given a medical examination by a doctor within 24 hours of admission.

The following warnings should be kept in mind while reading this appendix.

Drugs may be hazardous to your health. All of the medications listed in this appendix can impair your ability to drive a car or operate machinery.

Pregnant women should inform their obstetrician or other physician immediately if they plan to take psychotropic medication since the safety of these drugs during pregnancy has not been established.

Anyone who has *glaucoma* should advise his doctor of this problem immediately, since psychiatric medication may aggravate the condition.

If these medications are given at *high dosages* or *for long periods of time,* the possibility of serious permanent adverse effects increases.

It has been reported that the *concurrent use* of two or more psychotropic medications in the same drug class (*i.e.,* two major tranquilizers) is dangerous and may increase adverse effects. There is no scientific evidence to support concurrent use. The medical literature indicates that concurrent use is not in keeping with sound medical practice.

It has also been reported that the use of an *antiparkinsonian drug* for more than three months is generally not indicated. The current medical literature suggests that antiparkinsonian drugs lose their therapeutic effectiveness after this period.

Most of the drugs listed in this appendix can cause a *psychological dependency*. When going off these drugs, it is advisable to do so gradually to minimize the effects of a psychological withdrawal.

I. MAJOR TRANQUILIZERS OR "ANTIPSYCHOTIC" DRUGS

These drugs are the heaviest tranquilizers (see Drug Chart at the end of this appendix). In other words, a person would feel the effects of these drugs more strongly than most of the other tranquilizers. Thinking is slowed down; emotions are blunted.

Because you may be taking an "antipsychotic" drug does not mean you are "psychotic." If you want to know your medical diagnosis, ask your doctor.

The most common of these drugs are:

1. Thorazine (the most sedation)
2. Mellaril (moderate sedation)
3. Stelazine (low sedation)
4. Trilafon (low sedation)
5. Haldol (low sedation)
6. Prolixin or Permitil. (This is often given by "depot" injection. The effects of the injection can last for two weeks.)

Side effects. Some side effects of "antipsychotic" drugs are temporary; others are not. Again, if you experience any unpleasant side effect, tell a doctor. *Serious* side effects can occur with these drugs, even at low dosage. In addition, there may be hazards in taking these drugs for extended periods. In our view, if a person is going to use these drugs, he should take them on a short-term basis only. If a person decides that long-term use is necessary, the lowest possible controlling dose should be used. In addition, long-term patients should have their eyes and blood checked periodically. Where rapid tranquilization is being done (up to 200 mg. per hour the first day of "treatment"), the literature has *not* mentioned *serious* side effects during this several-days-to-one-week period.

Motor restlessness: There is a lot of tension and a need to keep walking constantly. You can't sit still. Insomnia has also been reported. The restlessness can resemble the original "neurotic" or "psychotic" problem. The dosage can be reduced or an antiparkinsonian drug can be taken. Two tablets usually control the symptoms in an hour.

Pseudo-Parkinsonism: Symptoms include tremors, shuffling walk (the "Thorazine shuffle"), drooling, and a stiff-looking face. A slow tremor of the hands has been reported. As for motor restlessness, an antiparkinsonian drug can control these symptoms.

Dystonias: Spasm of the neck muscles, progressing sometimes to tremor or rotation of the head are other side effects. Rigidity of the back muscles has been reported. The head can tend to turn to the side. Patients can become bent over backward (rare). The foot can become twisted into one position. Painful contractions and spasms of the face can develop. In addition, the eyes can become "stuck" in an upward gaze. Discontinuation of the drug or the use of an antiparkinsonian drug will bring relief.

Sexual problems: Many psychiatric patients have reported changes in libido (sex drive) on psychoactive drugs. The usual effect of these drugs on the sex drive is to lower it, although occasionally the drive is increased. Inhibition of ejaculation in males can occur. The treatment of this type of drug-induced sexual problem is to lower the dosage or to change medication. Mellaril is the big offender on inhibition of ejaculation. It has also been reported that female sexual response is lowered.

Orthostatic hypotension: Some patients may feel faint or dizzy when standing up. Others have been known to fall. This is more likely to occur when the drug is combined with alcohol, or in older persons with heart disease.

This effect is most likely to occur during the first few weeks of drug treatment. This problem can decrease if the dosage is lowered. Similar symptoms have been reported with *tricyclics* as well.

Sensitivity to sunlight: Another side effect is an allergic type of sunburn when unprotected skin is exposed to sunlight. This occurs most often in patients taking high doses of these medications. If you have this problem, you will have to avoid the sun, clothe exposed skin, or use a protective cream. Ask the druggist for the strongest cream he has. In addition to the above, a skin rash can develop unrelated to exposure to the sun.

Initiation or aggravation of "psychotic" symptoms: This is rarely seen with major tranquilizers. Occasionally, persons on high doses of tricyclics (Elavil, Tofranil, etc.) become confused, rambling, or incoherent. Adding a major tranquilizer and lowering the dosage of the tricyclic is recommended. Some persons can become more irritable on tricyclics, although this is not commonly seen.

Leucocytopenia: This is a relatively rare effect in which there is a moderate reduction in the number of white blood cells. Anyone with a sore throat or other infection should have his or her white cell count checked. Serious infections secondary to the above may occur, but are rarely fatal.

Grand mal seizures: A grand mal seizure causes the patient to lose consciousness and move uncontrollably. Epileptic patients should have higher doses of anticonvulsants if needed. It should be pointed out that grand mal seizures have been known to occur in healthy patients on steady doses, but this is uncommon.

Other side effects: These include but are not limited to dry mouth, blurred vision, urinary disturbances, constipation, lack of menstruation, fatigue, reduced or increased appetite, weight gain, and false positive pregnancy tests.

Permanent side effects. There is one severe permanent effect from "antipsychotic" drugs that was first recognized approximately 20 years ago. It is called "tardive dyskinesia" ("tardive"—late occurring, "dyskinesia"—abnormal muscle movements). It is estimated that anywhere from 2 to 25 percent of all inmates of mental hospitals who have been taking "antipsychotic" drugs for some as yet unknown period of time have this disorder. Older persons and women are more prone to get it. The damage affects the part of the brain used for control and coordination of muscle movement (the basal ganglia.) One doctor has described this brain damage:

Its (tardive dyskinesia's) manifestations include involuntary movements especially affecting the lips and tongue, hands and fingers, and body posture. Consequently, speech may be seriously affected, the face may become distorted and subject to uncontrolled expressions, and sustained normal posture may become impossible.

Another doctor has written:

Tardive Dyskinesia . . . consisted of slow, rhythmical movements in the region of the mouth, with protrusion of the tongue, smacking of the lips, blowing of the cheeks, and side-to-side movements of the chin, as well as other bizarre muscular activity.

Involuntary movements of the eyes, chewing movements of the mouth, and movements of other parts of the body may also be involved—swaying and rocking of the body, shoulder shrugging, foot tapping, and simple movements of the arms and legs. Rarely, a person may get respiratory dyskinesia, involving irregular, involuntary, forceful contractions of the diaphragm and thoracic muscles—which may interfere with speech and breathing.

The problem with determining whether a person has tardive dyskinesia is that it cannot be accurately diagnosed while a person is still taking the "antipsychotic" drug. In other words, the drug masks its symptoms. One way to find out if someone has it is for her/him to stop the drug and see if the signs show up.

If a person does get tardive dyskinesia, it is important to stop taking the drug. There is no known cure for this disorder. To prevent it there are a few helpful alternatives:

1. Stop taking any "antipsychotic" drug permanently.
2. Take a vacation from the drug for several months on a regular basis.
3. Lower the dosage.

If you think you may have tardive dyskinesia, tell your doctor immediately.

Another disturbing *permanent effect* from long-term use of "antipsychotic" drugs is clouding of the lens of the eyes with tiny granules. To identify this condition, users should receive at least annual eye examinations. Again, since there is no known cure, the drug should be stopped if the condition develops.

It's a good idea not to drink alcoholic beverages while taking "antipsychotic" drugs—their effect is magnified. Also, if you find that you are drowsy, do not drive a car or operate heavy machinery.

Withdrawal: Sudden discontinuance of major tranquilizers or antidepressants can produce withdrawal symptoms. The following have been reported with major tranquilizers: dizziness, tremors, nausea, vomiting, tension, and fever. Withdrawal from antidepressants is similar. These drugs should be reduced *gradually* to avoid or minimize the above. This type of withdrawal is indicative of a physical dependency, but not a dangerous and progressive addiction.

Tolerance to side effects: Some side effects can go away by themselves, others are persistent. This applies to both major tranquilizers and antidepressants.

Finally, it is suggested that instead of taking the more sedating drugs right before bedtime, take them two hours before to minimize "hangover." The blurring of near vision can be corrected with bifocals or reading glasses.

II. ANTIPARKINSONIAN DRUGS

These drugs help combat the temporary, muscular side effects of "antipsychotic" drugs. Often the side effects of the "antipsychotic" drugs disappear within a month or so, making the antiparkinsonian drugs unnecessary. They do not relieve symptoms of tardive dyskinesia. These drugs include:

1. Artane
2. Cogentin
3. Kemadrin
4. Akineton

Common side effects: Dryness of mouth, blurred vision. Confused thinking and speech can occur even at moderate dosage, but they are more likely at higher dosage.

Overdosage: Overdosing on these drugs can lead to an organic brain syndrome. There is the possibility of additive side effects when anti-parkinsonian drugs are taken with major tranquilizers and or tricyclics. This can manifest itself as increased dry mouth and blurred vision, among other side effects. Alertness necessary for driving a car may be impaired.

III. LITHIUM CARBONATE

Lithium carbonate is considered a major tranquilizer, as are the "antipsychotics." The amount of lithium required to produce the desired effect is close to an overdose, so persons taking it must have frequent blood tests to measure the amount of the drug in the body—at least once a month after the desired level is reached. Also, urine should be checked frequently, as there exists a possibility of kidney damage.

Side effects: Common, temporary side effects of lithium carbonate are nausea, nervousness, tiredness, tremor of hands or jaw, loss of appetite, muscle weakness or rigidity, twitching, thirst, and excessive urination.

When there is too much lithium carbonate in the body the symptoms are blurred vision, abdominal pain, diarrhea, vomiting, weight loss, drowsiness, dizziness, and severe muscular rigidity. With a large overdose, convulsions, coma, or death may occur.

With regular use, a person often develops a goiter (enlargement of the thyroid gland in the neck). This effect disappears when the drug is stopped. Lithium carbonate should not be taken by persons on salt-restricted diets, or by those taking drugs that increase the amount of urination.

IV. ANTIDEPRESSANTS

These drugs are used, as the name indicates, to relieve depression. They are stimulants—"uppers."
   A. *Tricyclics*
1. Tofranil, Presamine
2. Norpramin, Pertofrane
3. Tegretol
4. Elavil

5. Aventyl
6. Vivactil (least sedating)
7. Adapin, Sinequan (most sedating)
8. Triavil or Etrafon (these two are a combination of Trilafon and Elavil)

Oversedation: This can be controlled by switching to a less sedating drug such as Tofranil or Vivactil. The tendency to sedation can wear off in a few weeks.

Common persistent side effects: These include dry mouth, blurred vision, fine tremor, orthostatic hypotension (see I. Major Tranquilizers). This type of hypotension is more of a problem with the elderly, who are more likely to fall.

Tofranil can cause sweating, flushing, and feeling warm. Lowering the dosage or switching to another drug will help.

Other side effects: "Schizophrenic" people may develop increased symptoms of a "psychosis." "Paranoid" people may also have an aggravation of such symptoms. The combination of Elavil and Placidyl (a sleeping pill) can produce delirium. Other side effects are: pseudo-parkinsonism (see I. Major Tranquilizers), which is uncommon, ringing in the ears, insomnia, nightmares, constipation, skin rash, hives, blood disorders, and increased or decreased libido. The above is not a complete list. These drugs should be used with caution in patients with a history of seizures.

B. *Amphetamines*
1. Benzedrine
2. Dexedrine
3. Desoxyn (Methedrine)
4. Ritalin (related compound)

Side effects: Common, temporary side effects of amphetamines and Ritalin are: restlessness, dizziness, tremor, tenseness, irritability, weakness, inability to sleep, confusion, increased sexual desire, panic states, headache, chills, fast or irregular heartbeat, low or high blood pressure, excessive sweating, dry mouth, nausea, vomiting, diarrhea, loss of appetite.

Tiredness and depression usually occur after the stimulation caused by the drug.

C. *MAO Inhibitors*
1. Nardil
2. Marplan
3. Niamid
4. Eutonyl
5. Parnate
6. Furoxone
7. Eutron

It is important with these drugs to get a careful list of what you shouldn't take with them. This should be a list of *drugs and foods*. If a patient sees a doctor or dentist who is not aware of the patient's use of these drugs, the doctor should be so informed. Any tricyclics that are being taken should be mentioned as well. Also, one expert has stated that these drugs should not be given to people over 60 years of age.

V. ANTIANXIETY DRUGS OR MINOR TRANQUILIZERS

These drugs (also called the "minor tranquilizers") do not have the strong effects associated with "antipsychotics."

A person can become physically addicted to meprobamate (Equanil, Miltown). If someone stops taking meprobamate at high dosages (3.2 grams on up), there will probably be unpleasant withdrawal symptoms—tremors, inability to sleep, nausea, anxiety, possibly convulsions and coma.

Valium and Librium are muscle relaxants. They also can be physically addictive, and common withdrawal symptoms are depression, agitation, inability to sleep, loss of appetite, and more anxiety. These anti-anxiety drugs include:

1. Librium
2. Valium
3. Miltown or Equanil
4. Serax
5. Tranxene
6. Vistaril or Atarax

Side effects: Common, temporary side effects of antianxiety drugs (less intense and less frequent than with "antipsychotic" drugs) are drowsiness, depression, mental confusion, low blood pressure (with high doses), skin rashes, nausea, dizziness, constipation, menstrual irregularity, irregular uncoordinated muscle movements.

Infrequent temporary side effects of antianxiety drugs are fainting, bronchial spasms, headache, stimulation of appetite and weight gain, a reversible form of hepatitis, decrease in white blood cells, muscular side effects, loss of sexual desire and abilities, involuntary rapid movement of eyeballs, nightmares, increased agitation.

These drugs also magnify the effects of alcoholic beverages, so it's not a good idea to drink while taking them. They may also make you too drowsy to drive a car.

Overdosage: With these drugs there is the danger of "creeping overdosage," i.e., some people gradually take increasing amounts and feel "stoned" and start nodding out, then tend to fall easily, and finally pass out completely. On an overdosage, one thinks and talks incoherently, "crazily." The above happens most frequently with Valium and occasionally with Librium and Miltown.

VI. SLEEPING PILLS

These drugs are sometimes used on a one-dose basis to calm people down or to help induce sleep. They inhibit (depress) the central nervous system. They are physically addictive, so if someone takes them on a regular basis, the drug should be withdrawn gradually to minimize withdrawal symptoms. Also, in excessive doses they can make a person become unconscious, and even stop breathing. These drugs include:

1. Noludar
2. Placidyl
3. Chloral hydrate
4. Dalmane
5. Doriden
6. Various barbiturates.

These drugs tend to change the nature and quality of sleep. Research is being done now to discover exactly how. Although serious side effects from these drugs are rare at recommended dosage, many people experience an urge to increase their dosage, which can lead to addiction. Recent research at a sleep laboratory has shown that in less than a month, a person can develop a high tolerance to sleeping pills. Therefore it is recommended that these drugs be taken as infrequently as possible so as to maintain their effectiveness and prevent addiction.

NOTE: The combination of these medications and alcohol is particularly dangerous and can cause death!

Withdrawal. A person who has been taking large doses of minor tranquilizers or sleeping pills (sedatives) for a period of time runs the risk of a grand mal seizure (see I. Major Tranquilizers) if the drug is suddenly stopped. True physical addiction can occur with large doses of minor tranquilizers or sleeping pills. In the case of sleeping pills, tension, restlessness, and insomnia can occur, in addition to seizures. These drugs must be stopped gradually if large doses have been taken.

All drugs have possible side effects. Some people experience side effects—some do not. The information in this appendix is not intended to frighten, but is provided to help one understand what is happening to one's body. It does not contain a complete list of all possible side effects for the drugs listed. If you experience any unpleasant side effect, tell your doctor.

The following drug chart will help to identify drugs, dosages, and drug categories.

DRUG CHART

Major Category	Minor Category	Brand Name	Average Adult Dose Range per Day	Special Instructions
"Antipsychotic" Drugs (major tranquilizers)	Phenothiazines	Thorazine	100–800 mg.	
		Stelazine	2– 20 mg.	
		Mellaril	30–800 mg.	
		Prolixin (Permitil)	25 mg.	1 shot every 2 wks.
		Trilafon	6– 64 mg.	
		Repoise	15–100 mg.	
		Serentil	30–400 mg.	
		Sparine	150–800 mg.	
		Quide	20–160 mg.	
		Vesprin (Vespral)	30–300 mg.	
		Compazine	15–100 mg.	
		Dartal	10–120 mg.	
		Tindal	30–120 mg.	
		Etrafon	2–50, 16–100 mg.	Combined antipsychotic and antidepressant
	Butyrophenones	Phenergan	20– 50 mg.	Once to sleep
		Haldol	1– 25 mg.	
	Thioxanthenes	Navane	3– 30 mg.	
		Taractan	75–200 mg.	

211

DRUG CHART (continued)

Major Category	Minor Category	Brand Name	Average Adult Dose Range per Day	Special Instructions
Antiparkinsonian drugs (to combat muscular side effects of "antipsychotic" drugs)		Artane	3– 20 mg.	
		Cogentin	5– 8 mg.	
		Kemadrin	2.5– 20 mg.	
		Akineton	2– 8 mg.	
		Benadryl	150–200 mg.	
		Tremin	1– 20 mg.	
Antianxiety drugs (minor tranquilizers)		Librium	15– 100 mg.	
		Valium	2– 40 mg.	
		Serax	30– 120 mg.	
		Meprobamate (Equanil, Miltown)	600–1600 mg.	Some say should only be used once to calm
		Vistaril (Atarax)	75– 400 mg.	
		Ultran	600–1600 mg.	
		Tranxene	15– 60 mg.	Once to calm
Antidepressant drugs ("uppers")	Tricyclics	Imavate	50– 200 mg.	
		Elavil	40– 200 mg.	

212

DRUG CHART (continued)

Major Category	Minor Category	Brand Name	Average Adult Dose Range per Day	Special Instructions
		Vivactil	15– 40 mg.	
		Tofranil	50– 300 mg.	
		Norpramin (Pertofrane)	75– 200 mg.	
		Aventyl	20– 100 mg.	
		Sinequan (Adapin)	25– 300 mg.	
		Triavil	2–25, 16– 100 mg.	Combined anti-psychotic and antidepressant
		Loxitane	20– 100 mg.	
	Amphetamines	Benzedrine	5– 15 mg.	
		Dexedrine	5– 15 mg.	Some say not for psychiatric use
		Desoxyn (Methedrine)	2.5– 15 mg.	
	Related Compound	Ritalin	2– 30 mg.	
Antimanic-depressive drugs		Lithane (Lithium Carbonate, Eskalith, Lithonate)	900–1800 mg.	
Sedative-hypnotic drugs (sedating and sleep drugs)	Nonbarbiturates	Placidyl	100– 600 mg.	Once to sleep
		Doriden	125– 750 mg.	Once to sleep
		Noludar	150– 400 mg.	Once to sleep

DRUG CHART (continued)

Major Category	Minor Category	Brand Name	Average Adult Dose Range per Day	Special Instructions
		Quaalude (Parest, Sopor, Somnafac, Optimil)	150– 300 mg.	Once to calm or sleep
		Chloral Hydrate (Beta-Chlor, Noc-Tec)	500–1000 mg.	Once to sleep
	Barbiturates	Dalmane	15– 30 mg.	Once to sleep
		Seconal	30– 100 mg.	Once to sleep
		Tuinal	50– 200 mg.	Once to sleep
		Luminal (Phenobarbital)	30– 600 mg.	Once to calm
		Amytal	15– 200 mg.	Once to calm or sleep
		Nembutal	30– 180 mg.	Once to calm
Drugs with special uses		Methadone (Dolophine)	40– 150 mg.	Heroin substitute
		Antabuse	250– 500 mg.	For alcoholism
		Anectine (Succinyl-choline	20– 40 mg.	Once with shock therapy
		Premarin	.2– 7.5 mg.	Estrogen replacement
		Dilantin	100– 600 mg.	Anticonvulsant
		Tridione	300–2400 mg.	Anticonvulsant
		Mysoline	150–1500 mg.	Anticonvulsant

Appendix C

Advocacy Systems

One of the primary reasons for the inadequacy of the mental health system in America is its preoccupation with buildings and its neglect of human service link-ups. Even the community mental health movement shares this preoccupation and neglect. In many states, "community mental health" means little more than taking a large and remote institution, reducing it in size, and relocating it in a residential community. Studies in California have shown that very few ex-hospital patients use these community facilities—they simply stay in their rooms in welfare hotels, wander the streets, or sit on park benches. The community mental health centers in California are being utilized, even overutilized, but by an almost entirely new category of persons—essentially middle-class "neurotics"—who never were, and never would have been, hospitalized.

Mental health professionals are beginning to realize that they are going to have to leave their buildings and go out into the communities where ex-patients actually live. They are going to have to meet their clients in the parks, in the hotels, and on the streets. So long as these contacts are discreet and voluntary, we believe they are desirable and appropriate.

There is also a growing awareness that many of the problems faced by ex-patients are not mental health problems, but welfare problems, Medicaid problems, landlord-tenant problems, child custody problems, and so on. Those problems create stress, cause depression, and lead to hospitalization. A truly useful "mental health" system would pay at least as much attention to resolution of these problems as it would to the individual's "mental health."

For these and similar reasons, many governmental and private organizations, including the National Institute for Mental Health, the National Association for Mental Health, and the American Bar Association Commission on the Mentally Disabled are beginning to experiment with various types of "advocacy" or "ombudsman" systems or models. These systems vary greatly. Some offer advocacy in the institution, others in the community. Some are staffed by lawyers or social workers, others by retired "foster grandparents," and still others by ex-patients. Some have only the power to recommend solutions for problems, others the power to order and enforce solutions, and still others the power to file lawsuits seeking solutions. Some are financed by the state, others by private organizations. But they all share a common feature: the recognition that a skilled advocate may be more useful to a patient or ex-patient than a psychiatrist, psychologist, or traditional mental health professional.

We believe providing advocacy services to patients and ex-patients on a voluntary and individualized basis would be a useful and desirable development, and would significantly reduce the incidence of involuntary hospitalization.

The following organizations are currently active. This list, by no means exhaustive, includes groups that together comprise the mental patient movement described in Chapter 1.

Advocates for Freedom in Mental Health
c/o 928 North 62nd Street
Kansas City, Kan. 66102

Alliance for the Liberation of Mental Patients
112 South 16th Street
Suite 1305
Philadelphia, Pa. 19102

American Association for the Abolition of Involuntary
  Mental Hospitalization
c/o Post Office
University of Santa Clara
Santa Clara, Cal. 95053

American Bar Association Commission on the Mentally
  Disabled
1800 M Street N.W.
Washington, D.C. 20036

Center for the Study of Legal Authority and Mental Pa-
  tient Status
Box 277
Hartford, Conn. 06101

Center for the Study of Psychiatry
4628 Chestnut Street
Bethesda, Md.

Citizens Commission on Human Rights
(Church of Scientology)
1610 New Hampshire Avenue, N.W.
Washington, D.C. 20036

Elizabeth Stone House
128 Minden Street
Jamaica Plains, Mass. 02130

Federation of Parents Organizations for the New York
  State Mental Institutions
2175 Wantagh Avenue
Wantagh, N.Y. 11793

Institutional Legal Services
5308 Ballard Avenue
Seattle, Wash. 98107

Mandel Legal Aid Clinic
6020 South University Street
Chicago, Ill.

Mental Health Advocacy
Department of the Public Advocate/State of New Jersey
10–12 Stockton Street
Trenton, N.J. 08618

Mental Health Information Service
NYCLU
(New York only; inpatient only)
27 Madison Avenue
New York, N.Y. 10010

Mental Health Law Project
1220 Nineteenth Street, N.W.
Washington, D.C. 20036

Mental Health Law Project/NYCLU
84 Fifth Avenue
New York, N.Y. 10011

Mental Health Law Project of the Legal Aid Society
    of Metropolitan Denver, Inc.
912 Broadway
Denver, Colo. 80203

Mental Patients' Advocacy Project
Northampton State Hospital
Northampton, Mass. 01060

Mental Patients Association
2146 Yew Street
Vancouver, British Columbia
Canada

Mental Patients Liberation Front
Box 156
West Somerville, Mass. 02144

Mental Patients Liberation Project
Box 158
Syracuse, N.Y. 13201

Mental Patients Liberation Project
Box 1745
Philadelphia, Pa. 19105

Mississippi Mental Health Project
Box 22571
Jackson, Miss. 39205

National Association for Mental Health
1800 North Kent Street
Arlington, Va. 22209

National Association for Retarded Citizens
2709 Avenue E
Arlington, Tex. 76011

National Center for Law and the Handicapped
1235 North Eddy Street
South Bend, Ind. 46617

National Committee on Patient Advocacy
1800 North Kent Street
Arlington Va. 22209

Network Against Psychiatric Assault
2150 Market Street
San Francisco, Cal. 94114

Network Against Psychiatric Assault/Los Angeles
P.O. Box 5728
Santa Monica, Cal. 90405

Network Against Psychiatric Assault/Santa Cruz
(contact NAPA in San Francisco for information)

Network Against Psychiatric Oppression
c/o The Free Association
5 West 20th Street
New York, N.Y. 10011

Patients' Rights Organization
2108 Film Building
Room 707
Cleveland, Ohio 44114

Project Release
202 Riverside Drive
Apt. 4E
New York, N.Y. 10025

Women Against Psychiatric Assault
2150 Market Street
San Francisco, Cal. 94114

For more information about advocacy, see S. Alinsky, *Rules for Radicals* (Vintage Books, 1972); *Citizen Advocacy and Protective Services for the Impaired and Handicapped*, W. Wolfensberger and H. Zauha, eds. (National Institute on Mental Retardation, 1973); *The Organizer's Manual* (published by the O.M. Collective, New York: Bantam, 1971); *Let Our Children Go: An Organizing Manuel for Parents and Advocates* (Human Policy Press,

1974); G. Sharp, *Politics of Non-Violent Action* (Porter Sargent, 1972).

The following is a list of publications produced by ex-patient organizations:

Action Magazine
Shirley Burghard, Editor
B 1104 Ross Towers
710 Lodi Street
Syracuse, N.Y. 13203

In a Nutshell
Mental Patients Association
2146 Yew Street
Vancouver 8, British Columbia
Canada

Madness Network News
Network Against Psychiatric Assault
P.O. Box 684
San Francisco, Cal. 94101

Silent No Longer
Project Release
202 Riverside Drive
Apt. 4E
New York, N.Y. 10025

Skywriter Magazine
Dolores Warner, Editor
P.O. Box 32391
Jamaica, N.Y. 11431

State and Mind
P.O. Box 89
West Somerville, Mass. 02144

Welcome Back
3206 Prospect Avenue
Cleveland, Ohio 44115

For a listing of currently active ex-patient groups, contact Network Against Psychiatric Assault in San Francisco.

Are you
a member?

The ACLU needs the strength of your membership to continue defending civil liberties. If you have not renewed, we urge you to do so today. If you are not a member, please join.

Fill out the membership form below and send, with the mailing label on the right, to: American Civil Liberties Union, 22 East 40 Street, New York, N.Y. 10016. Att: Membership Dept.

If you have already renewed, give this issue to a friend and ask them to join.

	Individual	Joint
Basic Membership	☐ $20	☐ $30
Contributing Membership	☐ $35	☐ $50
Supporting Membership	☐ $75	☐ $75
Sustaining Membership	☐ $125	☐ $125
Life Membership	☐ $1,000	☐ $1,000
☐ $5 Limited Income Member		☐ Other $_____

Enclosed is my check for $_____.
(Make your check payable to the American Civil Liberties Union.)

PLEASE PRINT
☐ Renewal of membership
☐ New membership

NAME_____

ADDRESS_____

CITY_____ STATE_____ ZIP_____

ACLU-H

DISCUS BOOKS
DISTINGUISHED NON-FICTION

A SELECTION OF RECENT TITLES

ERNEST HEMINGWAY: A LIFE STORY Carlos Baker 50039 $4.95

THE EXECUTION OF CHARLES HORMAN
Thomas Hauser   49098 $2.75

THE BIOGRAPHY OF ALICE B. TOKLAS
Linda Simon   39073 $2.95

TO DANCE Valery Panov with George Feifer 47233 $3.95

TOO STRONG FOR FANTASY Marcia Davenport 45195 $3.50

BUDDHISM Alexandra David-Neel   46185 $2.75

GAY AMERICAN HISTORY Jonathan Katz   40550 $3.95

GERMANS George Bailey   44917 $2.95

EINSTEIN: THE LIFE AND TIMES Ronald W. Clark 44123 $3.95

THE PASSIONATE SHEPERDESS:
APHRA BEHN 1640-89 Maureen Duffy   41863 $2.95

POE, POE, POE, POE, POE . . . Daniel Hoffman 41459 $2.95

DELMORE SCHWARTZ: THE LIFE OF AN
AMERICAN POET James Atlas   41038 $2.95

GEORGE SAND: A BIOGRAPHY Curtis Cate   43778 $3.50

MUNGOBUS Raymond Mungo   42929 $3.95

QUASAR, QUASAR BURNING BRIGHT
Isaac Asimov   44610 $2.25

THE CONCISE ENCYCLOPEDIC GUIDE TO
SHAKESPEARE Edited by Michael Rheta Martin
and Richard C. Harrier   16832 $2.65

THE FEMALE IMAGINATION
Patricia Meyer Spacks   28142 $2.45

CORTÉS AND MONTEZUMA Maurice Collis   40402 $2.50

DIVISION STREET: AMERICA Studs Terkel 40642 $2.50

THE RADICAL THEATRE NOTEBOOK
Arthur Sainer   22442 $2.65

THE AWAKENING OF INTELLIGENCE
J. Krishnamurti   45674 $3.50

DRT 6-80

DISCUS BOOKS

DISTINGUISHED NON-FICTION

THE CONCISE ENCYCLOPEDIC GUIDE TO SHAKESPEARE Michael Rheta Martin and Richard A. Harrier	16832	2.65
CONSCIOUSNESS AND REALITY Charles Museous and Arthur M. Young, Eds.	18903	2.45
CONVERSATIONS WITH JORGE LUIS BORGES Richard Burgin	11908	1.65
CORTES AND MONTEZUMA Maurice Collis	40402	2.50
DISINHERITED Dave Van Every	09555	1.25
DIVISION STREET: AMERICA Studs Terkel	22780	2.25
EINSTEIN: THE LIFE AND TIMES Ronald W. Clark	44123	3.95
ESCAPE FROM FREEDOM Erich Fromm	47472	2.95
THE FEMALE IMAGINATION Patricia Meyer Spacks	28142	2.45
THE FEMINIZATION OF AMERICAN CULTURE Ann Douglas	38513	2.95
FRONTIERS OF CONSCIOUSNESS John White, ed.	48850	2.95
GAY AMERICAN HISTORY Jonathan Katz, Ed.	40550	3.95
GERMANS George Bailey	44917	2.95
GERTRUDE STEIN: A COMPOSITE PORTRAIT Linda Simon, Ed.	20115	1.65
THE GREAT POLITICAL THEORIES, VOL. I Michael Curtis	23119	1.95
THE GREAT POLITICAL THEORIES, VOL. II Michael Curtis	49858	2.50
THE GREEK WAY Edith Hamilton	37481	2.25
GROTOWSKI Raymond Temkine	12278	1.65
THE HEBREW GODDESS Raphael Patai	39289	2.95
HENRY JAMES: Five Volume Biography Leon Edel	39636	14.75
HOMOSEXUAL: LIBERATION AND OPPRESSION Dennis Altman	14214	1.65
THE HUMAN USE OF HUMAN BEINGS Norbert Wiener	21584	1.95
THE INCAS Garcilaso de la Vega	45542	3.50
INTERPRETATION OF DREAMS Freud	51268	3.95
THE LIFE AND DEATH OF LENIN Robert Payne	12161	1.65
THE LIFE AND WORK OF WILHELM REICH M. Cattier	14928	1.65
LIFE IN A CRYSTAL PALACE Alan Harrington	15784	1.65
THE LIFE OF JOHN MAYNARD KEYNES R. F. Harrod	12625	2.45
LOUISA MAY: A MODERN BIOGRAPHY Martha Saxton	48868	3.50
MALE AND FEMALE UNDER 18 Nancy Larrick and Eve Merriam, Eds.	29645	1.50
POE, POE, POE . . . Daniel Hoffman	41459	2.95
MAN IN THE TRAP Elsworth F. Baker, Ph.D.	18809	1.95
MAWSON'S WILL Lennard Bickel	39131	2.50